A Fife Parish

Dalgety in the 17th Century

Robin G K Arnott

Matador
Unit E2 Airfield Business Park,
Harrison Road, Market Harborough,
Leicestershire. LE16 7WB
Tel: 0116 2792299
Email: books@troubador.co.uk
Web: www.troubador.co.uk/matador
Twitter: @matadorbooks

ISBN 978 1803130 064

British Library Cataloguing in Publication Data.
A catalogue record for this book is available from the British Library.

Printed and bound in the UK by TJ Books Ltd, Padstow, Cornwall
Typeset in 11pt Sabon by Troubador Publishing Ltd, Leicester, UK

Matador is an imprint of Troubador Publishing Ltd

For my grandchildren
Finlay and Audrey; James, Jessica and Eleanor

The 'Troubles' which tormented Scotland during the middle years of the seventeenth century were the final episode of a social revolution deeply rooted in a long feudal past.

Dr Walter Makey *The Church of the Covenant 1637–1651*

Contents

Fife

Fife

St Andrews

Dalgety Parish

Kirkcaldy

Beath

Culross

Dunfermline

Burntisland

Aberdour

Inverkeithing

Not to scale

Foreword

In this book Robin Arnott has brought to life a turbulent period of Scottish history through the lens of a small parish and a great man. The turbulent period is the seventeenth century; the small parish is Dalgety in west Fife; the great man is Andrew Donaldson, minister of Dalgety between 1644 and 1694/5. By making Donaldson the focus of his book, Robin has found a way of guiding the reader clearly and safely through the complexities of a period when radically different religious traditions fought over the body and soul of Scotland. Donaldson was both an agent and a victim in this struggle, so his life represents a microcosm of his times, a fact which Robin exploits to the full.

He portrays Donaldson as embodying the spirit of the Presbyterian tradition: stern, unbending, prepared to sacrifice himself for his principles in his deeply held belief that his religion would make the world a better place. Yet the very depth of that conviction sometimes undermined its goal, a fact which Robin does not shy away from. One case in point were the witch-hunts with which the reformed Kirk was so obsessed. There was an especially vicious year in Dalgety – 1649 – under Donaldson's watch, so his complicity cannot be doubted, although he may have been instrumental in confining the persecution to that one year.

One of the many strengths of this book is Robin's use of primary sources, which he quotes at length in their original Scots. In this way, while explaining their context, he allows the reader to hear the voice of the age itself.

Amidst all the religious and political strife, Robin never forgets Dalgety itself. He himself is deeply rooted in the parish, his family having lived there for over 250 years, and this rootedness expresses itself in the meticulous attention which he devotes to the ordinary folk of Dalgety and the often grim and difficult conditions in which they lived.

This book is therefore not only a political and religious history of the life and times of Andrew Donaldson, but also a portrait of the ordinary people who, throughout all the strife, had to conduct their own struggle to survive at the most basic level.

National history is made up of a patchwork of local histories and individual lives. Robin has written a book which is eloquent testimony to this. I commend it therefore not only to the people of Andrew Donaldson's parish but also to anyone with an interest in seventeenth-century Scotland.

Simon Taylor
Aberdour
April 2021

Preface

To most people, the name 'Dalgety' is synonymous with the 'new' town of Dalgety Bay, construction of which started in the mid-1960s. As a parish, Dalgety had been in existence for centuries. Its origins are obscure and the date of the establishment of a church is unknown, although one must have been one in existence prior to 1178. In that year, the first documented reference to there being a church in Dalgety (*Fig 1*) is recorded in a Bull, issued by Pope Alexander III to Walter, Prior of Inchcolm.

In the Bull, the Pope confirms that the Priory is under "the protection of St Peter" and that "whatever possessions and goods which the same Church already rightly and canonically possess or shall in time to come manage to obtain by the help of God, whether through episcopal concession, the gift of Kings and princes or by offerings of the faithful, shall remain in the firm and secure possession of you and your successors. We thought it right to enumerate these in express terms: ... The Church of Dalgetty with its appurtenances... [Ecclesiam de Dalgathin cum pertinentiis suis]".[1] Such wealth as there was in the parish flowed into the coffers of the Priory.

The Priory, upgraded to Abbey status in 1235, held an important place within the Augustinian order of canons, with a wide sphere of influence. Apart from an incident in 1420, when a secular priest, John de Bullok, had been installed in Dalgety by Robert de Cardeny, Bishop of Dunkeld "to the no little loss and harm of the Abbot, to whom the presentation rightly belonged",[2] the pre-Reformation Church in Dalgety *(Appendix 1)* was of little significance. Post-Reformation (1567) a Mr Peter Blackwood was admitted as minister of Aberdour but with Dalgety, Auchtertool, Carnock and Saline also under his charge. Readers and exhorters then occupied the pulpit until Mr William Paton was admitted in 1598.

As the seventeenth century dawned both church and parish entered uncertain times. The parish was a *Quoad Omnia* parish which meant that the Kirk Session was, literally, "responsible for all things". It was a parish for both civil and religious purposes and covered a wide scope of activity in relation to pastoral work and the administration and organisation of such as Poor Relief and education.

Records for the parish for that period are incomplete or missing altogether,[3] sometimes contain information of dubious quality and for the most part rarely refer to local inhabitants in any detail; as such, it is difficult to provide a complete picture of the parish. For Dalgety, the situation is compounded by the fact that the parish probably consisted of no more than some fermetouns, (nothing that could be granted Burgh status) and with its scattered dwellings lying off the main thoroughfare between Inverkeithing and Aberdour there was little of interest for people to record. Such information as there is comes from extant Dalgety Kirk Session records, Dunfermline Presbytery and Fife Synod minutes, references in the Records of the Privy Council of Scotland and various other sources. Acts passed by the General Assembly of the Church of Scotland and the Parliament of Scotland often had a direct effect on life in the Parish.

My intention with this book is not to give a complete history of the period but to give a glimpse of life and events in Dalgety Parish in the seventeenth century, highlighting aspects that had an impact on its inhabitants and how they were affected by national and local events. For the mid to latter part of the century, I have made Mr Andrew Donaldson, admitted as minister of Dalgety in 1644, a focus. Donaldson held to the high ideals of the Covenanters, even to the extent of facing conditions on the battlefield. He was staunch in his support for Presbyterianism, a faith that placed God at the centre of life and one that, to him, demanded that children be educated and the poor looked after. He was a man strong in his support for the weaker members of the community and a man not afraid to speak out against injustice. At the same time, he reflected the age he lived in and did his best to clamp down on vice and licentious living. For half a century, he influenced life in the parish and the privations he suffered in defence of his faith were indicative of the situation at that time.

To understand how the lives of people in the parish were affected by the events of the period, it has been necessary to start the book with a brief overview of how, post-Reformation, the political and ecclesiastical landscape of the country was shaped. The decisions and actions of monarchs affected every church, parish and person in the land. Dalgety was no exception and felt the full effect, for both good and ill, of these actions.

For the residents of the 'new' town of Dalgety Bay there is a rich history on the doorstep, a glimpse of which I hope I have provided in these pages.

Timeline

*Key dates and events (those in **bold** refer to Dalgety Parish)*

1542	Mary, Queen of Scots born
1560	Reformation in Scotland; The Scots Confession; First Book of Discipline
1566	James VI born
1567	Mary abdicates, succeeded by her 13-month-old son as James VI; Church of Scotland established in law
1578	Second Book of Discipline
1584	The 'Black Acts' passed; episcopal authority re-established
1592	Presbyterian system of Church government authorised and approved by Parliament
1593	**Alexander Seton, Lord Fyvie, purchases Dalgety House and its lands**
1598	**Mr William Paton, admitted as minister of Dalgety Parish**
1600	Charles I born in Dunfermline
1603	Union of the Crowns; James VI also becomes James I of England
1610	Episcopalianism restored by General Assembly
1610	**Mr William Paton bribed to attend 'Angelical' General Assembly**
1611	Authorised or King James Version of the Bible printed
1611	**Dalgety, Aberdour and Beath parishes joined under one minister**

1614	**Mr William Paton moves residence to Aberdour**
1618	Five Articles of Perth approved by General Assembly and in 1621 by Parliament of Scotland
1622	Alexander Seton, 1ˢᵗ Earl of Dunfermline dies; is buried in Dalgety
1625	James VI & I dies; succeeded by Charles I
1629	Charles I dispenses with Parliament and embarks on eleven-year period of personal rule
1635	**Andrew Donaldson studies at University of St Andrews, graduated Master of Arts in 1638; continued his theological studies until 1640**
1636	Book of Canons published
1636	**Mr Robert Bruce admitted as minister,** to Dalgety, Aberdour and Beath
1637	Book of Common Prayer imposed by Charles I; riots at St Giles
1638	National Covenant signed; General Assembly of the Church of Scotland held in Glasgow; Presbyterianism re-established
1639	First Bishops' War; start of the Wars of the Three Kingdoms; Pacification of Berwick-upon-Tweed
1640	'Short' Parliament meets; Committee of Estates established in Scotland; Second Bishops' War; Peace treaty at Ripon; The 'Grand Remonstrance'; 'Long' Parliament starts sitting
1641	General Assembly passes act concerning conventicles
1642	First English Civil War starts
1643	The Solemn League and Covenant signed; Presbyterian system of Church government established; Westminster Assembly of Divines meets and continues until 1653
1643	**Dalgety parish separated from Aberdour and Beath, becomes kirk in its own right;** Mr Robert Bruce continued as minister of Aberdour
1644	Battle of Marston Moor, Royalists defeated; Marquess of Montrose starts campaigns
1644	**Mr Andrew Donaldson admitted as minister of Dalgety**
1645	**Donaldson accompanies Charles Seton, 2ⁿᵈ Earl of Dunfermline as a military chaplain**
1645	Plague and famine; Battle of Kilsyth; defeat of Montrose at Philiphaugh

1646	Charles I surrenders to Scottish Army; Montrose flees to Norway
1647	'The Engagement'
1648	Second English Civil War starts
1648	Engagers defeated by Cromwell at Battle of Preston
1648	**Donaldson marries for first time**
1649	Third English Civil War starts
1649	Charles I executed; Charles II proclaimed King of Scotland; Act of Classes passed by Parliament of Scotland; Patronage abolished
1649	**Schoolmaster appointed in Dalgety; Witch-hunt; Lady Callendar incurs wrath of Kirk Session**
1650	**Donaldson assigned to Lawers' Foot as a military chaplain;** Battle of Dunbar; Montrose executed; 'The Remonstrance'
1651	**Battle of Inverkeithing, Cromwell's troops ransack Dalgety Kirk; Donaldson protests against lawfulness of General Assembly**
1651	Charles II crowned at Scone; start of Cromwell's rule; Battle of Worcester ends English civil war; Charles II exiled to France
1653	Cromwell becomes Lord Protector; General Assembly meets for last time until 1690
1658	Oliver Cromwell dies; succeeded by his son, Richard
1659	Richard Cromwell resigns as Lord Protector
1660	Charles II returns from exile and monarchy restored
1661	Oath of Allegiance approved by Parliament of Scotland; Rescissory Act introduced; Episcopacy re-introduced
1664	**Donaldson deposed as minister of Dalgety**
1669	**Mr John Corsair, Episcopalian minister installed; dies in 1680**
1670	**Conventicle at Hill of Beath,** Mr John Blackadder preaches
1673	Test Act passed by English Parliament
1674	**Donaldson 'put to the horn' and declared a rebel; Fines levied against parishioners**
1676	**Donaldson intercommuned**
1678	**Donaldson imprisoned**
1679	Archbishop James Sharp murdered; Battles of Drumclog and Bothwell Bridge; Covenanting rebellion suppressed; start of 'the Killing Time'
1679	**Donaldson released from prison**
1680	**Mr John Lumsdain, Episcopalian minister installed**
1685	Charles II dies; succeeded by James VII & II

1686	**Mr John Row, Episcopalian minister installed**
1687	**Mr George Gray, Episcopalian minister installed**
1688	James VII & II deposed in the 'Glorious Revolution'
1689	William of Orange and his wife, Mary, crowned as monarchs of Gt. Britain and Ireland; Presbyterianism established in Scotland; Battle of Killiecrankie; Jacobite forces routed at Battle of Dunkeld
1690	**Donaldson restored as minister; James Seton, 4th Earl of Dunfermline, outlawed**
1690	General Assembly meets for first time in thirty-seven years
1690s	**Darien scheme affects the parish;** famine hits Scotland
1694/5	**Donaldson dies**
1696	**Mr Archibald Campbell admitted as minister;** dies in 1714
1707	Act of Union

Chapter 1

Introduction – Dalgety
and the National Context

Feudalism and Reform

Underlying the turmoil of the seventeenth century were two aspects which helped the Scottish nation to mature during those turbulent times. The first was a Scotland moving out of an age of superstition and medieval feudalism into the beginning of what is now termed the 'early modern era'. The seventeenth century was a transition phase as the country moved, albeit slowly, from its various hierarchies of monarchy, nobility, and priesthood into a (slightly) more equitable structure. The groundwork of the Scottish educational system, which by that date already had four universities of international acclaim, was in the process of being laid with the establishment of a school in every parish, leading, eventually, to Scottish education becoming very highly regarded and ultimately laying the foundation, in the following century, for the Scottish Enlightenment and the flowering of literature, art and science, as well as philosophical thinking and reasoning.

The second aspect hanging over it like a dark shadow was the Reformation, a religious revolution that had started in Germany in 1517 when Martin Luther reputedly nailed his ninety-five theses, railing against corrupt practices in the Roman Church,[1] to the door of the Castle Church in Wittenberg. The Reformation overturned centuries of Christian thought and development –

gone was the Roman Catholic dogma, with its rituals and superstitions, the sensory approach to worship, the Saints' days, the priestly hierarchy, and the blind obedience to the dictates of the reigning pope. In its place was a focus on 'The Word', the scriptures of the Old and New Testaments, and a rigour and discipline introduced through Kirk Sessions that saw lay people exercise power on a level footing with ministers of the gospel.

John Knox and Mary, Queen of Scots

One of the initial architects of the Scottish Reformation was John Knox. Born in Haddington around 1514, he had originally trained for the priesthood and then been influenced by early Scottish Reformers such as George Wishart, who was executed for heresy[2] in St Andrews in 1546. Following a period as a slave in a French galley, Knox obtained a post in Mary Tudor's Catholic England but, fearing for his safety, he fled to Geneva, the home of John Calvin, the French-born reformer. His thinking on Protestantism having developed alongside Calvin, he returned to Scotland in 1559. The Protestant cause was greatly helped when the devout Roman Catholic, Mary of Guise, Regent of Scotland and mother of Mary, Queen of Scots, died in June 1560. Knox and five other Protestant ministers were then invited by the Parliament of Scotland to draw up a Confession of Faith (*The Scots Confession*) outlining the beliefs of a reformed Church in Scotland. The Reformation in Scotland had started.

In August the following year, Mary, Queen of Scots, after the sudden death of her husband, Frances II, King of France, returned to Scotland. She was advised to recognise the fledgling Church of Scotland with its Presbyterian system, but her Catholic upbringing brought her into conflict with Knox and supporters of the new faith. Her disastrous liaisons and marriages, first to Henry Stuart, Lord Darnley (which produced an heir in a son, James) and after his murder, to Earl Bothwell, turned her nobles against her and in 1567 she was forced to abdicate and flee to England.

James VI

Ascending to the throne of Scotland at the age of thirteen months, James inherited a country in a state of political and ecclesiastical unrest. Given his age, he could not rule directly, and the kingdom fell under the control of successive Regents. In his youth, James was strongly influenced by his tutor, George Buchanan, who instilled in him a love of learning as well as a deep regard for the Protestant faith. Under Buchanan's tutelage, James received a broad and sound education and it became clear that he was an intelligent man, although perhaps lacking a degree of common sense. One well-known epithet applied to him was that he was 'the wisest fool in Christendom'; a more recent opinion suggests that he was 'an intelligent idiot'.[3]

James regarded himself as an intellectual amongst European monarchs and was firmly of the view that monarchs ruled by divine right and that he was accountable to no one but God.[4] He was outwardly Protestant but with a Roman Catholic mother and a Protestant upbringing he had a dichotomy in his life. While he retained some sympathy for the unreformed Church, tensions often arose, throughout his life, between these two positions. By the time he was of an age to rule without interference, pressure on James to fully commit to the reformed Church was strong. In 1601 he called a General Assembly to meet in St Andrews, rather than Edinburgh, where the plague was raging. As circumstances would have it, he had injured himself in a hunting accident and, as he was staying in Burntisland, he moved the General Assembly to the parish church[5] there, where it met on 12th May.

At that assembly he vowed that "he would, by the grace of God, live and die in the religion presently professed in the realm of Scotland, defend it against all its adversaries, minister justice faithfully to his subjects, reform whatever was amiss in his person or family, and perform all the duties of a good and a Christian king better than he had hitherto performed them".[6] His intentions did not last and, while he may have made a commitment to the Church of Scotland, "as soon as his fit of devotion, and perhaps of remorse, wore off, he returned to his course, and continued to prosecute his measures for the subversion of that Church which he so often swore to maintain".[7]

Various other matters were transacted in that assembly, including "a proposal to review and improve the common translation of the Bible, and the metrical version of the Psalms." Work did not start on a new translation for a few years and the Bible that we know as the Authorised or King James Version was not published until 1611.

Andrew Melville

After Knox's death in 1572, his mantle was taken up by Andrew Melville. A more radical reformer than Knox, he had one of the finest theological minds of his day and brought an intellectual rigour to the Reformation.

In 1578, and less than twenty years after Knox's *First Book of Discipline* had been published, the General Assembly authorised a revision. The *Second Book of Discipline*, strongly influenced by Melville, made clear that the Church did not expect to be subservient to the State. It outlined the boundaries of both Church and civil policy and promoted the view that governance should be exercised, not through a hierarchy but through ministers and elders, all with equal standing, meeting together in committees (presbyteries) and in general assembly to conduct their business.

James, still in his mid-teens, was not in agreement, but at the General Assembly held in Glasgow on 20th April 1581, Melville's view prevailed, and it was resolved to divide the then six hundred congregations in the Church of Scotland into fifty presbyteries, with several presbyteries grouped together to form Synods. The General Assembly minutes indicate the establishment of "… The Presbitrie of Dumfermling" to which 'Dalgettie' was then allocated, along with sixteen other churches.

Falling foul of the king for speaking his mind, Melville was forced to flee to England. Taking advantage of his absence, the Government, in 1584, passed what became known by the Kirk as the 'Black Acts'. These 'Black Acts' re-established episcopal authority and declared James to be head of the Kirk and the State. In 1592, however, the 'Black Acts' were overturned and Melville, who had by that time returned to Scotland, saw his views for a full Presbyterian system adopted both by the Church and the Parliament of Scotland.

His relationship with James remained fraught, as much of James' thinking was often at odds with the current climate, as Melville was not slow in pointing out. On one famous occasion, at Falkland Palace in 1596, he called James "God's silly [weak] vassal" and reminded him, "I mon tell yow, thair is twa Kings and twa Kingdomes in Scotland. Thair is Chryst Jesus the King, and his Kingdome the Kirk, whase subject King James the Saxt is, and of whose kingdome nocht a king, nor a lord, nor a heid, bot a member!"[8] To James, Melville's assertion that Christ was Head of the Church, and that a general assembly should wield ecclesiastical power, was regarded as limiting his regal authority. Melville's claim saw him banned from the General Assembly, and after James assumed the

English throne in 1603, he imprisoned Melville in the Tower of London and then exiled him to a theological post in France, where he died in 1622.

Andrew Melville was a towering figure of the early Kirk and, more than anyone at that time, he laid the base for an enduring Presbyterian system of Church government. "It was mainly thanks to him that Scotland became a firmly Presbyterian nation".[9]

Presbyterianism

A product of Presbyterianism was an educated clergy whose main focus was the development of the early Reformers' original aim of building a godly Society. That the Church maintained an iron grip on daily life and activities was without question, but it only managed to do so because of the superstitions of the time. The Age of Reason, the scientific revolution, the understanding coming from biblical scholarship, were far in the future. The here and now was the Church trying to finally eradicate 'popish' tendencies by replacing the corruption of the Roman Church with a set of ideas that placed Biblical truth and subservience to God at the centre of belief. Ministers encouraged this and permitted little argument in directing people along the 'right' path. Writing more than one hundred years ago, William Lecky, an American historian, examining the rise and influence of the spirit of rationalism in Europe, saw a country that "cowered in helpless subjection to her clergy".

"Scottish ministers [in the seventeenth century] succeeded in overawing all opposition, in prohibiting the faintest expression of adverse opinions, in prying into and controlling the most private concerns of domestic life; in compelling everyone to conform absolutely to all the ecclesiastical regulations they enjoined; and in directing the whole scope and current of legislation. They maintained their ascendancy over the popular mind by a system of religious terrorism, which we can barely conceive."[10]

As part of that apparently repressive system, Mr Andrew Donaldson served as minister in Dalgety from 1644, until he was deposed in 1664, and from his re-instatement in 1690 until his death around 1694/95. Donaldson was a man of the Covenants. He was a hard-line minister with strong views on matters of faith, education, and morality. A strict Presbyterian, he was probably closer to Puritan ideals[11] than many. He brooked no backsliding and his great desire was to see people live a life in which God was at the heart. Donaldson, if the evidence is to be believed, appeared to be as much a man of compassion as repression and, while an uncompromising minister, he appeared to care for people as much as he did for principles.

Emerging Into the Early Modern Era

As the seventeenth century dawned, it was evident that medieval feudalism in Scotland was coming to an end. Lingering on though, for probably another generation until memories had faded, were the precepts of Roman Catholicism, the mystery and remoteness of God and the sinful nature of Man, all of which had 'hudden doon' the population. The corruption which had been so evident in the Roman Church still existed to a degree and the freedom brought by the Reformation had yet to be fully grasped.

The actions of Church and State were almost indivisible for much of the century, and acts of general assemblies often found themselves enshrined in legislation. The church of repression came to the fore when it combined with the State to ensure that banishment to the plantations in America was seen as a fit punishment for various crimes; but the church of compassion actively encouraged care of the poor and the sick and not only advocated education but positively ensured that schools were set up and properly qualified schoolmasters were employed.

The seventeenth century was a period of huge turmoil in Dalgety Parish, as it was throughout Scotland. Religion, certainly, played a large part, as did economic development through the increase in the number of coal mines and salt pans and the expansion of international trade with the Low Countries and the Baltic. Scotland and England were united through the crowns on the death of Queen Elizabeth I and the realisation that the "auld enemy" was an enemy no more, but a valuable trading partner, was not yet fully understood.

The struggle for democratic supremacy between Parliament and successive monarchs took nearly the whole century to resolve, with Parliament's view that the monarch was subservient to the people overcoming the absolute rule of monarchs and their belief in the divine right of kings. The struggle was a bloody one and people in Dalgety shared in the pain and sacrifice deemed necessary for the national good. Men of character and principle emerged to make their mark and sustain a community through difficulties and privations. Men of the Covenant faced challenging times.

Chapter 2

Early Days in
Dalgety Parish

Mr William Paton, Minister of Dalgety 1598–1634

Dalgety was ill-served by its early ministers. Since the Reformation there had been a dearth of Protestant ministers, and Readers and Exhorters had occupied the pulpit in Dalgety until Mr William Paton, previously minister of Orwell parish, was admitted in 1598. He had been educated at the University of St Andrews, graduating Master of Arts in 1585.

His ministry in Dalgety was largely of little consequence except for two incidents which showed the measure of the man. Mr Patrick Carmichael was admitted as minister of Aberdour in 1602 and he petitioned the General Assembly that year, complaining that Mr Paton had the whole stipend belonging to Dalgety and Aberdour as well. He requested that half of the stipend belonging to the two parishes should be given to him, but Mr Paton put forward some technical objections and the Assembly ruled in his favour, with Mr Carmichael having to be satisfied with only the Vicarage dues.[1] The fact that Paton was receiving a full stipend but only doing half the work did not appear to concern him.

In 1610, he was nominated by James VI & I to be a member of the General Assembly that was to meet in Glasgow, in June of that year. The Assembly was an attempt by James to direct the Church to his way of thinking and is widely regarded as one of the worst and most corrupt assemblies ever to have been held. Bribery was rife, as "the Earl of Dunbar was sent from London as King's Commissioner, well provided with golden persuasives to use in lack of better arguments". Paton was a beneficiary, receiving 50 merks' worth of 'golden persuasives' for his support. The assembly overturned previous decisions and re-established Episcopalianism. "Thus did this packed, and intimidated, and bribed convention (often called the *Angelical Assembly*, in allusion to the gold coins (*angels*) used in bribing the mercenary prelatists) consent to the introduction of the corrupt and corrupting prelatic system of church government."[2]

Unlike Paton, not everybody attending that Assembly succumbed to temptation, although the majority did, with "some five thousand pounds Scots being distributed and… certain of the discontented sort did interpret it to be a sort of corruption, giving out, that this was done for obtaining the Ministers' voices."[3]

Mr Paton, no doubt well-pleased with himself at gaining financial benefit, returned home to Dalgety to discover that his elders were complaining that the kirk box, which stood in his house, was missing 50 merks. They challenged him to discover the offender, but he refused. The elders complained to the Bishop who, after his visit to Dalgety, ordered Mr Paton to replace the money – as it had been taken while in his care. Mr Paton, as it turned out, was no 'angel'.

In 1611, because of the shortage of ministers, the churches in Aberdour and Beath were also placed under his charge. As Aberdour was regarded as a more prestigious parish than Dalgety he transferred his residence there in 1614. He retained the benefits of the parishes of Dalgety and Beath, apparently expending little effort in return. He died as a result of a fall in 1634.

Alexander Seton – Chancellor of Scotland and 1st Earl of Dunfermline

James VI & I was a shrewd political operator and with one or two exceptions, he was surrounded by courtiers who did not always provide him with the best advice. An exception was Alexander Seton, Lord Fyvie, who had been born in 1556, the fourth son of the staunchly Roman Catholic George, fifth Lord Seton. He was well-connected; his godmother was Mary, Queen of Scots who, as a baptismal gift, had given him lands at Pluscarden in Morayshire.

As befitted the place of a younger son, his father had mapped out a career for him in the Church and at the age of fifteen, he was enrolled in a Jesuit-run college in Rome where he received a first-class education. He subsequently studied law in Paris and in 1580 returned to Scotland, where he discovered that he had been deprived of his Pluscarden lands for failure to conform to the new Protestant Church.

By the 1580s, James was feeling more secure and had wrested power from his Regents to rule in his own right. Requiring men with wisdom and experience whom he could trust, he turned to Alexander Seton. James appointed him to the Privy Council in 1585 and in 1587 he involved Seton in preparing his legislative programme. Not unnaturally, there were "mutterings" at Court about his rising through the ranks and questions started to surface about his Roman Catholic upbringing. To counter any suggestion that he was disloyal to James, or indeed to the new Scotland, Seton renounced Catholicism and embraced the Protestant faith.

In 1593, Seton purchased Dalgety House and its grounds from the Abernethie family, who had been granted a charter to the land around 1463. In 1597 he bought a tower house at Pinkie near Musselburgh. The following year he was appointed Lord President of the Court of Session.

Three years after James and Anne of Denmark were married, he was placed in charge of managing the Queen's finances. His success in bringing them under control prompted James to appoint him to a group of eight men charged with managing all aspects of the royal finances. The men were suspected of leaning towards Roman Catholicism and this caused a degree of consternation in the Kirk. At the General Assembly in Burntisland in 1601 some of the commissioners wanted to remove from the Court and management of his affairs "… eight lords (commonlie for that called the King's Octavians), all almost either papists known, or inclyning to Poperie or malignancie, who had the wholl government of the estate, and all the king's liveing in their hands".[4]

Seton weathered that storm and established himself as an able administrator, adept at navigating his way round political obstacles, and with his Jesuit education and legal mind he was more than a match for his critics. His power continued to increase and in 1604 he was appointed Lord Chancellor (the roughly equivalent position today would be First Minister of Scotland) and in 1605 he was created Earl of Dunfermline. *(Fig 4)*

Five Articles of Perth

When Queen Elizabeth of England died in 1603, James ascended the English throne and transferred his Court to London. Ruling Scotland from afar meant he could still control events but not become embroiled in religious disputes. According to the Earl of Clarendon, James would often say that "his access to the crown of England was the more valuable to him as it redeemed him from the subjection to the ill manners and insolent practices of Edinburgh's turbulent and seditious ministers".[5]

James was intent on harmonising the ecclesiastical position north and south of the border and, partly to make that happen, Seton masterminded his return visit to Scotland in 1617. When he arrived, James called a meeting of the Parliament to discuss how his vision might be achieved and suggested that the Kirk of Scotland should make some changes to its method of worship, to conform with the English Church. When "the Parliament ended, the King, with advise of the Bishops, ordained some ministers to be written for to come to St Androes, that he might advise with them concerning some things belonging to the well[fare] of the Kirk. The day appoynted was Fryday the 10 of Julie 1617; yit the King, finding good pastyme in the park of Falkland, keeped not that day, but came upon the morrow, being Saturnsday, where the Bishops and sundries ministers were waiting on his Majestie, who first heard notable disputations both concerning theologicall and philosophicall theses; and then there were five Articles proposed:-

1. Concerning kneeling in the act of receaving the elements of the communion;
2. Privat Communion;
3. Privat Baptisme;
4. Fyve Holie anniversarie days to be keeped, viz. Yoole-day, or Christmas; Good Fryday, or the Passion-day; Pasch-day; the Ascension-day; and Whitsunday or Pentecost;
5. Confirmation or bishoping of children."[6]

The ministers persuaded the king that these matters, which to them smacked of 'Popery' had to be referred to a General Assembly, and over a year later one was called for Perth, in August 1618, but only very reluctantly did that Assembly approve the Five Articles. The Scottish Parliament did not ratify them until three years later, in July 1621. Slowly but surely, James was making it clear that he saw it as his right to rule the Church but there was an uneasy relationship between the various Protestant factions, between monarch and church, James and the reformers. This was a situation that would last until the end of his reign.

Seton's Death and Burial

One of Seton's strengths was that he was not overawed by the king. In November 1615, when he was summoned to London by James, he declined to go and pleaded the imminent birth of a [fourth] child, as well as old age. "For this present I can nocht enterprise that iornay, for my badfellow [his wife, Margaret Hay] is on the point to be broght to bed within werie few dayis... [the journey] will be maist difficill and hard to onye man to travel and I am now na chikkin, drawing to three score...".[7] The roads were so bad that much travel to London would have been by boat and Seton, at the age of nearly sixty, clearly did not relish either a long horse-back journey or what could have been a week's sail in winter, in rough seas.

Seton had been married to Lady Lilias Drummond and then Grizel Leslie, both of whom had died leaving daughters but no male heir. His third wife, Lady Margaret Hay, was the only daughter of James de Hay, the seventh Lord Yester, and Lady Margaret Kerr. In 1607, at the age of fifteen, she married Seton who was then fifty-one years of age. *(Fig 5)* She provided him with a son, Charles, born in 1608, and two daughters, Grisel[8] and Mary, born in 1609 and 1611, and possibly, as he explained to the king, a fourth child.

During James' reign, Seton guided him through many political and ecclesiastical minefields and was to remain as his principal adviser until his death at Pinkie House in 1622. His body was embalmed and transported across the Forth and with great ceremony he was laid to rest in the family vault at Dalgety Kirk, with the following inscription on a metal plate on his coffin:

ALEXANDER SETONIUS, FERMELINODUNI COMES, SCOTIAE CANCELLARIUS, OBIIT 66 ANNO AETATIS SUAE, 16 JULY 1622. *(Fig 6)*

(Alexander Seton, Earl of Dunfermline, and Chancellor of Scotland, died 16th July 1622, aged 66 years.)

His death robbed James, and Scotland, of a man of unrivalled significance. He was widely regarded as "an able lawyer, an impartial judge, a sagacious statesman, a consistent patriot, an accomplished scholar, a discerning patron of literature, a munificent builder, a skilful herald and an ardent lover of archery and other manly sports, Lord Dunfermline, may certainly be regarded as having been versatile and many-sided, in no ordinary degree. His title to fame, however, mainly rests on his judicial and political reputation. Up to the beginning of the seventeenth century he was unquestionably the greatest lawyer that had been privileged to preside in the Court of Session; and in the successful discharge of his duties of the higher office of Chancellor, or 'keeper of the royal conscience', which he filled for the long period of eighteen years, he was probably not surpassed by any other of the distinguished men who held the same important position."[9]

Alexander Seton left a considerable estate. Charles, his son by his third wife, Margaret Hay, inherited a substantial fortune of 10,000 merks gold and became the 2nd Earl of Dunfermline. Until his majority, he was left in the care of the Chancellor's nephew, George, 3rd Earl of Winton, who proved to be a good steward. "He [Winton] left him at the expiring of the said tutory, the estate free of all debt whatsomever, with all his jewels and silver plate..."[10] For his wife, Margaret Hay, he provided life-rent of his property in Dalgety.

Death of James VI & I

With the voice of reason and common sense no longer there, James entered the last few years of his life trying to manipulate the churches in Scotland and England, as well as dealing with recalcitrant parliaments and overseas alliances that were no longer straightforward. James remained intent on controlling the Church and tolerated no dissent. In 1622 he published a tract, *Directions Concerning Preachers*, ordering clergy not to be controversial in their sermons and in trying to smooth relations with Spain, he relaxed the laws against Roman Catholics. There was still doubt as to where his real sympathies lay.

James died on 27th March 1625. The funeral sermon and eulogy were given by Bishop Williams of Lincoln and in them he commented on the life of a remarkable king. He regarded James as an intellectual, a man of learning who had brought peace to both kingdoms; a man who had upheld the discipline of the Church and under whom trade had prospered throughout the country. Yet this did not tell the whole story and the ecclesiastical struggles which James had endured, both with the Church of Scotland and the Church of England, had not been resolved, as his son Charles I was to discover to his cost.

Charles I

Dunfermline had long been the capital of Scotland and while the centre of power was now focused on Edinburgh, the Royal palace remained as one of the hubs of royal life. It was there in November 1600 that Charles, the second son of James VI and Anne of Denmark, entered the world, the last British monarch to be born in Scotland. It was never intended that he should be king. That position had been reserved for his elder brother Henry, who had been born in Stirling Castle in 1594. Henry died in 1612 from an illness, later thought to be typhoid fever, and Charles found himself, unexpectedly, thrust into the limelight.

Charles, in almost every way, was a complete contrast to his father. While he had inherited from him his belief in the divine right of kings, he lacked his father's pragmatism and ability to keep differing factions in a state of relatively peaceful co-existence. Unlike his father, he pursued this belief with tenacity, determined to exert his power and influence over government and the Church in Scotland as well as in England. His marriage in 1625 to the Roman Catholic princess Henrietta Maria, the youngest daughter of King Henry V of France, only fuelled people's suspicions as to his true intent.

Book of Canons

In 1633, eight years after his accession to the throne, Charles arrived in Edinburgh, when he was duly crowned King of Scotland. He was accompanied by William Laud, then Bishop of London, later to be installed as Archbishop of Canterbury. Laud was widely believed to hold anti-Calvinist views and to be aligned to the Arminian faction,[11] a position he later denied. Charles' visit did not meet with universal approval nor did his action of admitting

Episcopalian supporters, including Laud, to the Privy Council. Charles then decided that he could run roughshod over everything to achieve episcopal domination. This culminated in him devising the *Book of Canons* which, to his critics, was 'strictly popish in character' and proclaiming, by royal mandate, in 1636 that it be received throughout the country.

The *Book of Canons*, a book of Church laws based on the 'Five Articles of Perth', was widely rumoured to have been influenced by Laud. It made no mention of presbyteries or Kirk Sessions and insisted that the king had complete control over all Church matters. It stated that only prelacy was biblical and that Church rules could only be made with the king's permission. Charles reintroduced Confession, provided directions about how the Sacraments should be administered and what Church furniture was allowed. Ministers were prohibited from delivering their own prayers: these would have to be read from the *Book of Common Prayer* which Charles planned to introduce the following year. Critically, he indicated that any man wishing to enter holy orders had to subscribe to these Canons.[12]

In December 1636, the Privy Council proclaimed that all ministers should "before Easter" purchase two copies of the Liturgy for each parish "on pain of horning".[13] The proclamation only indicated that the liturgy should be purchased and made no reference as to whether it should be used. As a result, it would appear unlikely that it ever saw the light of day in most parishes.

Mr Andrew Donaldson

For someone like Andrew Donaldson, intent on entering the ministry, the dilemma about the *Book of Canons* was a severe blow to freedom of religious thought and observance. How could he and his fellow candidates for the ministry square the circle of being Presbyterian and yet acknowledge the *Book of Canons*?

Donaldson had been born in Perthshire around 1615–20 and studied at the University of St Andrews where he matriculated at St Salvator's College on 27th January 1635. He graduated Master of Arts on 5th June 1638 and over the next two years undertook his theological studies at the New College, St Andrews, graduating in 1640. During Donaldson's time at university most people in St Andrews supported the prelates, perhaps not surprising since this was the seat of the archbishopric. Consequently, the St Andrews' colleges were less liberal than they might otherwise have been and that would have given Donaldson first-hand insight into how restrictive church life could be under an episcopal system. We will never know, but perhaps he developed the seeds of protest, the desire to worship in a Presbyterian manner and the fervour to serve in a reformed Church, here in St Andrews, taking heart from Andrew Melville who had walked these same college grounds less than thirty years before.

While Donaldson was studying, there would have been discussion, no doubt heated at times, between the students and their lecturers. The principal was Robert Howie, previously Principal at Marischal College, Aberdeen, who had, in 1607, followed Andrew Melville in the post. Howie was academically well-qualified, but his appointment had not been well received by the students, who had wanted the return of Melville. Although Howie was a Presbyterian minister, it is recorded that, from 1610–1638, he was also a supporter of Episcopalian rule.[14] His thinking must have been an influence on Andrew Donaldson.

Running alongside Academia in St Andrews, the Ecclesiastical hierarchy, at that time, was under the control of Archbishop John Spottiswoode, who had been installed as archbishop and Primate of all Scotland in 1615, as successor to George Gladstanes. Originally a supporter of the reformed faith (he was Moderator of the notorious 1610 'Angelical' General Assembly), he decided that his future lay in supporting the King and embraced Episcopalianism. A contemporary pamphlet described him as a "deepe and subtle Disembler, who had discouraged and extirpated by degrees, and under divers pretexts, most of the faithful ministers there" [St Andrews].[15] With friends in the right places, he was later elected Chancellor of St Andrews university.

Unlike Melville, who had been a man of integrity with a strong, unwavering faith, to men like Howie and Spottiswoode personal survival appeared to be more important than principles of faith. To Donaldson, principles of faith were paramount.

Chapter 3

Covenants
and Wars

Book of Common Prayer

As his later actions testified, what became abundantly clear to Donaldson, during his time at university, was that the Presbyterian system of Church government was what had been ordained by the Reformation and the teachings of Calvin, Knox and Melville. The episcopal system, with its formalised structure and overtones of Roman Catholicism, ran counter to his beliefs.

Formality of structure was evident in the use of a prayer book, not in itself a new concept within the Reformed Church. King Edward VI had introduced a book of common prayer in England in 1549 and it was being widely used in Scotland, certainly by 1557–58,[1] although there was disquiet about its content. James VI had to an extent recognised the difficulties that the prayer book had encountered and in 1615 he discussed the matter with Archbishop Spottiswoode, who is reported to have responded by saying, "there is lacking in our Church a form of divine service; and whiles every minister is left to the framing of public prayers by himself, both the people are neglected and their prayers often prove impertinent". The climate was such that in 1616 the General Assembly meeting in Aberdeen "ordained that a uniform order of liturgy, or divine service, be set down to be read in all kirks".

By the time Charles came to the throne, the general view in Scotland was that an updated liturgy framed to Scottish requirements, by Scottish ministers, was what was required. Charles demurred, but by 1634 he had apparently softened his stance and encouraged the Scottish bishops to compile a more suitable liturgy. What was finally published, two years later, was widely believed to be an English prayer book with Laudian insertions to appease Scotland.[2] Whether that was true, or not, the people believed what they wanted to believe – and that was not having an English episcopal prayer book foisted on them.

Charles, learning no lessons from the introduction of the *Book of Canons*, issued a Royal proclamation in December 1636 imposing the *Book of Common Prayer* on the Church of Scotland and instructed that it be read in churches throughout the land. "When the nixt Sabbath, Julie 23 [1637], came, the Bishop of Edinburgh, about 10 o'clock brought in the Service Booke to the pulpit and his Dean [James Hanna] satt in the reader's seat with his Service Booke before him, in the Great Kirk of Edinburgh. Now so soone as the Bishop did open his Service Booke and began to read thereon, and the people perceiving the Dean also opening his booke; all the commone people, especiallie the women, rose up with such a lewd clamour and uproar that nothing could be heard; some cryed 'Woe, woe', some cryed, 'Sorrow, sorrow! For this doolefull day, that they are bringand in Poperie among us!'"[3]

That event has been recorded in popular history as the day Jenny Geddes threw her stool at Dean Hanna, supposedly shouting, "Daur ye say Mass in my lug?" Whether this happened or not is a matter of conjecture, although various sources describe a Janet Geddes or 'Gutter Jennye' as being a kaile-wife with a stall near the Tron Kirk.[4] It was clear that women played a major role in the riot and what occurred was an organised demonstration orchestrated by forces opposed to the introduction of what was perceived to be an Episcopalian prayer book. This was more than just a few women shouting insults.

Opposition to Charles' ecclesiastical reforms had now reached a critical point. By September, petitions for withdrawal of the liturgy had originated from a broad area extending from Ayrshire through Clydesdale, Stirling, the Lothians and Fife to the more accessible areas of Perth and Angus.[5] Accompanying the well-organised petitions to Edinburgh were large crowds of demonstrators who left the king in no doubt as to their views. Charles recalled the Privy Council but his response was to do nothing except give the petitioners twenty-four hours in which to leave the city. This did nothing to quell the unrest.

Did Andrew Donaldson travel from St Andrews to Edinburgh on that day in July? There is no way of knowing. Spottiswoode was reputedly in St Giles that Sunday and would have experienced the mood of the congregation at first-hand. Seven months later, and adopting a pragmatic attitude, Spottiswoode saw which way the wind was blowing and declared that "[it] will be in the mind of all good clergy men to lay aside the book and not to press the subjects with it anymore". The Privy Council took his advice and suspended the new service book.[6]

The imposition of the Prayer Book, and the subsequent riot, were, arguably, the start of the process that would put an end to Charles' attempts at absolute rule. In all likelihood the Prayer Book was the last straw, and the feelings its introduction engendered were a precursor to the signing of the National Covenant, the Wars of the Three Kingdoms, the English Civil War and the decades of violence and unrest that lasted until the end of the century.

National Covenant

While Andrew Donaldson continued his studies in St Andrews, events were unfolding which would influence his views and have a significant impact on his later life. St Andrews was a hub of ecclesiastical life, with more than a hint of political intrigue coming from Archbishop Spottiswoode. Donaldson would have been aware of what was happening throughout the country, where the mood of the people, but not the king, was for change. To make their voice heard a "general invitation" was issued to those "who supported the cause of freedom" to gather in Edinburgh to sign a National Covenant.[7]

Covenants were not a new idea; they went back to Biblical times. Pre- and post-Reformation a number of 'local' covenants had been signed as a means of binding people together to support the Presbyterian cause. The National Covenant was intended "to recover the purity and liberty of the Gospel" with the prayer "that religion and righteousness may flourish in the land to the Glory of God, the honour of our king and peace and comfort of us all." There was little that people could take exception to, as it was neither anti-Royalist nor anti-Government. With great enthusiasm, the

National Covenant was signed before the pulpit in Greyfriars Kirk on 28th February 1638 and then taken into every corner of the land to give people the opportunity to sign it.

Charles was very much against this turn of events and attempted to counter it by considering military action to subdue the Covenanters. With little money and few men, his attempt failed. He was forced to call a General Assembly which met in Glasgow Cathedral on 21st November that year. Proceedings were, initially, acrimonious, with disagreements with the Marquis of Hamilton, the King's Commissioner in Scotland,[8] over the election, membership, and powers of the Assembly. The upshot was that Hamilton dissolved the Assembly on 28th November. He appealed to the Privy Council to confirm and justify his action, which it did. Despite that, the Assembly continued to meet and was supported by the presence of the powerful Earl of Argyll, along with seven other Privy Councillors.

With the Covenanters in the ascendant, little opposition and no representative of the King present, the Assembly proceeded to nullify all the acts of General Assemblies between 1606 and 1618. The *Book of Canons* and the *Book of Common Prayer* were deemed unlawful and on 8th December Episcopacy was abolished, as were the 'popish' Five Articles of Perth. Of the Scottish bishops, eight were excommunicated, four deposed and the remaining two renounced their episcopal orders and were 'declared capable of officiating'.

"The Scots instead of a Common prayer booke, joined in a Covenant, which when Spottiswoode saw he said, 'the bottome of their business was broken out' and for his part, he thought it seasonable to repaire into England, which he forthwith did and with grief died a Martyr to this Designe".[9] His death in 1639 cleared the way for Donaldson to have a more 'enlightened' approach to theological studies in St Andrews, with an apparent clear Presbyterian direction now set out.

1st Bishops' War

The 1638 General Assembly was a watershed moment in the life of the Church and the country, and many saw it as the 'dawn of the second Reformation'. It changed the ecclesiastical and political debate in the country, as the Covenanting Party had seized power and Presbyterianism had been re-established.

The debate, however, between Episcopalians and Presbyterians was by no means over and Charles was not to be persuaded that Episcopalianism was not the proper form of religious observance throughout all his kingdoms. Not for the first time did those in power fail to recognise that Scotland was not like England. It was a country that saw itself pursuing a different course, more suited to the needs and wishes of its people. This was of little import to the King and he lost no time in mobilising his forces.

Charles had misread the situation. The Covenanters had not only succeeded in becoming the predominant religious force in Scotland; they had also achieved political supremacy. Rising against the Covenanters saw Charles, effectively, declare war on Scotland. He had little money; and because most Puritans in England supported the Covenanters, he had difficulty in raising an army and what he did gather was poorly trained.

Scotland, on the other hand, had a significant number of highly trained soldiers who had spent some years fighting in Europe during the Thirty Years' War, under the banner of protestant King Gustav Adolphus of Sweden. They were led by Lt. General Alexander Leslie, later ennobled as Earl of Leven, who was enticed by the Committee of Estates[10] to return to Scotland, along with his army. Leslie took control of Edinburgh Castle, seized the Scottish regalia along with the King's arsenal and ensured that the main ports were in Covenanting hands. Apart from areas of the country such as Aberdeenshire (which remained strongly Episcopalian) and some of the Scottish nobility (e.g. Marquis of Hamilton), Scotland was largely supportive of the Covenanters, with a desire for Presbyterianism and an end to the absolute rule of King Charles.

The early part of 1639 saw a few skirmishes between the opposing forces with General Leslie gaining the upper hand and forcing King Charles to the negotiating table at Berwick-upon-Tweed. While Charles reluctantly agreed that Scottish Church matters should be handled by general assemblies, he refused to accept the outcome of the Glasgow Assembly but did agree that an assembly should be held in August and that the Parliament of Scotland should meet thereafter. Relations between Charles and the Covenanters deteriorated further after that Assembly agreed that "acceptance of the Covenant should be enforced" and it passed again all the legislation agreed at the Glasgow assembly. When Parliament convened it passed an Act abolishing episcopacy, thus nullifying rule by divine right.

2nd Bishops' War

Charles, believing that he could rule without political interference, had, in 1629, dismissed the English Parliament and undertaken a period of 'personal rule'. What he could not rule without was money. To pursue military action against the Covenanters he required funds, and these could only be granted by a parliament. To assist him in his endeavours, Charles recalled Lord Wentworth, one of his chief advisers, from service in Ireland and promptly created him Earl of Strafford. On Strafford's advice, a parliament was called at Westminster and started sitting on 13th April 1640, the first time in eleven years. Since many of the Puritan parliamentarians supported the Covenanters, it refused Charles' appeal for funds to fight the Scots. Making no progress with any of his requirements, he dissolved the parliament on 5th May. Sitting for just three weeks, it became known as the 'Short' Parliament. Charles still had no funds and he appealed to Spain and the Pope for assistance, while his wife approached her brother, the King of France. None of them had any desire to help.

It was clear to most people that the 1st Bishops' War had not settled the matter and a second war was inevitable. Feelings were running high in Scotland and by August 1640 the Covenanting army, which had not fully disbanded after the first war, marched on England under the command of Lt. General Leslie. Once again, he was more than a match for the English forces and winning the Battle of Newburn, he then proceeded to occupy Newcastle. Charles was, for the second time, forced to the negotiating table and the Treaty of Ripon was signed on 14th October, bringing the 2nd Bishops' War to an end.

The terms of a permanent settlement remained to be agreed and ratified and Charles had no option but to call another parliament. This started meeting in November 1640 but, unlike its short-lived predecessor, sat for twenty years, subsequently becoming known as the 'Long' Parliament. Not only did it refuse to grant Charles any funds, but it had also built up a list of grievances (The Grand Remonstrance) against him and his key advisers, as a result of which the Earl of Strafford, who had made many enemies, particularly with his Irish campaigns, was executed for treason. Archbishop Laud was impeached, imprisoned, and later executed in 1645. To undo the damage, as parliament saw it, that had been caused by Laud, it called for "A General Synod of the most grave, pious, learned and judicious divines of this island, assisted with some from foreign parts professing the same religion with us, who may consider all things necessary for the peace and good government of the Church."[11] The outcome of this motion was to be the Westminster Assembly of Divines, which sat from 1643 until 1653. It was to have a direct, and continuing, influence on the Church of Scotland.

English Civil War Starts

It was clear that the views of Charles and the English Parliament as regards governance were not in harmony. Charles was determined that his view should prevail, and he refused to accept 'The Grand Remonstrance', instead suggesting that it was the Puritans who had been stirring matters up and inciting the Scots to rebellion. He formed the opinion that five of their number,[12] under the leadership of John Pym, were plotting against him and had to be arrested and put on trial. On 4th January 1642, against all precedent, Charles entered the House of Commons, the first monarch ever to do so, only to discover that the suspects, given warning, had fled.

Charles declared that parliament was "in rebellion" and, fearing for his safety, left London and resettled his court in Oxford. With the Royal presence absent, parliament proceeded to enact its own laws, one of which gave it control of the London militia. With the King raising an army and London and the English Parliament under the protection of the militia, there could only be one outcome, and when Charles raised the Royal Standard at Nottingham in August 1642, the first English Civil War started. Events unfolded which were to have a severe impact on the life of Andrew Donaldson, the parish of Dalgety and the nation of Scotland.

The Solemn League and Covenant

Over the next twelve months, battles and skirmishes took place, with neither the Royalists nor Parliamentarians gaining any material advantage. The Battle of Edgehill in October 1642 was inconclusive, and the English Parliamentarians concluded that, if they were to succeed, they needed support from the Scots. The Scots were not averse to supplying troops, but they were not so much interested in a military pact as gaining a religious covenant that would bind the two countries together in a Presbyterian alliance. The outcome was the Solemn League and Covenant. It was signed in 1643 and attempted to satisfy the required political, military, and religious requirements of both sides. It failed to impress Charles and much of the nobility of Scotland, including James Graham, 1st Marquess of Montrose. He had been a strong Covenanter but found himself abandoning his Covenanting stance and changing sides in favour of the King.

Charles Seton, 2nd Earl of Dunfermline

Support for the Covenanters was strong in the County of Fife and Charles Seton, 2nd Earl of Dunfermline, a Presbyterian, became one of General Leslie's trusted commanders. He had signed the National Covenant in 1638 and in 1641 had been sworn a Privy Councillor. He had been one of the Commissioners to the General Assembly of the Church of Scotland which met at St. Andrews in July 1642.

Commanding part of the army of the Solemn League and Covenant, a combined force of English Parliamentarians and Scottish Covenanters, Seton had tasted victory at the Battle of Marston Moor in July 1644, helping to defeat the Royalists under the command of King Charles' nephew, Prince Rupert.

He had also been the colonel in command of a regiment (Fife (Dunfermline's) Foot) at the siege of Newcastle and had been one of the eight Scottish commissioners negotiating the treaty of Ripon, following which he was appointed as governor of Durham. As the Civil War progressed, Seton became ambivalent about the Covenanters and found himself supporting the Royalist cause,[13] even to the extent of approving the Engagement (*see Ch.* 5). Due to his allegiance to the Engagement, he was debarred from holding any public office and as a result, in 1649, fled to exile in the Netherlands with Charles II. Returning to Scotland in 1650, he had a change of mind and repented for his role in the Engagement.

After Charles was defeated at Worcester in September 1651, Seton accompanied him to exile in France and when Charles was restored to the throne, Seton was rewarded with his appointment as a Keeper of the Privy Seal, a position he held until he died in 1672.

Seton had married Lady Mary Douglas, daughter of William, 7th Earl of Morton, in November 1632. Of his children who survived, Lady Henrietta married twice, first to the 5th Earl of Wigton and then to the 18th Earl of Crawford. He had three sons; Charles, who died in a sea battle against the Dutch in 1672, Alexander, who succeeded to the title after his father's death, and James, who became the 4th Earl in 1677, on the death of his brother at the age of thirty-five.

Chapter 4

Donaldson's Training
and Ordination

The Exercise and Andrew Donaldson's Trials for Ministry

While the struggle for ecclesiastical supremacy was underway and significant events were happening throughout the nations, Andrew Donaldson was completing his university education at St Andrews and by 1640 was ready to embark on the final stages of his theological studies.

An Act of the General Assembly of 1638 required candidates for the ministry to subscribe to the *Scots Confession of Faith* of 1560; preach in public; study Latin texts and debate their content; be examined of their skill in Greek and Hebrew and bring a testament of their life from their college. Donaldson's testament was satisfactory as he was appointed by the Presbytery of Perth to deliver his exercise on the text "But let us who are of the day be sober, putting on the breastplate of faith and love, and for an helmet the hope of salvation". *(1 Thessalonians Ch. 5 v. 8, KJV)*

From the time of the Reformation, ministers and elders had regularly met together for the study of passages from the Scriptures. The act of interpreting a passage of Scripture, the exercise of prophesying, became known as 'The Exercise' and this, latterly, was the name of the meeting at which such interpretation was undertaken. Presbyteries arose out of 'The Exercise' and ministers, the brethren, were accustomed to starting such meetings, which usually began in the morning, with an opening study and examination of a passage of Scripture.[1] A minister would expound on a biblical text and another would add his interpretation, before they were subject to questioning and criticism from other ministers. It was a means by which Presbytery could be satisfied that wayward views were corrected and the message that was preached conformed to reformed doctrine.

Exercising, or studying the Scriptures, was not just the prerogative of ministers. The *First Book of Discipline* (1560) was at pains to lay down policy for the developing Church and ensure that proper instruction was given to people: "We think it a thing most expedient and necessary that every Kirk have a Bible in English and that the people be commanded to convene and heare the plaine reading and interpretation of the Scripture, as the Kirk shall appoint. …Every Master of household must be commanded to instruct, or cause to be instructed his children, servants and family… Moreover, men, women and children would be exhorted to exercise themselves in Psalmes…"

The *First Book of Discipline* continued under the heading, "For Prophecying or Interpreting of the Scripture": "To the end that the Kirk of God may have a tryall of men's knowledge, judgements, graces and utterances, as also such that have somewhat profited in God's word, may from time to time grow in more full perfection to serve the Kirk, as necessitie shall require, it is more expedient that in every towne where Schooles and repaire of learned men are, there be one certaine day every week appointed to that exercise which St. Paul calls prophecying".

The Exercise was also a means of ensuring that ministers did not preach for an excessive length of time. In 1587, the Presbytery of Edinburgh "be reason of the greit prolixity and langsumnes of sum brethren" levied a fine of 18*d*. for any preacher "quho pass the hoir glass in making exerceiss".[2]

Successfully completing his private Exercise, Donaldson was then "entered on trials for the Exercise of Perth on 17th June 1640 and was appointed to handle these words, in Latin, 'For the grace of God that bringeth salvation hath appeared to all men' *(Titus Ch. 2 v.11 KJV)* for the brethren made an ordinance that all who enter on their trials hereafter shall have one trial in Latin and they begin with this young man."[3]

The record does not specifically show what his trials consisted of but based on the exercises that the Presbytery of Perth would normally have undertaken he would have been expected to preach. Following that public exposition, Presbytery would then have retired to consider what had been said. Alexander Henderson's treatise of 1641 provided a good summary of seventeenth-century practice: "The exercise... ended in publick, the people depart and the Minister and Elders, with others who are permitted to bee present, goe to the private place of their meeting, where... the Moderator having begun in prayer, the doctrine delivered in publick is examined." Donaldson would have faced rigorous questioning. This was not a paper exercise; this was, as the *First Book of Discipline* made clear, "a thing most necessarie for the Kirk of God this day in Scotland. For thereby, shall the Kirk have judgement and knowledge of the graces, gifts and utterances of every man within their body". Any departure by Donaldson from accepted teachings would have resulted in an admonishment and the likelihood that he would have had to undergo further instruction before his exercise could be approved. As it was, he had no difficulty, and his trials were sustained on 12th August 1640.

The minute of Perth Presbytery of that date continued: "He was posed before the Presbytery whether it was lawful to read prayers: because there went a report of him that he disdained reading of prayers altogether. He declared he was never of that mind, but thought them lawful, though to conceive was better." This was a direct reference to the *Book of Common Prayer* which had proclaimed the reading of prayers as the only course of action, with ministers forbidden to extemporise. The prayer book had not been accepted for common use and ministers had become accustomed to delivering their own prayers. Perth Presbytery was trying to clarify where Donaldson stood on the matter.

From private trials Donaldson, and other candidates for the ministry, had to undergo public trials. Entries in the minutes of the Presbytery of Perth indicate, for example: "September 9, 1640 Mr And: Plaifair exercised and Mr Andro Donaldson added; both approved. Mr Andro Donaldson appointed to mak, Mr Alex^r Petrie to add; January 12, 1641 Mr Andro Donaldson exercised, Mr Rob: Moray added – both approved."

From these extracts, "it is abundantly evident that the Presbytery of Perth discharged their duty in a most faithful way to candidates for the ministry, the public and private trials of Andrew Donaldson extending over a period of not less than seven months. ... We may conclude that, soon after the date of the last minute [we have given], Mr Andrew Donaldson was licensed to preach the Gospel."[4]

Dalgety Becomes a Kirk in Its Own Right

At the time Donaldson was studying, Dalgety shared a minister with Aberdour and Beath. In 1641, it was suggested to John Row, minister in Carnock, that he take over the three parishes, a proposal that did not find favour as "he could not be induced by all their persuasions and arguments to take on the three kirks, alledging, that one small charge wes too weightie for him".[5] William Paton, minister in the early part of the century, had set the standard as he "contrived to make the burden of these kirks far from weighty by acting on the principle of neglecting two of them and paying indifferent attention to the third."[6]

It was becoming evident that the sharing of a minister among spread-out parishes could not continue. At its meeting on 9th April 1641 the Synod of Fife resolved to: "Recommend to Parliament the parishe of Aberdour:- The deplorable estate of a great multitude of people living, in the mids of such a reformed shyre, as verie paganes, because of the want of the benefit of the Word, there being thrie kirks far distant under the cure of ane minister, to wit, Aberdour, Dagetie and Baith, the remeid whereof, the Synod humblie and earnestlie recommendis to the Parliament".[7]

Parliament, after a lengthy delay, set up a committee to investigate, to which was appointed John Row. The Kirk Session records of Carnock, for 29th January 1643, note his absence from that parish, "... the Presbitrye had ordenit me to go to Edinburgh to attend the committey of the Parliament appointed to see that the Kirkes of Aberdour, Dalgety and Baithe might be disjoined. Quhairupon I attendit many days and dyetts and, in end, the Lords of the Committey disjoined them, and a decreit was gifine...". The current minister of the three churches, Mr Robert Bruce, continued as minister of Aberdour, as that had the cachet of being the 'principal' parish.

Ordination of Andrew Donaldson

Once the disjunction had been completed, the Kirk Session of Dalgety was now able to proceed with the calling of its own minister. John Row was again appointed by Presbytery to attend Dalgety, as he reported to Carnock Kirk Session on 19th February 1643: "...Presbitrye appointed me to preache in Dalgatie Kirk, quheir there had been no preaching many yeiris befor. I also taught on Wedinsday thairefter at the visitation of that kirk of Dalgatie with my Lord of Murrayis consent, their wer six persons leited to be sent to the King that he might chuse ane of them for that kirk".

With a shortlist of six candidates to choose from, time was taken up in checking background and credentials, hearing the candidates preach and exercise and making sure their theology was sound reformed doctrine. But even so, despite Presbytery's actions and John Row's work, it was another eighteen months before Andrew Donaldson was selected and admitted and Dalgety could look forward to a period of settled ministry.

The day of ordination, 28th August 1644, saw a packed church with Presbytery in attendance along with "cottars from various farm towns and colliers from Fordell, and well-to-do farmers, several lairds and even one or two noblemen". The Moderator of Presbytery, Mr George Cowden of Kinross, preached on the text "Ye are the salt of the earth; but if the salt has lost its savour, wherewith shall it be salted? It is thenceforth good for nothing but to be cast out and to be trodden under the foot of men." *(Matthew Ch.5 v.13, KJV)* [8]

As minister of the parish, Donaldson had to be provided with a manse and a stipend and it was the responsibility of the heritors to provide both. His stipend would have been paid in a combination of cash and grain. The Statistical Account of Scotland for Dalgety, written by the Rev. Peter Primrose in 1795, records the position as it was a few years after Donaldson's appointment: "The stipend, by a decreet granted in the year 1650, consisted of 67 bolls, 2 firlots, 3 pecks and 1 lippie of grain and 37l. 6s. 5$^{4/12}d$. Sterling. *(Fig 7)* The glebe consists of about 12 acres."

Receiving a stipend in grain was no guarantee of a fixed amount as in the latter half of the seventeenth century weights and measures were not universally agreed and short measures were often the order of the day. In February 1688, the Guildry in the Burgh of Inverkeithing tried to ensure fairness in trade and defined each measure used in the burgh. *(Appendix 2)*

Fasting as a Means of Humiliation and Penance

Andrew Donaldson had arrived in Dalgety at a time of great turmoil in the country. War was raging throughout the three kingdoms of England, Ireland, and Scotland, placing a terrible burden on communities. The

Church of Scotland, through its strict adherence to Biblical precepts, felt that Scotland had a unique relationship with God, and war was as a result of that relationship having been disrupted because of the sinful nature of the country. Penance had to be paid and the Church set days aside for fasting.

Donaldson was a man who would go to great lengths to keep God in front of the people, direct them in the 'right' path and do everything in his power to save their souls. Fasting was a reminder to people that moral standards had to be upheld and the relationship with God had to be maintained. With the country at war and pestilence rearing its ugly head, the wrath of God had to be appeased. In July 1644 "a solemn fast and humiliation was kept throughout Scotland on account of backsliding from the Covenant, and the prevalence of vice and godlessness".[9]

Barely three months later, on 1st October 1644, the Synod of Fife met and ordained, "Seeing the Lord our God, heighlie provockit by our sinnes, hath called in the sword and smyten this shyre in special, the Assembly think it fitt that the inhabitants thairof be stirred up to humiliation and reformation beyond others." The Synod then instructed the Presbyteries to keep the last Sunday of October, and the following Wednesday, as "days of solemn humiliation". They were also instructed to ensure that "every minister enter to visite the families of his charge, exhorting them most earnestly to repentance, and pressing the performance of prayer in families". Andrew Donaldson on 20th October then intimated to Dalgety Kirk Session that "a solemn fast, be keiped by ordinance of the provincial Assembly".

The General Assembly, at its meeting on 12th February 1645, warned the "whole Nation of their present dangers" and encouraged people to humble themselves before God. It decreed that "this warning be forthwith printed and published and sent to all Presbyteries in this Kingdom and that each Presbytery immediately after receipt hereof, take speedy course for the reading of it in every congregation within their bounds, upon the Lord's day after the forenoon sermon and before the blessing."[10]

Dunfermline Presbytery duly carried out the Assembly instructions and on 29th June 1645 Andrew Donaldson "did intimate ane solemne fast to be keiped the Thursday following, and did exhort the people to deal with God for preparation of heart, that all might be enabled to stand befoir God for the turning away of wrath that was kindled in an extraordinary manner against the land, as the bloodie sword and devouring pestilence did more nor abundantlie evidence; and, for their better informatione and preparatione, a printed paper was read, laying open the reasons wherefor the people of God at this time suld be deeplie humbled and lay in the dust before God."[11]

The message was clear – war, plague, famine and storm were the fruits of a community's dissension and moral uncertainty; the relationship with God had been broken. A period of fasting, with a focus on prayer and humiliation, tempered the body, and by abstaining from meat, strong drink and sex, the balance of the relationship would be restored and the country would prosper.

Chapter 5

———

Donaldson
and War

The Wars of the Three Kingdoms

Donaldson had inherited a parish with some eminent families. Apart from local lairds such as Henderson of Fordell, Spittal of Leuchat and Mowbray of Cockairnie, James Stuart, 4th Earl of Moray, owned property at Donibristle and Charles Seton, 2nd Earl of Dunfermline, maintained Dalgety House as one of his residences. Donaldson and Seton, despite the ten-year age difference, struck up a friendship. This was one reason why Andrew Donaldson found himself on 3rd August 1645 under instruction from the Synod of Fife "to accompany Lord Dunfermline's regiment for a period of three months". Dunfermline was recruiting quite widely and men who failed to obey the summons to take up arms faced, as they discovered in Burntisland, a severe punishment as "some of the men who ought to have joined the Earl of Dunfermline's regiment, and did not do so, were made to stand at the Kirk door with rock and spindle, and then banished".[1]

Lord Dunfermline's regiment (Fife (Dunfermline's) Foot) had originally been commissioned in 1643 and consisted of men recruited in the Kirkcaldy and Dunfermline areas. The regiment had served with the Earl of Leven in Northumberland and by the time Donaldson arrived it was conducting garrison duties in Carlisle and northern England.[2]

Donaldson's connection with Lord Dunfermline was only one factor in his recruitment as a military chaplain. Earlier, in April, Lt. General Baillie, commander of the Angus Regiment, had become concerned about keeping his troops in order and had enquired about the number of chaplains who were with the army. Ministers were reluctant to serve, so he picked up his pen and wrote to one of his brethren: "You cannot be answerable to God if you do not your best quickly to send up an able minister to every regiment and at least one half-dozen of the most gracious, wise and courageous ministers of the Kingdom".[3]

His role as a chaplain was quite clear. He was expected to conduct morning and evening prayers and on Sundays and holidays to preach to the whole regiment, a complement of about 550 men, both morning and afternoon. Penalties were in place for those who absconded from prayers or sermons and punishments were meted out to soldiers who blasphemed, swore or committed scandalous acts. There was "a complete system of ecclesiastical jurisdiction established in the army. Church discipline and military discipline were to flourish side by side in it".[4]

When the 1st Bishops' War had started in 1639, Scottish soldiers were well-armed with swords, muskets, and pikes and well-supplied, with shirts, breeks, stockings and blue bonnets. The officers were better provisioned with items that included hats, silk stockings and buckskin gloves. The officers lived in tents and the ordinary soldier, very often, in timber huts. Donaldson, ranking with the officers, would have been living a reasonably comfortable life under the circumstances and would have been well-clothed, well-fed and received payment during his time with the army, although regular, timely payment was always a bone of contention for those in the army.

At some later date, Donaldson found himself called up for further army service with Lawers' Foot. The laird of Lawers had received a commission in February 1642 from the Privy Council and the regiment had been an efficient force, although it was almost wiped out at the Battle of Auldearn (1645). Donaldson served in the rebuilt regiment for a short period (June-July 1650), during which time the regiment engaged in "successful skirmishing against Cromwell's troops in late July in Holyrood Park, Edinburgh."[5]

Marquess of Montrose

While Donaldson was with Lord Dunfermline, Montrose was proving his loyalty to King Charles by fighting the Covenanters. Some skirmishes had taken place during 1644 with Montrose usually on the winning side; and that pattern was continued at Auldearn in May 1645 and at Alford in July. After his significant victory over the Covenanters at Kilsyth in August, the Committee of Estates took fright and fled the country to Berwick-upon-Tweed. Montrose was *de facto* in control of Scotland.

Also fleeing from the Kilsyth battlefield was Sir John Henderson, laird of Fordell. In late July, he had been nominated by the Committee of Estates to raise a levy of about 1,000 men from west Fife. They were placed in the reserve line of the Covenanter army but mainly fled before the battle. Henderson, who was colonel of his regiment (Fife (Fordell's) Foot) escaped from the field.[6]

After Kilsyth, Montrose travelled northwards to Aberdeenshire but found Royalist support was lacking and many of his troops, mainly Highlanders, deserted him. His failure to enlist support meant that his forces were not only under strength but deficient in training and discipline. He turned south, towards the borders, reaching Philiphaugh, near Selkirk, in September 1645, where there are conflicting accounts as to what happened. Unbeknown to Montrose, it would appear as though Lt. General Sir David Leslie had been informed about Kilsyth and to avenge that defeat had swiftly marched his troops from England, giving him the advantage of surprise over an unprepared army. Montrose was soundly defeated, and his forces suffered greatly and, consequently, in retreat, they were in no mood to be magnanimous. Local populations suffered from their ravages and sexual violence and in Dalgety the Session records note that on 15th March 1646 help was given "out of the boxe, to ane pure gentlewoman, that had been spoiled with the enemie, 24s 6d." The Committee of Estates, however, was once more in control in Scotland. Montrose retreated to Aberdeenshire and fled to Norway in September 1646.[7]

Compassion for Widows and Orphans

War was a debilitating experience for both parish and people and the Church recognised that. The outward face of the Church was strict and repressive but underlying it there was a degree of compassion and understanding and a realisation that men had lost their lives fighting for the liberty of the country and freedom of worship.

The Church nationally recognised that widows and destitute families had to be cared for. In October 1645, the Synod of Fife asked for "a list of the necesitous widdowes and orphanes within the shyre of such as have beene killed in the publick service" and six months later on 7th April 1646 the lists were "...delivered to the Committee of Parliament and to joyne their requeest for speedie help".

Pestilence

Donaldson's three months as an army chaplain extended to five and it was not until January 1646 that he returned to Dalgety, not to the happy parish that he had left but to one that had been neglected as "... after that lamentable fight at Kilsyth, ministers durst not hazard to come abroad [for fear of the enemy]; ... and after Philiphaugh (a day to be held in remembrance by God's people in this land), it pleased the Lord to visit this congregation with pestilence." The pestilence forced Donaldson, on 6th January, to preach his sermon in the fields. Midwinter or not, Donaldson was adamant, the Word of God was not to be held hostage to disease or the weather.

Meeting outdoors was a means of pacifying the congregation who had a fear that as some infected people had been in the church their infection would be passed on. The Session ordered fires to be lit in the church so that it could be cleansed, and the Session records indicate that those who assisted with the work were recompensed with drink money "given this day for ail, that they got that cleansed the kirk, 16s". On at least one occasion, the session ordered that a house be burned "because of infection". Fortunately for the owner, the Kirk Session paid compensation as the records reveal that "£3 Scots was paid as a contribution toward the cost of replacing the dwelling".

There is a suggestion that the pestilence took hold because the country was insufficiently robust to withstand it. "There had been a dearth the preceding year from deficient harvest, the drawing away of men for the army, the grievance of heavy excise to support it, the incessant harassment of many districts by hostile and plundering armies and the extreme anxiety and distress of mind occasioned by the civil war ... assisted, doubtless, by the generally depressing effect of incessant preachings, prayings, fastings and *thanksgivings*, [the italics are the original writer's] by which the whole sunshine of life was, as it were, squeezed out of the community."[8] A very sanguine view of the role of the church!

King Charles Surrenders

Donaldson may have returned from military duty, but the Scottish army remained in England, feeling unwanted and unwelcome. Despite the agreement with the English parliament that it would cover all the expenses of the Scottish army, the troops had not been paid and they were forced to forage for food and steal what they needed.

Their actions did not endear them to the local population and a letter from the Earl of Lauderdale, and others, to William Lenthal, Speaker of the House of Commons, made a plea for assistance: "Sir, ... when we consider the exceeding great wants of that Army... we do find a necessity laid upon us still to importune the Honourable Houses for sending a considerable Supply of money to the Army... that all differences which may arise between them and the Country, or the Parliaments Forces may be avoided."[9]

Nevertheless, the army continued its presence and its negotiations with King Charles I, who still had hopes that there might be foreign intervention, that he might garner enough support at home and that he might yet convince Parliament that it was on the wrong tack. Despite his failure to recognise that his intransigence and belief in absolute rule were still stumbling blocks he finally agreed to accept Presbyterian worship in England.

With his army under siege in Newark, Charles was persuaded to surrender and hand himself over to the Scottish army which he did, in May 1646. He then refused to sign the Solemn League and Covenant, reneging on his promise to have Presbyterianism installed in England. The Scottish army withdrew, and Charles was taken to Newcastle. As relationships with Charles were barely conducive to reasoned negotiation, the Scottish army left Newcastle and Charles in the hands of the English.

The Engagement

King Charles was taken by Parliamentary forces, under the command of Lord Fairfax and Oliver Cromwell, to Carisbrooke on the Isle of Wight, where his life now lay at their mercy. This prompted the Earl of Lauderdale, a strong Covenanter, to switch sides and become a committed Royalist. Along with the Earls of Loudon and Lanark, he attempted to 'engage' with Charles in December 1647 to broker a solution. The Engagement, it was thought, represented the policy of the Duke of Hamilton who had advised Charles "to buy off the Scots by ecclesiastical concessions".

"In the Engagement, the Scots expressed their desire that the king should be allowed to go to London in safety, honour and freedom and undertook to intervene on his behalf, in return for the establishment of Presbyterianism in England for a trial period of three years and participation in the commercial privileges of English subjects."[10] The venture failed and the 'Engagers', and the Engagement itself, were reviled as betraying Covenanting ideals.

Lauderdale's proposal "showed some sense of realism, and in a way foreshadowed the settlement which was, in the end, to be made in 1690. Scotland was to be Presbyterian, but the Scots grudgingly acknowledged that the people of England might have a say in the choice of a constitution for their own Church. Behind the Engagement lay the awakening of the Scottish aristocracy to the fact that in appealing to religious fanaticism they had conjured up a force which they could not control."[11]

Once more, Scotland was a divided country with a Church that was Episcopalian by government in a society that was Presbyterian by inclination. Part of the nation favoured Parliament, part supported the king and another part was a group of nobles, on opposing sides of the argument, who could not lay their differences aside and agree on what was best for Scotland.

It is easy to underestimate the effect of the Engagement on the country. Strong feelings were aroused, with the Covenanters very much against Engagers and the Engagement. The General Assembly denounced it and on 25th June 1648 Andrew Donaldson announced to his congregation that there would be a solemn fast for "the great backsliding of the land, which now hath come that length as the undertaking of ane wicked and sinful engadgement in warre against the kingdom of England".

In August, the Engagers were defeated in battle at Preston but still had hopes of the Engagement prevailing, as later in the year the Earl of Lanark's forces attempted to recruit in Fife. Their actions disrupted life in the parish as the Kirk Session minutes for 8th October 1648 indicate: "No Sessione keepit thir dayes by-gone [since Sept: 10th], becaus off the troubles by Lanerick and George Monroe's men, that came along from Stirling. The Sessione appoynts that tryall be maid iff any in the congregatione hes complyed with the malignant enemie."

The General Assembly had decreed, that men who joined the army in support of the Engagement were acting unlawfully and would be fined for their pains. On 26th November 1648 Dalgety went to some lengths to root out any Engagers and by early December the elders concluded "that they know none that have beine comoune souldiers in the laite sinfull engadgment, becaus the most part did give moneyes to comanders" [they paid a bribe to avoid being conscripted]. On 30th April 1649, however, William and James Henderson, sons to the laird of Fordell, appeared before the Kirk Session "having testified befor the congregatione, according to the Act of the General Assemblie, their sorrow for their going on in that unlawful ingadgment".

The Engagement had been disastrous for Scotland as many saw it as a betrayal of the Covenants. The General Assembly was keen to ensure that Presbyterianism won the day and it saw renewal of the Solemn League and Covenant as one way forward. Kirk Sessions throughout the land were instructed to ensure that all members of their congregations reaffirmed it. In Dalgety, the Covenant was renewed on 17th December 1648 "… and sworne by the whole congregation."

Some people found excuses for not signing but nobody evaded the observant eye of the Session. In January 1649, the minister reported that "he hes spoken with my Lord Doune [James Stuart, the Earl of Moray's eldest son] and his brother [probably Alexander, who became 5th Earl of Moray], and with the Earle of Murray and my ladie, and that they did declare that the reasone why they did not suffer their children to take the Covenant, wes their yongness, and that quhen they were more rype they suld most gladlie doe it. The sessione leaves the further consideratione of this for a time, till they be more clear what to doe in such a caise".

On 21st January 1649 the Kirk Session, ever watchful, "Compeirs James Peacocke and declaris that his going to Innerkeithing the day quhen the covenant was renewed, wes not out of contempt or any dissafection to the covenant, but because his wife did live there, and that he did take the covenant there with the rest, which declaration the elder off the quarter seconds: nevertheless, because many wes offended at his running away that day to another kirk, he's appoynted to renew the foirsaid declaratione befoir the congregatione."

Death of Charles I

While Scotland was wrestling with the impact of the Engagement, worse was to come south of the border as the English Parliament, from which Cromwell had had all the Presbyterian sympathisers ejected (the 'Rump' Parliament), passed a resolution that declared it was "high treason for the king to levy war against the parliament and kingdom of England". Charles was brought to trial in January 1649 and executed in London at the end of that month. In Scotland there was a feeling of revulsion against his execution, a feeling that also ran through much of England. Shockwaves reverberated around Europe.

Charles, despite his weaknesses as a king, was an educated man with an interest in the arts and had proved to have a high degree of self-belief. People's objections were not so much against Charles *per se* but against his belief in divine rule and his stubbornness in refusing to negotiate a compromise over ecclesiastical governance and worship. A master of dissimulation, he had failed to grasp the fact that subjects had rights as well as rulers. Although largely the architect of his own misfortune, Charles was, in many ways, unfortunate. He was in the wrong place at the wrong time and caught up in a religious revolution that was sweeping the country, one that he had started and over which he had lost control.

Chapter 6

———

The Kirk Session

Kirk Session's Boundaries of Responsibility

The Kirk Session was responsible for the pastoral care and spiritual discipline of people within the Parish of Dalgety. With no dissent in the parish, the whole population belonged to Dalgety Kirk. Every family and every individual, old and young, was under the jurisdiction of the Kirk Session, so far as religion and morality were concerned. People moving into the parish were expected to bring with them a testimonial from the parish they were leaving. In this way, the Session could judge the nature and character of incomers and whether they were in sympathy with Covenanting ideals.

With no testimonial, they were likely to be banished from the parish – even itinerant agricultural labourers or servants working at the 'big' houses were not exempt. An instance of this is recorded in the Session minutes of 8th May 1653, when "James Buchanan, ane servant to my Lady Murray [the earl was now dead] produced ane testimonial for him and his wife from Traquair, subscribed by the minister. The sessione having considered off it, doe refuse it: (1) becaus it specifies not the time quherin they lived there and when they came from that: (2) because they are informed that they are lying under grosse scandal in the next congregatione off Aberdour and therefore appoints the man and his wife to bring ane testimonial from Aberdour and suspend the receiving of them as members heir, till then."

The parish stretched from the coast up to Springhill, now part of the village of Crossgates. "[It] is situated in the county of Fife, and in the presbytery of Dunfermline. It is bounded by the parish of Aberdour on the East and North, by Inverkeithing on the West, and by a small part of the parish of Dunfermline on the North West: On the South, it is bounded by the Frith of Forth, along which it extends in a straight line about three miles; but as the coast in this place is intersected by many bays, its circuitous extent is considerably more. It is of an irregular form, but approaches nearest to the triangular, being about four miles from South to North, but in breadth gradually diminishes towards the North, and in some places it scarcely exceeds half-a-mile."[1] *(Fig 8)*

As Dalgety was a scattered community there was no focal point such as existed in Inverkeithing, which had been a burgh since at least the time of Malcolm IV (12th C.) with Royal licence conferred on the burgesses by David II (October 1363),[2] or Aberdour which had been upgraded to a Burgh of Regality in 1638. The status of a royal burgh was significant as it allowed a town to trade country-wide, and overseas – a privilege denied to other burghs. Lying off the main Inverkeithing to Aberdour road, Dalgety had no through traffic and lacking burgh status was at a severe disadvantage from a trading point of view.

Kirk Session

Donaldson had to understand the parish and its people and how better to do that than be instructed by his Kirk Session? Kirk Sessions came under the jurisdiction of Presbytery; in Dalgety's case that of Dunfermline, which, in turn, was governed by the Synod of Fife, with the ultimate authority resting with the General Assembly.

Kirk Sessions had been in place before presbyteries and in the early days of the Church consisted of worthy men (elders) who were elected by the congregation. In the major towns and burghs these were men often elected for who they were, or the position they held, rather than whether they were suitable for the spiritual and pastoral care of a parish.

In Dalgety, Donaldson found the Kirk Session to be a cross-section of the community. It was led by James Stuart, 4th Earl of Moray, along with

Sir John Henderson, laird of Fordell, and his cousin, Alexander Spittal of Leuchat. The remaining nine members, drawn from the various quarters of the parish, were tenant farmers or local tradespeople: Robert Anderson, Donibristle; William Cunningham, Little Fordell; James Murray, Fordell Moor; Alexander Baxter, Clinkhill; John Stenhouse, Otterston; William Logan, Cockairnie; James Dewar, Barnhill; William Anderson, Barnhill and David Currie, Dalgety.

Elders

Despite the *Second Book of Discipline* stating that "the eldership is seen as a spiritual office to be held for life", the General Assembly of 1597 had ordered "that all Sessiouns be electit with consent of their awin congregatiouns". Perhaps they were mindful of John Knox's view that "election of elders ought to take place every year, lest by long continuance of such officers men presume upon the liberty of the Church". The *Second Book of Discipline* pictured the elder as a man who was ceremonially ordained and thus set irrevocably apart from the community. Andrew Melville had envisaged the elder as a salaried professional wholly engaged in the government of a Church which, far from reflecting society, would seek deliberately to transform it. Inevitably, "the revenues of our church are so small that they cannot spare stipends to ruling elders" and elders remained as the early reformers had intended as "devoted amateurs".

Alexander Henderson, one of those who had been responsible for drawing up the National Covenant and who had been a commissioner to the Westminster Assembly of Divines, had written a short Treatise in 1641. In it he described the office of the elder at the time. "Such are chosen to be Elders as come nearest to the gifts and qualities required by the Apostles, and after they are chosen are at all occasions exhorted by the Pastor to be examples to the flock, and to watch over them faithfully against all corruptions in religion and life. The Elders do attend with the Pastor in catechising the people and assist him in visiting the sick, in admonishing all men of their duty, and if any will not hear them, they bring the disobedient before the Eldership ... but a principal part of their duty is to join always with the Pastor in the particular Eldership, (i.e. Kirk-Session) and in the other assemblies of the church..."[3]

By the mid-seventeenth century, the practice of electing men to the eldership had virtually died out and when the Session of Dalgety in late 1644 or early 1645 decided to increase its numbers, there was no evidence that any elections took place. Four more elders were appointed: Sir John Erskine, Otterston; John Henderson, younger of Fordell; John Moubray, portioner of Cockairnie and John Henderson, Fordell Green, factor on the Henderson estate.

Elders and ministers had to conform to reformed doctrine and were regularly inspected by Presbytery to ensure that they did so. Kirkcaldy Presbytery, for example, recorded that in the summer of 1636 visitations were carried out in all its churches, with ministers and elders individually examined on matters of doctrine and life.

One extract from the Presbytery minute reads, "Kirkcaldy, June 23, 1636, The whilk day… The Kirk of Kirkcaldie is appoyntit to be visited; Mr William Nairn, [minister at Dysert] preached. The Ministers [Mr James Symeson and Mr Robert Douglas] and Reider being removed for thair tryells the elders present praise God for them and approve them both in doctrin and in thair lyfes and conversatiouns. The elders also being removed for thair tryells, the ministers returning praise God for them also, bot desired them to be admonished to keip the sessioun better, whilk was done."[4]

Such inspections were often difficult, particularly for ministers whose faith may have been wavering or elders failing to be zealous enough and not carrying out their prescribed duties adequately. Over the next few years in Dalgety, some of the more prominent names disappeared from the Kirk Session as Donaldson's insistence on a strict pastoral care regime proved too rigorous for such men, many of whom were, for much of the time, absent from the parish on State, military or other duties.

Deacons

As well as elders, the *First Book of Discipline* had introduced Deacons as part of the governing structure of a congregation, allowing them "to assist in judgement with the ministers and elders" but the *Second Book of Discipline* restricted their activities to dealing with financial matters. Deacons flourished during the seventeenth century, after which the office gradually fell into abeyance.

When Donaldson arrived in Dalgety, there were no deacons in post. In 1649 the Kirk Session appointed: William Lithell, in Dalgety; Robert Henderson, Seaside; John Jameson, in Leuchat; John Cunninghame, in Letham; Robert Stenhouse, at Parkhall and John Colline, in Clinkhill. They were given responsibility for the Church box or "brod", a large metal chest made by "Richard Potter, ane wrycht". It had two keys, kept by different members of the Kirk Session.

To prevent theft or misuse of money, the Session, on 3rd June 1649 "appoynted that deacones onlie, and not elders, sall collect at the dores the peoples charitie and take the cair and charge off the boxe, tyme about. The key off the boxe given first to Robt Hendersone, and that two deacones sall collect ane whole moneth, and the first Sabbath off the following moneth give account to the Sessione, and then to be releived by other two, and this order to be keeped in all tyme coming."

The income for Church needs was generated by faithful parishioners putting their money in the "brod", from fines on members who failed to behave in an acceptable manner, or from those who had had to make repentance. Money also came from donations for special purposes. The output from the "brod" supplied all the parish needs from maintaining the poor, infirm and sick in the parish, to covering school expenses and books for poor children and providing funds for Communion.

The Kirk Session minutes record the amounts collected at the church door on the Sundays immediately after Mr Donaldson's ordination, on 1st September 1644, 51s 4d; 24 Oct (a fast day), 26s 6d. In two months £22 6s Scots was freely contributed. By January 1648 there was a surplus in the kirk box of £96 16s.

Disputed Stipend

Donaldson had a personal concern about money. His ministerial colleague in Aberdour, Mr Robert Bruce, who had previously ministered to the three congregations of Aberdour, Dalgety and Beath, turned out to have an avaricious streak. Mr Bruce felt that he had been unduly penalised by the loss of income when the other two churches separated from Aberdour in 1643. He petitioned parliament in 1646 and had "ratified, approved and confirmed the fact that he was lawfully entitled, during his lifetime, to the ministry of the kirks of Aberdour, Dalgety and Beath" and to "the constant stipend, teinds, fruits, rents, emoluments and duties thereof, with manses and glebes of the samen". The monetary value of his stipend in April 1642 was £40 Scots.[5] Dalgety Church and Donaldson were deprived of income as a result and the situation only resolved itself on Bruce's death, twenty-one years later.

Dalgety Kirk Refurbished

While Andrew Donaldson set about discussing matters of finance and education with his Kirk Session and attempted to persuade the heritors to part with their cash for building a manse, a school and paying a school master's salary, he also had other pressing matters to address. The fabric of Dalgety Kirk was in dire need of repair and given the lack of care paid to the parish by Mr Robert Bruce, and Mr William Paton before him, there was a high possibility that the church had seen infrequent use. In the early part of the century (1610) Alexander Seton, 1st Earl of Dunfermline, had extended the building with his burial vault and laird's loft. Probably not much had been done since.

Most parish churches, like Dalgety, were pre-Reformation buildings of medieval origin and as such not wholly conducive to Presbyterian worship. For many reasons, a good number of them were in a state of disrepair "owing to internal strife and invading armies as well as to neglect by many of the incumbents and the alienation of teinds".[6] Efforts were made by Reformers "to put [churches] into good if somewhat uncouth repair but their funds were limited. Thus, during much of the seventeenth and eighteenth centuries the medieval church buildings remained uninviting, dismal, cold places. The old buildings were usually small, narrow, dark and dank, rectangular in shape, with earthen floors, still often disturbed for burials leaving bones scattered about and a settled and prevailing odour of the dead."[7]

The *First Book of Discipline* had indicated that, "we think it neither seemly that the Kirk appointed to preaching and ministration of the Sacraments shall be made a place of buryall, but that some other secret and convenient place, lying in the most free aire, be appointed for that use". Numerous attempts had been made since the Reformation to keep church buildings free of burials, but none had been wholly successful. An Act of the

1643 General Assembly forbidding "all persons of whatsoever qualitie, to bury any deceased person within the body of the Kirk, where the people meet for hearing of the Word and administration of the Sacraments", appeared to have been the catalyst for change.

With that picture in mind, it does not take too much imagination to understand why in September 1644, a month after his ordination, Donaldson started to replace the earth floor in the church with "pathment stones". He also had the walls plastered and whitewashed, not only to increase the light levels but to remove any remaining traces of Roman Catholic decoration. The kirk box paid for the materials, the masons' wages and remuneration for James Thomson, the beadle, who supervised the work. After paving the floor, one of the first burials in Dalgety kirkyard, at the west gable end of the church, was that of a Bessie Steivson who died in 1644. *(see Chap. 14)*

Making the church building fit for worship was one thing but the need for a manse was outstanding and although Donaldson was not yet married, he required somewhere to stay. At that time the position with manses in Scotland was iniquitous as incoming ministers were held liable for the debts of their predecessor in relation to any manse expenditure. This was later changed by the General Assembly petitioning parliament, but with no manse in Dalgety, Donaldson did not have that aspect to worry about.

The Manse and Glebe

Heritors, rather than parishioners, were responsible for providing ministers with a manse and a glebe, as well as paying their stipend. The *First Book of Discipline* indicated that every minister should have "sufficient whereupon to keep an house and be sustained honestly in all things necessarie as well for keeping of his house and cloathes, flesh, fish, bookes, fewell and other things necessarie, of the rents and treasurie of the Kirke". A glebe, generally accepted to be in the region of 10 to 12 acres, was a reasonable amount of land on which to build a manse and still have enough for a smallholding. Andrew Donaldson would have required his glebe to include sufficient grass for grazing his horse, an area to grow vegetables and crops and, perhaps, space for a cow or sheep. The heritors, as bound by law, had provided land about a quarter of a mile to the west of the church. *(Fig 9)*

The manse was probably built in late 1646, as the Kirk Session records of

30th January 1647 show that, over and above what the parish had contributed, Andrew Donaldson "was far out off purse. They [the Session] ordaine him to draw up ane reference to the Presbitrye, and the heritours to subscrive it, that ane Act pas there for payment from the intrant of five hundredth merks, according to the practick and order."

Manses were not grand buildings and "like many other houses of the period, reflected the relative poverty of the country. Like the kirks, they were long and low, usually made of clay, turf and stone and thatched with heather." Around 1666 a manse in Aberdeenshire was described as "a house with stone to the height of the door, with a timber cellar and a loft above it, an inner chamber with a kitchen in one end, an outer chamber with a study in the end of it, having 'two windowes, hewen, glassed and cased' and 'two fixed beds joyned to the wall', a stable, a barn and 'ane brewing house' completed the major buildings."[8] The floor of the manse would likely have been covered with rush matting.

No description remains of Dalgety manse, but it remained in use until 1830. Rev. Peter Primrose recorded in the first Statistical Account of Scotland, in 1795, "The manse… is an old house, but there is a prospect that another one will soon be built."[9] Considering it lasted for nearly two hundred years, it must have been a reasonably substantial building, probably thatched with stone walls, although no doubt it would have been much altered with the passage of time and possibly had, at some point, a tiled roof.

Donaldson's Marriage

By the following year, everything appeared to have settled down, as in June 1648 Andrew Donaldson was able to bring his bride to the new manse. His wife was Helen Hamilton, the daughter of James Hamilton, laird of Meikle Parklie in West Lothian and his wife, Issobella Mauld, the daughter of William Mauld, merchant and burgess in Edinburgh.[10] He was marrying into a respectable family and, presumably, with its Edinburgh links, reasonably well-connected.

Chapter 7

―――

Parish
School

Education

Donaldson had been well-occupied in refurbishing the church, building a manse and marrying, but none of these activities deflected him from his desire to see a school set up in the parish. An Act of the Parliament of Scotland in 1633 had ratified the decision made in 1616 about the planting of schools and, as progress in establishing them was slow, introduced a tax on each ploughland. This improved matters slightly. Pressure was maintained on the authorities, and the General Assembly, which met in Edinburgh on 5th August 1641, ordained that, "Every parish would have a reader, and a schoole, where children are to be bred in reading, writing, and grounds of religion [the Three R's]". It was not until 1646 that a subsequent Act of Parliament made the position abundantly clear, "that there be a school founded and a schoolmaster appointed in every parish with the advice of the presbytery, and to this purpose that the heritors in every congregation meet amongst themselves and provide a commodious house for the school and modify a stipend to the schoolmaster".

Appointment of Schoolmasters

In late January 1647, Donaldson, impatient to establish a school, reminded the heritors of their duty and by 15th March several candidates had been interviewed for the post of schoolmaster and a Mr Gillies had been placed on probation. "Taken out of the boxe and given to Mr. William Gillies, quhoun the Sessione minds to keepe a whyle, and try iff he be fit to teache ane schoole – 5 *lib*. 8s." With a probationary teacher in place, a school, probably meeting in the church, or possibly in rented property at some cost to the parish, Andrew Donaldson began to lose patience with the heritors. On 29th March 1647 he threatened that if they did nothing, matters would be taken out of their hands and "… Presbyterie will go on to establish ane schoole heir, according to the said Act [of Parliament]."

Donaldson's tactics succeeded as the heritors were forced to meet. They did not immediately agree to build a schoolhouse but did agree that the present incumbent should be paid a salary of 100 merks per year and they took this to Presbytery for approval. The 1646 Act of the Parliament of Scotland had stipulated a minimum salary of 100 merks and a maximum of 200 merks and Presbytery clearly felt that, given the size of Dalgety parish, the heritors were erring on the parsimonious side. The heritors increased their offer but were "onlie willing to give ane hundred and ten merks".

Notwithstanding Andrew Donaldson's efforts, it was to be some years before the parish was able to fulfil the appointment of a permanent schoolmaster. Mr Gillies, whose position had not been confirmed, was "after a whyle… found wanting". A Mr William Campbell suffered a similar fate. In October 1649, Mr William Thrift offered himself for the position and the Kirk Session "delays ane answer to him, till they thinke upone it", but "… because off some ill reports off Mr William Thrift, doe refuse that he sall be schoolmaster." Eventually, Mr George Watson was appointed and kept under scrutiny.

While Donaldson had been successful in establishing a school and appointing a schoolmaster, the heritors continued to argue over the schoolhouse. None of them appeared willing to release land. While the heritors prevaricated, Andrew Donaldson provided a neat solution by offering a portion of his glebe. As this was part of his living, it was not only a generous gesture on his part to the community but an indication as to how fervent he was in establishing a school and teaching people to read with the aim of bringing them closer to God.

The Session, in March 1650, finally reported progress "considering that the want of a scool and house for the scool-master is ane great lett to the instruction of childring and that it will be longsome to get ground and ane place to build it on off the heritors and that it will stand commodiouslie besyd the minister's manse, doe ordaine ane house to be built there with all diligence." Like the manse, it was probably stone-built with a thatched roof and rush matting on the floor. It soon became a focus for the community, with children attending from all parts of the parish.

The School Day

The school day was long and records, from parishes in Fife, show pupils starting school at seven o'clock with classes until nine o'clock, then from ten o'clock until noon. In the afternoon classes started at two o'clock and finished at six o'clock. Spending all day in school was a strict lesson itself for young children and apart from a Sunday, there were no days off. The Privy Council had recognised, as early as 1598, that children needed some time away from school and it appointed Monday "to be a weekly pastime and exercising day over the realm" and instructed schoolmasters to let the children leave school after midday. In Fife, by the early 1640s it had become common for 'play days' to be Tuesdays, Thursdays and Saturdays.

Dalgety was not a burgh and as such, teaching was in the vernacular, as opposed to the Latin of the burgh grammar schools. Learning was by rote, memorising and reciting passages from the Bible, with corporal punishment meted out to those who failed to come up to the mark or who misbehaved.

As well as teaching pupils to read, schoolmasters had to teach them to write, a time-consuming and laborious exercise as, "it would be the duty of the master to make or mend his pupils' pens, 'rule their paper, cast their coppee, tak inspection particularly of everie one writing, point out their faults and learn thus by ocular demonstration his own practice before them how to mend. The master must lead the hands of young beginners, stand over their heid for their direction, and by goeing throuch all for their furderance'."[1]

School Attendance

The *First Book of Discipline* indicated that irrespective of social standing, wealth, or lack of it, children must be sent to school, "[the rich] must doe of their own expences because they are able. The children of the poore must be supported and sustained of the charge of the Kirk. If they be found apt to learning and letters, then may they not be permitted to reject learning, but must be charged to continue their studie…"

When the Synod of Fife met in Dunfermline in April 1647 it was not only at pains to reiterate these points but laid obligations on ministers and Kirk Sessions to compile a register of children aged between five and ten, ensure that children had at least five years of schooling and that they did not leave until they had become proficient [they were able to read the Bible].

The Kirk Session was aware that domestic and economic factors within the parish could prevent children attending school. Dalgety was largely an agrarian economy and there were specific times when labour was required on the land, springtime for ploughing and sowing and autumn for harvesting. At other times, cattle had to moved and milked, sheep had to be lambed and sheared and fuel gathered. A farmer's livelihood depended on the work having to be done and cottar families, and their children, whose lives were generally one of toil and poverty, would be employed to help with these seasonal tasks. *(Fig 10)* Nevertheless, penalties were put in place for parents who withdrew their children from school without authority or "in caise of slaknes". In June 1649 the Kirk Session issued an instruction: "considering that hirds, and such as are tyed to keip cattle in the summer season, grow up in much ignorance, by reasone of their not frequenting the Kirk on the Lord's-day and the dyetts of weiklie examinations, doe therefore appoint and ordeane that, in all tyme coming, the maister of the familie, where such are, sall caus relieve them everie 2nd or 3rd Sabbath, that they may come to the church."

Not every family obeyed the rules and the Kirk Session continued to take a dim view of absences. On 3rd October 1652 John Lillie was cited for "taking away his daughter from the schoole, without acquainting the Sessione" and he "promises to send his child to the schoole again and to keip her at it till she be able to read the bible."

The Session instructed elders to visit their quarters regularly to check on pupils, effectively acting as unpaid attendance officers. By January 1653 they were providing a list of absentees to the schoolmaster and issuing an instruction to parents "to caus send againe [their children] to the schools". Parents who did not heed these warnings were summoned before the Kirk Session and this was usually enough of a reminder for them, although it was not unknown for punishment to be meted out by the Session on recalcitrant parents.

School Inspections

The setting up of schools was mandatory and supervision of them was one of the responsibilities of the Session. In 1651, "The minister, John Moubray, Robert Andersone appointed to visit the schoole" and a week later, they reported that "the bairnes are in a good way of proficiencie".

Dunfermline Presbytery kept a close eye on progress. "Presbyterial visitations were concerned with much more than the educational state of the parishes, but at practically every visitation the parish schoolmaster's life and work was reviewed. The presbytery interviewed minister, elders and schoolmaster singly. The minister was asked, among other things, if his elders saw that the children were put to school; if his schoolmaster 'was careful to keep the school'; and the like. The elders in turn were asked to give their opinion of the schoolmaster's life and work. The subject of all these enquiries in his turn was then asked if he kept his school well; was invited to answer any charges made against him; and questioned about the amount of his salary and how regularly it was paid. It is plain that this visitation could be a very painful occasion for the schoolmaster."[2]

With all that was going on in the country at that time, Andrew Donaldson and the Kirk Session were not to be deflected from their aim of educating children and building a godly society. To them this was not just about education but an exercise in social reform, attempting to alter attitudes and patterns of behaviour and to change the culture of society to fit in with the Church's view on how life should be lived. It proved to be an uphill struggle and, while it could be argued that that approach was needed at that time and was successful in keeping God at the forefront of people's lives, ultimately, although long past the time of Andrew Donaldson, it did not succeed. Over the next few centuries, improvements in living conditions, developments enabling scientific progress and a deeper understanding of what it meant to be human, affected society and the way in which it behaved. The Church of Donaldson's time had none of these concerns; its intent was on driving people towards God.

Funding for Poorer Pupils

Dalgety was not an overly wealthy parish and while it had some noblemen and landed gentry, it also had its share of the poor. On 16th January 1646, the Kirk Session considered the case of some poor children whose parents were not able to maintain them at the school and "ordaines that they be maintained by the Kirk boxe both for their schooling fyes and also ordaines everie one of them to get twentie shillings to buy them buiks and other necessars presently".

Three years later the Kirk Session remained concerned about poor children and "thinks fit that poore people be helped and that therefor ane charitable collection be called for, once in the quarter, from the paroch for that end." The Kirk Session lost no time in collecting money, as on 21st November 1651 "gathered for the help of poore people's bairnes – to wit 16 *lib*". For poor children willing to show initiative, additional help was available, as on 5th December 1651 "John Henderson, ane pure boy at the schoole, desirous to tarie and learne to reid and altogether destitute of maintenance, the Sessione appoynts for him the Fryday's collection for a tyme."

Lack of money was not seen as a barrier to learning to read. In January 1654, "The Sessione appoynts that all who have learned to reid, buy bibles, and that, at catechising and visiting off families, people be exhorted to reid and learne the Scripture and that pure bodies who are not able to buy bibles, their caise to be presented to the Sessione, that they may be helped." Over the next few years, the Kirk Session minutes regularly records sums of money given to poor people to buy their Bibles: 5th February 1654 "Given out of the boxe, this day 18 *lib*. for nine bibles for poore bodies." By 1659 Bibles had become cheaper as "the price of a copy of the Scriptures had fallen to thirty-six shillings". If people could not afford the full price the Kirk Session encouraged them to give something towards a copy of the Bible.[3]

Payment of Schoolmasters

Salary was a continuing problem for schoolmasters. They were university educated, (usually graduating Master of Arts, and hence allowed to use the title Mr.) and one of the few 'learned men' in the community. The schoolmaster's salary was the responsibility of the heritors, but they often failed to meet their obligations and the salary had to be met from the Church box. For many schoolmasters, the salary was barely enough to cover his living costs and he would supplement it with fees from parents, or from the Kirk Session where additional teaching of poor pupils was involved. He was expected to act as session-clerk and possibly precentor and would receive a fee for those duties, as well as an additional fee for registering births, marriages and deaths. Dalgety Kirk Session minutes of 4th June 1652 records the fees as: marriage, 24s. (18s. to the clerk and 6s. to the beadle); baptism, 15s. (10s. to the clerk and 5s. to the beadle). As precentor, he would expect additional payment for his "extraordinary pains at the Sacrament" and that could add a further £5, or so, to his salary.

How long a schoolmaster remained in post is not always clear. For some it was a fixed term, for others open-ended, although blotting of the copybook always meant dismissal. Departures happened for several reasons and not always related to educational matters. As they were university graduates, many schoolmasters aspired to become ministers and would conduct their theological studies while in post, in the expectation of a church of their own when they had completed their course.

After the Restoration of the monarchy, Fife Synod in 1662 instructed its presbyteries to ensure that only schoolmasters who had taken the episcopal archbishop's licence were to teach either in public schools or privately and the Synod reiterated its instruction in 1663 and 1666. Mr Robert Wilson, who had come as schoolmaster to Dalgety from Dalkeith Presbytery, was in sympathy with Andrew Donaldson's views and, presumably as he was not licensed, did not declare his "loyalty and satisfaction with church government" to Presbytery. No more was heard of him.[4]

John Knox and the early reformers saw the value of schools in teaching children how to read and write and their approach laid the foundations for an educational system that would see Scotland become one of the European intellectual powerhouses of the eighteenth century, through the

Enlightenment. With his insistence that a school be set up in Dalgety Parish, and ensuring that teaching standards were high, and monitored, Donaldson made his contribution to building a Scotland that became admired throughout the world.

Chapter 8

———

Sunday
Worship

Keeping the Sabbath

Establishing a school was only one aspect of the care Donaldson paid to the parish. Before his admission there had been little activity of any kind for many years; pastoral care had languished, preaching had been virtually non-existent, and behaviour of parishioners left much to be desired. Donaldson was determined to bring the neglected parish into what he saw as a 'fit state' by bringing the 'Word of God' to the people.

The *First Book of Discipline* had indicated that preaching, ministering the sacraments and public prayers were "utterly necessarie" as "without the same there is no face of a visible kirk". It instructed that "Sunday must straitly be kept in all townes. Before noone must the word be preached and sacraments ministered, as also marriage solemnized, if occasion offer: after noone must the young children be publickly examined in their Catechisme in the audience of the people."

The order of service followed by Andrew Donaldson was that as specified in the *Book of Common Order* and the doctrine that he followed was contained in *The Scots Confession* of 1560. The Confession was regarded as "Doctrine groundit upon the infallibil Worde of God" and addressed not only the tenets of the faith but the "trew preaching of the Worde", the celebration of the Sacraments and the position of Civil Magistrates. "It is a simple, straightforward, frank document, stating in plain language their (i.e. the Reformers') general credal position and revealing conviction, determination and enthusiasm. In it our national religion from an attitude of mere protest passed to being positively articulate."[1] It was not a substitute for the Apostles' Creed, which all communicants in the Church of Scotland were expected to know.

In 1643, the Westminster Assembly of Divines had started its lengthy deliberations about matters relating to the 'substance of the faith'. In 1645, as one of its first acts, it introduced the *Directory for the Publick Worship of God* in an attempt to have uniformity of worship in both Scotland and England. The following year the Assembly produced the *Westminster Confession of Faith* and in 1647 the *Shorter Catechism*, both of which were adopted by the Church of Scotland. Over the next few years, Donaldson's reliance on the *Scots Confession of Faith* diminished as the Westminster version replaced it and became, and remains, the subordinate standard of faith of the Church of Scotland.

Each congregation in Scotland had to be informed about the Directory and the Session records of Dalgety show that when it should have been publicised Donaldson was in England, serving as a military chaplain with Charles Seton's regiment: 15th February 1646 "This day becaus the directorie wes not read heir quhen it was read in other churches, becaus of the minister's absence, the minister did read at lest those places that did concern most the congregatione to know." The Directory endeavoured to change the way in which ministers conducted Sunday worship, although, given the continuing religious upheaval, it did not gain universal acceptance and at the Restoration, Parliament annulled the Act which had introduced it.

The early Reformers saw that the path to God was through prayer and the preaching of the Word. No barriers were to be placed between God and the people – men, women and children, young and old, had to be instructed in the faith. There could be no exceptions. If a person's faith was lacking, they were unlikely to gain salvation at the Day of Judgement. The job of the Church was to save souls and transform society, and it was at pains to ensure that what it saw as the errors of the Roman Catholic Church were eradicated from Scottish society. Sunday was a key day in this respect and worship on a Sunday morning was a central part of the life of the parish.

While Sunday was a day of no work it is doubtful if it was a 'day of rest'. People, without exception, were expected to attend Church and it was an early start, particularly if you lived in the northern part of the parish, near Springhill, where you faced a three- or four-mile walk to the church along rough tracks. To remind them that Sunday was a day set aside from normal activity, the church bell would ring three times – firstly at seven o'clock, indicating that services would start in an hour; next at eight o'clock for a preliminary service, conducted by the Reader, and at nine o'clock when the minister would enter the pulpit and preach 'the Word'.

The bell that was hanging in the bell-cote of Dalgety Kirk at the time of Andrew Donaldson's ordination was possibly pre-Reformation. Its Latin inscription, in Gothic lettering around its base, although now defaced, carries Roman Catholic overtones with its wording: "O Mater Dei Memento Mei" – "O Mother of God, remember me". *(Fig 11)* The origin of the bell is unclear, but it may previously have hung on the west gable end of the kirk and been in use prior to the building of the Seton loft in the early seventeenth century and relocated to the new bell-cote at that time. It is possible that the bell may only have been installed when the loft was built. Most parishes had only one bell and many of them would had been cast by the Burgerhuys family of Middelburg in the Netherlands. Some of these bells may well still be sounding today.[2]

The Reader

In the early days of the reformed Church, as few people could read or write and fewer still had ever heard the Bible read aloud in their own tongue, there was felt to be a great need to let the people hear it being read in English. The *First Book of Discipline* had made the Church of Scotland's position clear; "We think it a thing most expedient and necessary that every Kirk have the Bible in English and that the people be commanded to convene and heare the plaine reading and interpretation of the Scripture. By frequent reading, this grosse ignorance which in this cursed Papistry hath overflowed all, may partly be removed." Introducing Readers was an innovative way of achieving this. A Reader, who had to be over the age of twenty-one years, may not have attended university but he was educated enough to be able to read the Bible and lead the congregation in prayer.

When Andrew Donaldson arrived in Dalgety, a Patrick Anderson[3] was recorded as holding that position and he would have conducted the eight o'clock service. The Reader's service lasted about one hour and consisted of prayer, readings from both the Old and New Testaments and the singing of a psalm. When the beadle rang the bell for a third time, Andrew Donaldson entered the pulpit and bowed[4] before embarking on another two-hours' worth of prayer, psalm-singing, admonition to penitents and a sermon.

None of Andrew Donaldson's sermons have survived but, as with most preaching at the time, they would have been based around the fundamental narrative of salvation. The established doctrine was that God was good, people were wicked but saved through the grace of God. The staple sermon highlighted the sinfulness of people and the agonies which lay in hell for those who failed to 'walk with the Spirit' but offered the promise of redemption, if only they were to turn away from their sinful lives. The morning could be long and last three hours or more and, apart from the Reader's contribution, was repeated in the afternoon, when catechising was also included.

As befitted the occasion, Donaldson would have been severely dressed as King Charles had decreed, "within our kingdom of Scotland... for all inferior clergymen we will that they preach in their black gowns, but when they read divine service, Christian burial or administer the sacrament of the Lord's supper they shall wear their surplices; ... all inferior priests and ministers shall at times and places use their square caps, especially in all our universities."[5]

Sermons were delivered from the pulpit. *(Fig 2)* Donaldson had a new one built in 1646 with the installation carried out by Richard Potter and his two sons, who were rewarded for their work with "drink money for the pulpit, 30s". It was on the south side of the church, set into a recess with a window just above head-height. During the sermon, with the light behind him, it not only provided illumination for the Bible or papers that Donaldson might have had in front of him, but it allowed him to observe the effect of his words on the congregation.

The pulpit was an important item of church furniture.[6] Below it was placed the repentance stool and slightly to one side, a lectern, from which the Reader would conduct early morning worship. Attached to the pulpit there may have been an hourglass, which the minister would have turned at the beginning of his sermon, and maybe several times before he had finished, and a bracket holding the baptismal bowl.

Baptism

Baptism had been declared to be one of the two sacraments of the Church of Scotland.[7] It is the sacred admission of a person into Christianity, signified by the sprinkling of a few drops of water on the head. An Act of the Scottish Parliament in 1621 decreed that baptism had to be carried out within a week of the baby's birth. Evidence exists in Kirkcaldy Kirk that this Act was enforced, as a fine of 40s was imposed on "those who kept their bairnes unbaptised for twa preaching Sundays". By 1672, the law extended the period allowed for baptism to thirty days.

The early Reformers' view that baptism was not a private event was supported by the Westminster Assembly which, in its *Directory of Public Worship*, indicated that it had to "take place, where the people most conveniently see and hear and not in places where fonts, in time of Popery, were unfitly and superstitiously placed".

Many baptismal bowls and fonts had been carried away or destroyed at the Reformation. Much church plate had disappeared and it is obvious this deficiency cannot have been made good, for it is significant to find an Act of Parliament of 1617 which ordains, "that all the Paroch Kirks within this Kingdom to be provided with Basins and Lavoirs for the ministration of the Sacrament of Baptisme; and of Cups, Tables and Table-Cloathes, for the ministration of the Holy Communion". The mention, in the Act, of basins and lavers for baptism is worthy of note, for it "indicates the normal reformed practice in Scotland from the sixteenth century till recent times. The medieval fonts were cast out and baptism was conducted, from a basin of silver or pewter attached by a wrought-iron bracket to the pulpit, in full view of the congregation."[8]

Before a father could bring his child forward for baptism, he had to satisfy the minister as to his character and religious knowledge. Those who failed the examination were declared ignorant, subjected to public disgrace, and were not permitted to present their own child for baptism. Some other godly person had to be found. In July 1655, the Session records show "David Greig, having a child to be baptised and grosslie ignorant and having beine keeped back from that benefite for a tyme because of his ignorance and now bro' to some sense of it, is appointed to acknowledge befoir the congregatione his sinne off ignorance, promises to take paines to learne and his child is to be baptised."

Baptisms were great occasions, and the baptism would be attended by numerous gossips[9] and witnesses. Over time, the number of gossips increased, as did the numbers attending the family celebrations. Parents were determined to 'keep up appearances' and became over-extravagant with what they provided for guests. In an attempt to ensure that families did not incur debt they were unlikely to be able to repay, the Scottish Parliament, in 1621, legislated on the matter such that at baptisms nobody was allowed to provide "any manner of wet or dry confectionery, or any food that was not grown in Scotland" on pain of facing a fine of 1,000 merks. Among the items banned were figs, raisins, almonds and confections with spices from overseas.[10]

Curbing people's enthusiasm for celebration was easier said than done and in 1645 the Synod of Fife had to instruct all parishes to reduce the number of gossips and guests at baptism, "...that in number thei exceede not six or seven." The authorities placed similar restrictions on most other parishes in the country.

Metrical Psalms

Sitting in Church from early morning and listening to long prayers and a two-hour sermon was enough to test the patience and stamina of even the best of parishioners. The early reformers were aware of the dangers of Roman Catholic services where the laity were mere observers. They were keen to engage the congregation in worship in ways which were meaningful, with words they could understand. In Roman Catholic churches, there had been no congregational singing and the Latin Mass had been sung by trained singers.

For the Reformers, worship had to be relevant and understandable and they cast their minds back to John Knox who had accepted Calvin's view that "nothing but what was biblical should be used in public worship". This opened the way to use the Psalms as "versified texts to melodies sufficiently easy to make congregational singing possible".[11] This prompted the printing of the *First Scottish Psalter* in 1564 and an Act of Parliament, 1579, ordained, "that all Gentlemen with 300 merks in yearlie rent, and all substantious yeomen, worth 500 pounds in lands or goods, be holden to have ane bible and psalme booke"[12]

The early translations of the psalms into metre were not successful and King James VI made his own effort to provide 'good' psalms. The Synod of Fife, meeting in St Andrews on 2nd October 1632, instructed its presbyteries that "the Psalmes of King David, translated in meeter by King James ...to be accepted and sung in all his Majesties [Charles I's] dominions...".

The original plan had been for each psalm to have its own tune and some tunes from France and England had retained their place in the 1635 Scottish Psalmody. As some of them were difficult many psalms were sung to the same tune. Throughout Scotland a number of tunes were devised locally[13] but these often met with limited success and were little used outside the immediate locality. They were generally written by the precentor but most did not survive the passage of time, unlike the 'great' Scottish psalm tunes such as 'Culross', written in 1634; or 'Dunfermline', from the Scottish Psalter of 1615 and attributed to the "good and meike Jhone Angus".[14]

The Congregation and Seating Within Dalgety Kirk

In many churches the congregation sat on forms or stools, and it was the custom for the men and women to sit separately, except in the lairds' pews. Many worshippers brought their own stool, others would have had to stand or sit on the cold stone floor, and part of the beadle's salary would have derived from him renting out stools to members of the congregation.

Early in Donaldson's ministry it was evident that the number of people attending Sunday worship did not fill the church, but two years later and space was at a premium. The Kirk Session minutes of 26th September 1646 record that the Laird of Fordell, after lengthy discussion, was given permission to "build ane loft upon the north side of the kirk, from Leuchat's ile westward, because he had ane great familie and could not be convenientlie eased upon the floore, without prejudice to the congregatione". Eight months later, in May 1647, the Session resolved to install four benches along the west wall.

An idealistic view of the congregation inside the church was painted for us by William Ross: "There are two doors on the south-side wall, by means of which admission may be gained [to the Church]. As we enter, we see the great bulk of the congregation occupying seats ranged along the floor – farmers in hodden-grey, with their broad blue bonnets reverently doffed; shepherds with their maud plaids; colliers with something of a grimy look, in spite of their ablutions; matrons with their sow-backed mutches, as white as the driven snow; young women with their hair neatly braided and bound with a snood; and boys and girls with bright eyes and happy faces. But there are various lofts and seats in which the rustling of silks and satins is heard.

The gallery at the east end of the church is the Earl of Murray's; and the seat immediately under it is where worthy John Moubray, of Cockairnie, and his family sit. The gallery at the west end is the Earl of Dunfermline's, the entrance to it being by the round stair on the north side. The laird of Fordell's gallery – the erection of which was the cause of so much contention and debate – is on the north wall, between Lord Murray's gallery and the north aisle. The arched vault on the north is the Otterston aisle; but Sir John Erskine having married Margaret Inglis, the heiress of Otterston, it goes by the name of Sir John's aisle. The Leuchat seat is immediately under Lord Murray's gallery, alongside of that belonging to Cockairnie, and the pulpit is on the north wall.[15] Everything connected with the fabric and fitting-up of the church is severely plain."[16]

With services long and in a crowded church, there was always the temptation to let the mind wander. As people worked hard during the week it is not too difficult to imagine them relaxing. But church was church and if people were expected to discuss the sermon at home later, then the beadle was at hand with his pole to prod those who had fallen asleep, who were chatting or not paying enough attention to the words of the minister.

On occasion, people like James Peacock were found out and "rebuiked for discoursing in time of hearing and admonished to make more conscience off hearing the word in tyme coming" and William Cunninghame, an elder, was appointed to "reprove Catherine Thomsone, in Little Fordell, for sleeping in the kirk, in tyme of hearing".

Chapter 9

Communion

Catechising

Communion Sunday differed entirely from normal worship. It was not to be approached as any other service. The Lord's Supper was a sacramental feast in which the congregation shared consecrated bread and wine. Unlike baptism, Communion was to be celebrated regularly and the *First Book of Discipline* suggested that should be four times per year. Admittance to the Lord's Supper was not meant to be as a matter of course; people had to prove they were worthy before they were allowed to attend.

Determining whether people met the criteria to take Communion required constant effort on the part of Donaldson and his elders. Parishioners were expected to read their Bible and gather for family worship every day and memorise the Ten Commandments, the Lord's Prayer and the Apostles' Creed. These were regarded as the fundamental building blocks of the Christian faith and without knowing them, there could be no salvation. In addition, they had to be able to respond to the questions in the *Shorter Catechism*. To ensure people were conforming, families were visited each month by their elder. With a dozen or so households[1] to look after, he had to "take notice of such as want familie worship, as mock prayer and the power off godliness, as are prophain and scandalous, that they may be brought to censure." He was also expected to "take especial notice off any that are gracious and seikers off God, that they may be strengthened and encouraged".

Living up to such standards was no easy task, even for elders, and many were not as assiduous as Donaldson would have liked. He had no compunction about taking them to task and exhorting them "that there be no slackness in visiting their quarters and regrets the want of familie worship in their own houses as ane hindrance off it in other houses."

The education of parishioners in matters of the faith was carried out by catechising, a means of learning by question and answer. The Catechisms that were used in Scotland originated from the Westminster Assembly and were introduced in 1647. Bearing in mind an earlier General Assembly resolution that ministers should be catechising "one day every week", the Kirk Session, in June 1654, appointed a Monday morning "for opening up the grounds of the Catechise to the people, and that the whole congregatione be exhorted to keip the diet weiklie, at 9 a cloak." For those who were working, this must have been an almost impossible demand to meet. To an extent, the Session recognised this and made allowances at specific times during the year. On 24th August 1653, "Examination laid by till the harvest be done, as also the weekly sermon and visitations."

For generations, until recent times, most Scottish children could tell you, at least, the opening question and answer of the *Shorter Catechism* – "What is the chief end of man?" "Man's chief end is to glorify God and enjoy him forever."

Trial and Examination

Catechising was not an end in itself, although that very often became the case. It was designed to instruct people in matters of faith and doctrine. To be eligible to take communion, was dependent on their knowledge and understanding of such matters and prior to each communion parishioners would be examined by the minister and elders.

Dalgety Kirk did its best to celebrate communion at least once each year but sometimes that was difficult. In December 1652, the Kirk Session records note that because of the troubles caused by Cromwell's troops since the previous summer, communion had not been celebrated for some time. They resolved to remedy that fact but first had to ensure that the congregation had been examined. The minute shows no fear or favour being given to any person and it also shows them exercising a degree of compassion towards those who were older and lesser-educated. It is worth noting in full:

December 31st 1652, "The Sessione this day, taking to consideratione the tryall and examinatione off people in order to communione, doe think fitte: 1. That people off all ranks within the congregatione be examined; and none admitted to come to that ordinance that refuisse to submitt themselves to tryall: 2. That some off the most judicious of the elders be appoynted, from tyme to tyme, to be concurring with the minister in this work, that such as sall in any measure be found qualified, may be admitted, and others laid by for the present till further paines be taken upon them: 3. That people be tryed (1) in their knowledge off the grounds of religione, whether they be such as in some measure are able to discerne the Lord's bodie; (2) in the point of prayer, whether they be aiming in any measure at the seiking off God, and, if they be heads off families, whether they have prayer and God's worship in their families, yea what care they have to bring up their children in the knowledge of the Lord, according to their solemn engadgment at baptisme, and how they carie themselves towards their servants in things that relate to godliness; (3) that such as can reid be tried what paines they take to reid the Scriptures for the knowledge off the things of God; (4) whether people sanctifies the Lord's day from morning to night, how they waite upon the public ordinances, and what use they make off the word after hearing; (5) how they walk in their stationes, whether they follow the duties of their calling, whether they live without scandal and offence, especially if they be free of drunkenness, of swearing and prophaning the name of God, off mocking and contemning the exercise of godliness &c, and if in some measure their conversatione and walking be suitable to the Gospell; yea, iff their endeavour and desire tend that way; and the sessione, however they resolve to use tenderness toward such as are now come to years, and have beine bred up in ignorance, iff so be they in any measure concerned, have any good affection to the way of God, are labouring for more knowledge and live soberlie, yet they think that such as are young and have had the means off a better educatione ought to be exactly tryed and no admitted to the communion till they be in some measure qualifies, least by the sudden rush admitting off them they be hardened in sin and ignorance."

The following week Andrew Donaldson, along with John Moubray and Mr William Thomson, the laird of Blair, and tutor to the Earl of Moray's children, started the process in the Dalgety proper district. The elders were kept occupied and it took the Session nearly three months to complete the "tryall and examination" but the "re-examinations delayed for the present, becaus off the minister's present sickness and weakness". They restarted on 9th May and this phase lasted until July, "the Sessione considering that now the people have beine thryse gone throw, and examined in order to the communione, and that there be mony desirous and longing for that blessed ordinance doe appoynt the first dyett off it to be on the Lord's day, 24th off this instant".

Attending for examination was not a voluntary act, as the Synod of Fife made clear in October 1630, when they instructed all ministers to make public intimation that "all householders of al qualitie present themselves with their families to the examination before the Communion, otherwise to be excludit and debard from the Holy Table." In 1652, the General Assembly took matters a stage further, when it ordained that ministers and sessions "debar from the Lord's Table all such persons as are found not to walk suitably to the gospel and being convinced and admonished thereof do not conform."[2]

Preparation

Fulfilling the requirements of the examination was only one aspect. Communion had to be approached with the right attitude and any disagreements which parishioners had with each other had to be resolved before the sacrament was celebrated. To help focus peoples' minds the 1645 General Assembly instituted a service of Preparation for the Saturday prior to Communion. On 5th April 1645, Andrew Donaldson warned his congregation that "the Lord's Day following, the Communion was to be celebrate; and exhorted the people to be cairfull, in preparation this week, befoire, as also to be present the Setterday next, about two hours in the afternoon, at the sermon of preparation, and all that wants [lacks] tokens, are forbidden to approach the table".

Also common was the practice of observing a fast-day. Although fasting was not a tenet of the faith, it was believed that it helped to overcome the inherent sin present in everybody and concentrate the mind on spiritual matters. On 9th June 1654, the Session agreed that "the Thursday before the comunione to be keiped in a solemne fast for the sin and ignorance off God in the congregatione. And the Lord to be dealt with and soucht efter for his presence to the ensueing comunione".

The church had to be specially prepared and in June 1646, the minutes record money given to "the beddell 3*lb*" and "to ane woman that keepit the comunione cloath, 12s. and for dressing the table and formes, 8s." She would have been responsible for washing and ironing the tablecloths (using "smoothing" stones) and making sure that the layout was as it should be. Organising a Communion service was a major operation. Permanent communion tables were not yet a feature of church furniture, and a long table had to be constructed from wooden planks and trestles. Bread and wine had to be sourced and purchased and, once it was over, everything had to be cleared away.

Communion Tokens

The established law of the Church of Scotland was that no person was permitted to take communion unless they had been provided with a token. Tokens were only issued to parishioners who had been examined and found worthy. The process of examination was time-consuming and demanding and over time slackness crept in, with some people lacking the discipline to satisfy the pre-Communion examination and some, given their status, feeling there was no need for them to be examined. On 11th July 1653, the Session warned that "this day, having looked throw the Communion roll, and taken notice of those in the severall quarters of the paroch, that upone tryall and examination, have been found in some qualification for the communion, appoints tokens to be given to them, and all others laid by for the present. As also ordaines that none presume to come to the table, off whatever rank, or degree, without ane warrand and token from the Kirk sessione."

Younger people were not exempt from examination. In June 1654, "some young men and young women not entered yet to the communion, appoynted to be present the next day and seriouslie exhorted to studie the knowledge of God and follow the exercises off pietie, and so to receive tokens".

As a general rule, tokens were issued to intending communicants by the minister and elders in church or in the place of examination, with a strict record kept as to who had been allocated a token. Metal tokens had replaced written 'tickets', which were open to forgery, around the beginning of the seventeenth century, and most Kirk Sessions had their own mould for producing lead, tin, pewter or, occasionally, brass tokens. *(Fig 12)* To prevent people taking the Sacrament without approval new tokens would be cast each year, usually by melting down and remoulding old tokens. In any event, it was the custom that new tokens were cast when a new minister arrived in the parish.

Communion

The early Reformers were keen to establish a sacrament that did not in any way resemble Roman Catholic practice. The *First Book of Discipline* stated "But plaine it is… we judge that sitting at a table is most convenient to that holy action". They affirmed the need for people to break and eat the bread and "drinke the cup of wine" together. It was "urged that the people sat 'weel back' and took a 'deep draught' and that this was done as a protest against the withholding of the cup from the laity prior to the Reformation".[3] Needless to say, a fair amount of wine was needed, as the cups were refilled many times from large flagons.[4]

For his first communion after ordination, Andrew Donaldson anticipated that a large number would attend as he informed the congregation on 12th April 1645, that "there would be two sermones in the forenoone, and therefore desyred that families wold divide themselves according to the two dyets, and appoynted these that were to come in the morning to be present at half sex [half-past five], at which time sermon wald begin".[5] At such an early hour, lighting, such as candle or torches, would have been required in the church.

With an increased size of congregation and multiple services, Andrew Donaldson required help and a Session minute of 7th June 1646 records, "this day the comunione is celebrate. Mr. Robert Key, minister at Dunfermline, preached the doctrine of preparatione the day befoir. Mr. Patrick Gillespie, minister at Kirkaldie, preached in the morning and efternoone, and the mid dyet served by our owin minister". The form of worship in Dalgety was similar to other parish kirks of the time. Andrew Donaldson, or the visiting minister, would conduct worship as usual from the pulpit and after the sermon move to stand at the communion table.

At this point in the service, elders would bring in the bread and wine from a temporary store outside the church. In April 1645 "William Logane and Robert Andersone, two elders, are appointed to sie [look out] for good wyne and bread and to be cairfull off it the day of the communion." Rather than using the gray bread, eaten by ordinary families, the bread would have been the more expensive white bread, probably baked specially for the occasion and made from wheat flour, procured specifically for that purpose. It would have been cut up and placed in large salvers or basins.

The wine was "claret unmixed with water and has been poured into the wide silver mazer provided by the heritors".[6] The wine used may either have been imported to Leith and fetched from there by boat or quite likely purchased from a merchant in Burntisland which, certainly by 1680, was importing 'wood from Norway, flax from Flanders [and] French wine'.[7] The elders were responsible for the quality of the bread and wine and it was not unknown for elders to have to 'taste' the wine beforehand to ensure it was good enough.

Donaldson would have issued an invitation to all who were contrite to communicate, and delivered a "stern warning to the impenitent, the unforgiving and the hardened sinners not to eat and drink damnation to themselves." The General Assembly in 1645 had decreed that the service was to be conducted in silence except "the minister making a short exhortation at every table ...onely when the minister expresseth some few short sentences, suitable to the present condition of the communicants in the receiving and while the tables are dissolving and filling there be alwayes singing of some portion of a Psalme, according to the custome". Nobody was "permitted to go forth whill the whole tables be served and the blessing pronounced, unlesse it be for cases of necessity".

The table would have run the length of the kirk and been solemnly fenced-off and guarded by a 'traverse' of stakes with an entrance at each end.[8] (Fig 13) Two elders would have stood guard at the entrances to the table to ensure that no unworthy person was admitted and with Dalgety Kirk having two doors on its south wall, they probably monitored the communicants by allowing those with tokens entry through one door and after communion, exiting through the other. A careful note was kept by the elders of those who had attended and those who failed to turn up. These lists were examined by the Session with 'delinquents' receiving a visit from the elder.

Given the infrequency with which communion was held in most churches many flocked from neighbouring parishes and provided they had the necessary testimonial from their own minister they were admitted to the table. On such occasions the kirk could not contain the numbers wishing to attend and those waiting outside in the kirkyard[9] would have been addressed by one of the visiting ministers, preaching to them from a 'tent'.[10]

In Aberdour, where Mr Robert Bruce was minister, the teaching and pastoral care were apparently of a lesser standard as some people were prepared to walk to Dalgety for spiritual food. Others clearly felt that Dalgety was getting above itself as Andrew Donaldson had to resort to complaining in Presbytery about the treatment visitors to Dalgety were receiving when, after Communion, they returned home through Aberdour. Mr Bruce was forced to investigate and Aberdour Kirk Session recorded the outcome: 16th June 1654, "The session resolve that whosoever in this parish shall calumniate those who go to the Communion of Dalgatie shall be punished exemplarily and shall be made to pay according to their ability."

To complete the communion season, a service of thanksgiving was generally held on the Monday, following which many ministers (and it is not known if Donaldson was one) celebrated with a 'sumptuous Monday dinner' at the manse, with leading parishioners as guests.

Communion Cups

In the early days of Donaldson's ministry, there is no record of what cups or plates were used. "The Church seems to have considered it of little import whether the Communion cups were vessels devoted at other times to secular purposes or reserved for ecclesiastical use… there was no particular reverence for vessels which had been used at Communion services."[11] Cups were often borrowed from landed proprietors or local hostelries. There was a practical aspect to using such 'common' cups as, following the Reformation, many of the pre-Reformation relics 'had a lowered sense of sanctity' and were sold to raise money for the 'common weal'. Some were destroyed, others were misappropriated or melted down and some were simply lost. With the church in a poverty-stricken state, there were no resources to replace them.

By the early seventeenth century some churches were beginning to commission Communion cups for their own use and Dunfermline Abbey had two silver cups made in 1628 and another two the following year. When Donaldson examined the need for Communion cups in Dalgety, he probably had in mind the 1617 Act of Parliament that required parish churches to acquire "vessels made of an appropriate fine metal". He commissioned two beaten-silver communion cups *(Fig 14)* and in April 1659 the Kirk Session paid "out off the Box for two Communion Cups brought from Edr, one hundred and nyn *libs*. eight *sh*."

The cups were made by Edward Cleghorn, one of Edinburgh's pre-eminent goldsmiths. Cleghorn had been admitted to the Incorporation of Goldsmiths, Edinburgh in 1649 and, prestigiously, held the office of deacon three times. *(Fig 15)* His items were generally regarded as "fine pieces of superior quality."[12] Dalgety's Communion cups bore the deacon's punch of James Fairbairne, admitted to the Incorporation of Goldsmiths, Edinburgh in May 1641. They carried an inscription, "FOR x THE x COMVNION x OF x DAIGETIE x KIRK 1659". The bowls of the cups were described as having a diameter of $6^{5/8}$ inches; depth of $2^{1/16}$ inches; height 7 inches; and diameter of foot 4 inches. The hallmarks on them were reported to be upside down.[13]

Chapter 10

———

Discipline
and Repentance

Discipline

Donaldson had no intention of letting his elders stray from their tasks, and keeping the pressure on families to catechise and attend worship was one way in which he attempted to ensure that there was no backsliding or straying from the path of righteousness. In the *Second Book of Discipline* the elders' duties included, "visitation of the sick, of prisoners and the poor, catechising in the homes, assisting at the sacraments and reading the Scriptures and prayers…". Alexander Henderson, in his 1641 treatise, considered that elders were also called "… for the exercising of disciplining and governing the whole congregation."

Keeping the Peace

Kirk Sessions throughout the land developed an unhealthy obsession with bringing to book those found wanting and Dalgety was no exception. 20th April 1645, "Compeared this day before the Session Cristian Lyall and Margaret Wilsone, who were summoned for flyeting and casting off ail upone other, immediatelie after the receiving off the communione, quho confessed their sinne. The Sessione, considering the miscariage to be great, ordanis them first to show their penitencie befoir the Session upone their knees, and the next Lord's-day to goe to the publick place of repentence that the congregatione may be satisfied; and upone their grief and penitencie they received againe as members thereoff."

Flyeting was a grave misdemeanour and for repeated offences, a person might find themselves placed in the 'branks', a device clamped over the head with a projection placed inside the mouth to prevent the person from talking or expressing opinions. It was used overwhelmingly on women. Often attached to the 'branks' was a chain to lead the woman in public with a view to teaching her a lesson but which, in fact, added further shame and disgrace upon her.

Where scandalous behaviour could be linked to another misdemeanour, the Kirk Session took full advantage. On 31st May 1646, "The Sessione having considered the mater betwixt John Cuninghame and Janet Blyth, and examined witnesses, finds that Janet Blyth has cursed the said John and his wyff in a vile, unchristian, and scandalous manner; therefor appoynts the said Janet publicklie to satisfie the next Setterday, being the day of preparatione before the communione, and John Cuninghame's wyff is put to private humiliatione befor the Sessione, becaus nothing is cleared [proved] against her but that once or twice, before the minister's admissione, she caused knock beir on the Lord's day. And the said parties are ordeined to be reconciled one to another before the comunione."

Reconciliation was a key theme for the Kirk Session, and it endeavoured to ensure that there was harmony in the community. In June 1648, John Clerk and Helene Scot were cited "for refuising reconciliation with their neighbours, before the communion, and therefor suspending themselves." The Session decided to investigate and the following month, John Dyck and his wife, the aggrieved neighbours, were rebuked, in private, by the Session but John Clerk and Helen Scott were forced to make public repentance "for their slighting of the communione."

The Session was diligent in keeping the peace, as on 28th June 1646, "Compeirs Barbara Stennous in Barnhill, and acknowledges her breach off the Lord's day, in carieing foules." On 6th September 1646, "The Sessione considering that the Lord's day is profaned in the efternoone by people coming to the towne loanes and sitting or standing there, in idle and unprofitable conferences, ordeanes that every elder go throu his quarter and see this curbed: that all keip their families for repetition of sermones, prayer and other spiritual dueties: and that, efter admonition, quhoever sall continue in such fruitless exercises and conferences, sall be delated as prophaners of the Lord's day."

In common with other parishes in Fife, the Sabbath, in Dalgety, was sacrosanct. Records indicate that Sabbath-breaking was an item high on the Kirk Session's agenda and heavily punished, along with sexual offences and verbal assaults, including flyeting and swearing. Sabbath-breaking was often of more concern to the elders than more serious offences. Aspects such as drink, violence and communion absence trailed far behind in the Session's attention, as did disobedience and religious ignorance.

Sexual Offences

If flyeting was a grave misdemeanour, adultery was a serious offence and offenders were heavily punished, although punishment was often a one-sided affair. In April 1666, in a case recorded by the Synod of Fife, "As for that woman who lay in adultery with John Auchterlonie and was deprehendit in the bed with him… [the Synod] declared, that the woman with whom John Auchterlonie fell in adultery, was sent away to Barbados". John Auchterlonie, presumably, went free.

Fornication was prevalent. It was regarded as less serious than adultery but still a matter of censure and often did not come to light until the woman showed signs of pregnancy. The Session was keen to ensure that sex outside marriage was firmly dealt with as, apart from the sinfulness of the act, it often led to single-parent families, with their concomitant poverty and dependence on the parish for support. 16th October 1698, "John Johnstone and Margaret Henderson in Otterstoun compeared before the congregation and were rebuked for the sin of fornication before marriage." Where the Session felt they needed advice recourse would be made to Dunfermline Presbytery or the Synod of Fife. In October 1633, the Synod refused permission for a widower to marry [his mistress], "because he committed adultery twyse with her, and children procreat by her in his wyffs time, quhen schoe was living and hes committed fornication with her also since the death of his umquhile wyff."

Civil Magistrate

Every so often, the Session would issue a blanket warning to the congregation. In early March 1646, they had drunkenness in their sights, "the Sessione this day taking into consideratione the abuse of drunkeness, do estatute and ordaine, that quhosoever sall be found guiltie heirefter, for the first fault sall be brought befoir the Sessione, there to be rebuiked and gravely admonished, and that thereafter, *toties quoties*, they sall be bro[t] to publick repentance in case they sall fall again in that abuse".

Two weeks later and swearing and blaspheming were a cause for concern and a week after that the cat fights among women caught their attention where, "scolding among women wes ane great abuse and scandall in the congregatione, thocht fit that besyd publick repentance each one that sall heirafter be guiltie of the said scandal sall pay *toties quoties* 10s. and recomends it to the magistrate".

Civil magistrates in parishes had come into force as a result of an Act of the Parliament held in Perth in 1645, "[where] it was enacted that swearing, drunkenness, and mocking of piety should be dealt with as civil offences; and at the same Parliament it was provided that magistrates and justices should be appointed in every congregation for the purpose of carrying the Act into effect."[1] The General Assembly of 1648 recommended congregations to make use of these Acts, and magistrates and justices were appointed in the parish of Dalgety.

The Kirk Session had no legal power to fine parishioners for crimes which they may have committed. It could enforce 'public repentance' and levy a fine for moral sins but where the cases were outwith its bounds, it had to report them to the civil magistrate. On 11th February 1650 "Alexander Reid compears and gives in a bill on William Steinstone, reporting that he did sclandour him in calling him a trewker lowne, &c. The Sessione delays their answer to it whill the civill magistrat plays his part, sieing there hes beine blood betwixt them."

Performing Repentance

The punishment for misdemeanours depended on the severity of the incident. As well as fines, it could require a person to be dressed in sackcloth or linen and sit, kneel or stand, on the repentance stool *(Fig 16)* at the foot of the pulpit, be reprimanded by the minister and face the public humiliation of the congregation. It could mean a period in the 'branks' or in the stocks or 'jugges', a form of iron collar, chained to the Kirk wall. Wilful boys would often feel the birch, although it would be up to the civil magistrate, the laird of Fordell, to mete out the punishment.

An Act of the Parliament of Scotland in 1593 pronounced that prisons, stocks and 'jugges' were to be provided at every Parish Kirk, so that idle beggars and wrongdoers could be placed in penitence, and those attending Sunday services could witness them. In bringing people to repentance in such a public manner, shaming or humiliation was not the Church's prime aim, although that was a definite by-product of its actions. Its desire was to make people acknowledge their sin, repent of it, and allow them to be fully restored to God, the Church and their fellow community members.[2]

A high standard of moral behaviour and good conduct was particularly expected from elders and deacons but even they succumbed to human weakness, sometimes with serious consequences. In October 1650, the Session had to consider "a scandellous rayiotte acted by James Dewar, Elder, and John Jamesone, Deacone, who on the last Lord's day, quhen the congregatione was coming to divyne service, did fall out ane with another to foull words, and efterwards did fall a streaking ane another. The Sessione before they medle with it apoynts the minister and ye rewling elder to represent it to the presbitry, and to seek their advyse in that mater".

The miscreants were called before the Kirk Session to account for their behaviour but "James Dewar callit upon compeirs not, is apoynted to be cited *pro secundo*. John Jameson compeirs and confesses his scandillous carriage; John Stinstone is callit upone for his accessioune to y[e] rayiott, compeirs, goeing about to denay the same is at last convinced; James Danskeine compeirs and confesses his accessioune y[e] to and the sessioune considering y[e] laird of Blair's part in that rayiott, esteims him in som degree to be guiltie".

The Session had no fear or favour in administering justice. Elders, deacons and lairds who overstepped the mark had to face the same punishment as ordinary members of the congregation. Riotous elders forced to appear 'on their knees', bare-headed, bare-footed and dressed in sackcloth or linen was a severe punishment. In a community where everybody wore some form of headgear, appearing without a hat indicated subservience, going barefoot allied them with the poor and wearing sackcloth completed the humiliating experience.

With exercising discipline in the parish, supporting the minister in his work, visiting parishioners every month, looking after the school and its pupils and caring for the poor of the parish, the Kirk Session was kept occupied. Donaldson expected much from his elders, most of whom were working men, but no more than he was prepared to give himself. As a man of the Covenant, he was determined that his parish would be well-schooled in matters of faith and morality and that his parishioners would walk closely with God.

Lady Callendar Admonished

Reproving parishioners was one thing, dealing with the nobility was another. Lady Margaret Hay was the widow of Alexander Seton, 1st Earl of Dunfermline who had died in 1622. She had continued to live for part of the year at Dalgety House – latterly, with permission from Charles I, by a letter dated 4th June 1635 in which, "she was allowed to 'retaine the place dew to her as Countess of Dunfermline'."[3] Dalgety House lay just to the north of the Kirk, and was described as "repaired and beautifyed with gardens by chancellor Seaton, Earl of Dunfermling".[4] In a writ of 1611 it was described as the "Manor place of Dalgatie" and in 1677, it was noted that while the garden and walks were in very good order "the house is little and very low, having no chambers in it, though the few rooms there are, are in indifferent good order."[5]

Eleven years after Seton's death, Margaret Hay remarried. (*Fig 5*) Her second husband was James, Lord Livingston of Almond,[6] the third son of the first Earl of Linlithgow. As part of an arrangement between King Charles I and the Covenanters to suppress details of a potential Royalist *coup d'état,* Livingston had been created first Earl of Callendar in 1641. He was one of the Scottish army's commanders, although he had an undistinguished military record and a slightly untrustworthy reputation.

A high social standing did not help avoid the scrutiny of the Kirk Session and on 17th June 1649, when Lady Callendar decided to "tarry at home on the Lord's day" the minister and an elder were appointed to call on her "and admonish her". Normally, the Session would have summoned people to meet them, and by visiting her they were probably aware of the sensitivity of her position, but the Session was making it clear that regardless of her status Lady Callendar was not above its jurisdiction.

She treated the Session with a certain disdain as, when the minister called, he discovered she had moved to one of her other residences. Perhaps, she did not relish the prospect of a reprimand by those she would have classed as her social inferiors. There was also the suggestion that she absented herself because her husband was fighting in England on the side of the forces of the Engagement, a position Andrew Donaldson and the Covenanters opposed. Four months later, Lady Callendar returned to Dalgety and the minister and the laird of Blair were again appointed to visit. On 24th October she was "admonished for not keeping the Kirk [and] is referred to Presbyterie".[7]

Lady Callendar was clearly not intimidated by the Kirk Session as that same month she decided to embellish the decorations in the Seton loft with painted images in the windows. The loft had been built by Chancellor Seton and amounted to what was almost a small Scottish tower house at the west end of the church. The lower part of the extension was the family burial vault, while upstairs there was a large room with a viewing platform into the body of the kirk and off that, facing the sea, was a small with-drawing room, complete with fireplace. In both rooms, there were panels on the walls and above the windows, one of which (probably the one on the gable end of the church) was "rudely emblazoned [with] the heraldic arms" of the Earl of Dunfermline.[8] There would have been other painted panels and tapestries or wall-hangings and possibly rugs or carpets on the floor.

The wrath of the Kirk Session was aroused with her painted images and the laird of Blair was appointed on 1st November 1649 to call on her "… and desire that no novelties be put upone her loft, till the presbytrie be acquainted with it." Presbytery recoiled at the thought of such images appearing in a Protestant church and retribution was swift. Just over two weeks later the Session "appoynts the minister and ruling elder to represent the mater of my ladie Callendar's casements, in the foir part off her loft, the idolatrous and superstitious images in the glasse windows, that they may caus take them doune."

To the Presbyterian mind of that time, religious images were no more or less than evidence of leanings towards Roman Catholicism. Chancellor Seton, through his upbringing, had always had Roman Catholic tendencies, but he had foresworn those in favour of Presbyterianism and service at the court of King James VI. Memories ran long and deep and the Session probably held more than a suspicion about his widow.

She continued to live in the parish until "The Lady Callendar, the E. of Dunfermlings mother depairted this life at Dalgety in Fyfe and was interred Jan. 20 [1660] in the daytime, att Dalgety."[9] She died at the age of sixty-eight and was buried in the Seton vault, along with her first husband. Her son, Charles, second Earl of Dunfermline, was also laid to rest there in 1672.

Chapter 11

Witchcraft
and Superstition

Witches

With significant events happening locally and nationally, 1649 was proving to be an eventful year. Lady Callendar was the least of it, as the spectre of witchcraft had raised its ugly head. Witchcraft had been banned since 1563, when an Act of the Parliament of Scotland had made both the practice of witchcraft, and consulting with witches, capital offences. Through the efforts of the General Assembly this Act was strengthened and in 1649 a new witchcraft act not only ratified the 1563 Act but extended it. Those who consulted with the "Devil and familiar spirits" were now subject to capital punishment.

Witchcraft was seen as a supernatural evil throughout Europe, and many countries shared common elements of witch-beliefs where "individual witches [are regarded as] evil persons and individual acts of witchcraft are specific evil acts which are performed through supernatural powers. The characteristic ingredients of an act of witch-craft are that the witch should feel malice towards an individual who has offended her and that through cursing, incantation, sorcery, or the sheer force of her ill will, should cause illness or death to livestock, family or person of the individual concerned."[1]

A witch[2] was predominantly a poor, middle-aged, or elderly woman, generally near the bottom of the social structure, living a normal life in the villages and burghs. She was often regarded as someone who knew various charms and who could heal different ailments. As such she was a valued member of the community but at the same time one who was feared because of her seeming 'supernatural' powers. From being healers and charmers how did they come to be regarded as demonic forces?

Superstitions abounded as to the reasons people became ill or animals died, and the devil became a focus for the cause of such events. Much of the reformed Church's early belief centred on its position that Jesus Christ had overcome forces of evil in the world and that the works of the devil had been superseded by the power of God. Good had to prevail over evil, in both thought and practice, otherwise the forces of darkness would prevail.

The Church, supported by the nobility and perhaps encouraged by them, was determined to make sure that was the case. In its desire to achieve the godly society, the Church had introduced a "system of religious terrorism" which suppressed all opposition, frowned upon any form of enjoyment, "numbed the intellect"… to such an extent that its "teaching necessarily created the superstition of witchcraft".[3]

The Session minutes record many cases where people were rebuked for their behaviour and for making accusations of one kind or another. What seemed to be a common trait throughout the country was that people accused of witchcraft had a sharp tongue aligned with a quarrelsome nature.

In Scotland, witch-hunting reached almost epidemic proportions at various points during the seventeenth century, generally during periods of national panic, with 1649 ranking as the worst. Fife was a hotbed of witch-hunting with Dunfermline Presbytery recording the most activity. Unlike Inverkeithing, which had a history of witch-hunting going back to the 1620s, Dalgety had never been an area of persecution.

Dalgety's Witch-hunt

Dalgety's witch-hunt was short-lived, starting on 22nd April 1649 when the Kirk Session, "hearing that one Robert Maxwell [of Little Fordell], put from the communione for ignorance, hes beene confessing some things that looks like witch-craft, appoynts him to be examined by the minister and four elders." The investigation is duly carried out and the following week, "the minister reports that, Rob[r] Maxwell having confessed witchcraft and paction with the Devill, he hes the last Presbytrie day read the depositions to the Presbytrie and is appoynted to use means to procure ane comissione off estaits, to some gentlemen, for the further tryall and judging off the said Robert".

The process of trying a witch was complicated. Although Kirk Sessions may have been prime instigators in searching them out and bringing them forward for questioning, the power of life or death lay with a Commission set up by the Privy Council. Commissions to local landowners and officials were the most common way of trying a witch. They would receive information from a Kirk Session, take evidence and question suspects and witnesses and then pronounce judgement. In Robert Maxwell's case, the Commissioners were notable people: Sir John Henderson, the laird of Fordell, Sir John Erskine of Otterstone, Alexander Spittall, laird of Leuchat, Andrew Dickson, Alexander Henderson, Robert Logan, William Oliphant and John Scott.[4]

Maxwell was found guilty and sentenced to death and in his final confession before his commission implicated others. He accused Isobel Scogian, Margaret Orrock, Isobel Bennet and Isobel Kelloch, wife of Archibald Collier, who had already been accused by women who had been burned as witches in Aberdour. The Kirk Session wasted no time in investigating and under questioning Isobel Scogian claimed that she had been suffering a "sore and vehement paine in her heid" ever since she had borrowed a courche from Isobel Kelloch. Kelloch, meanwhile, had sought her forgiveness and "sate down upon her knees and said thryse oure, Lord, send the thy health" after which, Isobel Scogian confessed she was "much eased".

This was of little import to the Kirk Session and they concluded that "… taking to consideratione that Issobell Keiloch, spous to Archibald Colzier in Daigetie, hes bene this mony years under ane evill report for witchcraft, and that now she hes been delated by Rob[r] Maxwell, late Warlock… he avowing that he hes sene her at meetings with the devil… do recomend it to my ladie Callendar, lyfrentrix off Daigetie, and William Lithell her officer, to cause put her in firmance that she may be tryed and brought to confessione".

In another example of the character of the woman who had defied the Session, Lady Callendar, on whose land Isobel Kelloch lived, refused to pay any costs associated with her imprisonment or trial, as the records of 17th June 1649 indicate; "The Sessione appoynts ane comissione to be procured for the further tryall and judging of Issobell Keiloch, confessing witch, since the Presbytrie hes seine her confessions, and have found them such as may bring her to ane assysse; and becaus she is ane pure bodie the charges to be taken out off the boxe, as the ladie Callendar, on whose ground she lives, refuses to bear them." The Kirk Session is forced to pay the costs and on 1st July 1649 the records note that these amounted to 24*lib* 4*s* 4*d*. *(Fig 17)*

Executing a witch was a costly business, although Isobel Kelloch's fees were relatively inexpensive. The imprisonment, trial and execution of Margaret Dunham in Lauder in 1649 came to 92*lib* 14*s* Scots but as she had savings of 27*lib* she was forced to pay these towards the cost of her own execution.[5] For some, like the witch-pricker, the carter, the hangman and the watchmen, witch-hunting was good business. The morality of witch-hunting was of little concern to them.

With the number of cases coming before Kirk Sessions within Dunfermline Presbytery and with the baillies of Inverkeithing having appealed to the Synod of Fife for "help in examining and bringing witches to confession", the Presbytery in May 1649 took the unusual step of petitioning Parliament: "… humbly supplicates we, the moderator, other brethren and ruling elders of the presbytery of Dunfermline, and more particularly the parishes of Inverkeithing and Dalgety…"

Their intention was to have a blanket commission that would cover all witchcraft cases instead of making an application for each individual case – and they did not want to have to pay for them; "that standing commissions shall be supplicated for in such emergencies, or at least it may please your lords that we may have commissions gratis least through the want of monies this work which the Lord has so miraculously begun and so wisely heretofore carried on".[6] Presbytery was of the opinion that witch-hunting was a divine instruction with the brethren carrying out the Lord's work. The supplication was refused.

These commissions had the power to approve the use of torture, a form of medieval barbarism. It was widely used, with sleep deprivation as the most common form. In Inverkeithing, a Commission hearing the case of Marion Durie, daughter of George Durie, Town Clerk, opposed the use of torture in any shape or form. As a result, Dunfermline Presbytery found "the people much wronged and the worke of God in the descoverie of witchcraft much obstructed". The Church would go to any lengths to gain a confession and Presbytery sent the minister, Mr William Bruce, to Edinburgh to have the decision overturned. Presbytery won the appeal, but the Committee of Estates ordered it to be sparing in the use of torture.

Many so-called witches faced degrading treatment including the use of 'brodder's' needles for the purpose of discovering 'the devil's mark' – a place on the body that was insensitive to pain. The witch-pricker would use his needles to find such a numb spot, often no more than a mole, and thereby 'prove' the person was a witch. John Kincaid was a noted, and notorious, witch-pricker, from Tranent, who was recorded as working in Dunfermline Presbytery in 1649 and may have been involved in some of the Dalgety witch trials. He was known to be in Dirleton in June of that year as he provided a testimonial to the Privy Council, boasting of his prowess; "I, John Kincaid, had some skill and dexteritie in trying of divellis marke in the personis of such as wer suspect of witchcraft…"[7]

Another Commission was granted in July 1649 "for the trial of 'certaine personis guiltie of the cryme of witchcraft' within the parish of Dalgety". Apart from these women, whose names are unknown, two final cases arose in Dalgety, those of Christian Garlick and Isabel Glen. The former had already appeared before the Session, as recently as 24th June where, as she had been previously admonished, she was ordered to be rebuked and reported to the civil magistrate for further action.

Isabel Glen's case was highlighted by Richard Pickston, a servant to the Earl of Moray. Pickston was facing a reprimand from the Kirk Session for having visited some of the accused witches in prison and he told the session "… that he had, some time before this, bought a cow from Isabel's husband; and that as his wife was milking the said cow, a few days after she was brought home, in an instant the animal fell down dead, without being known to be under the influence of any disease". In his statement, Pickston implied that Isabel Glen had bewitched the cow, a view seemingly corroborated by his wife, who had hinted that some of the neighbours had said that "Isabel was not well pleased that they should have got the cow".

On such superstitious comments – headaches caused by a head covering or a cow dying during milking – human life hung in the balance.

Condemned witches faced a death that "… was almost too revolting to bear description. The wretched creatures were first strangled on a gibbet, around the foot of which were piled heather, turf, wood, and sometimes coals and gunpowder; and then the pile was fired and their bodies burned to ashes".[8] Burning witches alive was not a common occurrence and, as far as is known, did not happen in Dalgety. The site of witch-burning in Dalgety is reputed to be on the southernmost approach to Fordell Castle at a place called "The Witch Knowe".

Margaret Henderson, Lady Pitadro

In the neighbouring parish of Inverkeithing, the minister, Mr William Bruce, in July 1649 accused the wives of the town's baillies and Margaret Henderson, sister of Sir John Henderson, laird of Fordell, of witchcraft. Her brother was one of Andrew Donaldson's elders and Donaldson would likely have had some discussions with Sir John and Mr Bruce over this case. Mr Bruce's unhealthy attitude to witch-hunting not only incurred the wrath of the Burgh Council but made him neglect his parish duties to the extent that the following year he was deposed by Dunfermline Presbytery for "gross neglect of the special duties of his ministry".

In many ways, despite coming from a good family, Margaret Henderson was unfortunate. Her marriage dowry to her husband, Sir William Echline of Pitadro, in 1597, was recorded as 4,000 merks and her marriage contract was signed by no less than the Earl of Mar.[9] She seemed set for a good marriage, but her husband incurred huge debts and as a result he lost his lands. He died in 1623, leaving his widow to a life of penury.

Lady Pitadro, fearing that the accusation would lead to her punishment if she remained in Inverkeithing, moved to Edinburgh, where she was subsequently apprehended and placed in the Tollbooth to await trial. The Committee of Estates, following a supplication from the General Assembly, issued a command to Mr Thomas Nicholson, His Majesty's advocate, to proceed with her arraignment before the justice-general and "if she be guilty of the said crime, to convict and condemn her, pronounce sentence of death against, cause strangle her, and burn her body, and do every requisite sic cases."

Her end was both sad and unexpected: "after remaining in prison for a time, [she] being in health at night was upon the morning found dead. It was thought and spoken by many that she wronged herself, either by strangling or poison; but we leave that to the judgement of the great day."[10]

In December of that year, Inverkeithing Kirk Session placed information before Dunfermline Presbytery regarding the burial of Margaret Henderson. Witches were not accorded burial in consecrated ground, but it appeared as though Lady Pitadro had been, and Presbytery instructed a committee to investigate the circumstances. In January 1650, her brother the Laird of Fordell and two others, "declarat thair sense of oversight" and six others "were made sensible off their fault for countenancing the burial of Margt Hendersone, sometime Ladie Pittadro, under the scandal of witchcraft".[11] Blood ties had proved to be too strong, even for Dunfermline Presbytery.

Superstitions

Much of what was determined as witchcraft then would now be regarded as mere superstition but in the seventeenth century superstitions were not to be taken lightly and even extended to such as bonfires and burials. On 4th April 1648, the Synod of Fife records concern about "the kindling of bonfyres upoun superstitious nightis, viz., Midsomer and Alhallowmes" with the result that "the Assemblie ordaines, that the severall Presbytries tak exact notice of abuses in that kynd within ther boundis; and that the severall heretouris, and in ther absence the principall tenentis, with the concurrance of the elderis in eache paroche, cairfullie observe delinquentis, that they may be censured according to the acts of the Kirk".

As far as burials were concerned, once a person had died, it was the belief that, "the body should not utterly perish but rise againe" and the fate of a person depended on whether they had found salvation and departed life "in the faith of Christ Jesus", or died "in unbeleefe" to face the wrath of God. Prayers for the dead were viewed by John Calvin as "without warrant in Scripture" and the *First Book of Discipline* expanded that view when it stated that masses, and other rites, should be avoided, as well as "all other prayers over or for the dead, which are not onely superstitious and vaine, but are also idolatry and doe repugne to the plaine Scriptures of God".

It regarded a funeral sermon as nourishing superstition and rejected singing or reading at the graveside; "we think it most expedient that the dead be conveyed to the place of burial with some honest company of the kirk, without either singing or reading". That sentiment was reinforced by the *Directory of Public Worship* (1645) where it stated, "praying, reading and singing, both going to and at the grave… are in no way beneficial to the dead and have proved many ways hurtful to the living. Therefore, let all such things be laid aside."

This may explain the Synod's view of 3rd April 1650 as it tried to determine the circumstances surrounding another burial associated with the Henderson family. "The Presbiterie of Dunfermline, being removit for censure, are approven. And because some information was given to the Synode anent some superstitious rites usit in the burial of the late Laird of Fordell,[12] the Presbiterie of Dunfermline are ordinit to inquire thairanent".[13]

Superstitions continued to abound but the pain, misery and suffering of witch-hunting in Dalgety had been short-lived and by the end of July 1649 it had run its course. Witches had been tried on nine occasions, on two of these with more than one unnamed person involved. Thirteen witches were burned in Dalgety, while in Scotland, over three hundred people were executed in 1649, most of them in Fife.

With all that, and with suspicions about which side people were on and where their loyalties lay, it was no wonder there was a degree of panic and some unrest. There were good reasons why the population was unsettled and good reasons why people should seek to take their frustrations out on the less fortunate in their midst – witch-hunting provided just such an outlet.

(Fig 1) A church in Dalgety has been in existence since at least 1178 when it was allocated to the Augustinian Priory on Inchcolm. The earliest surviving stonework is thought to date from the thirteenth century, but it has been so extensively altered [to make it suitable for Presbyterian worship] that there is little trace of any medieval aspects. The Seton loft and burial vault at the west end of the kirk were added in the early part of the seventeenth century.

(Fig 2) The pulpit recess is on the south wall where remains of plasterwork can still be seen. The light from the window would have illuminated the minister's papers. The colonnaded memorial to the left is that of Lady Janet Menstrie.

(Fig 3) This headstone shows a symbol of immortality in the form of a winged soul. The crown above a hammer is an indication that the man was a member of the Hammermen's Guild, a blacksmith.

(Fig 4) Alexander Seton, Lord Fyvie, Chancellor of Scotland from 1604–1622. He was created 1st Earl of Dunfermline by James VI & I in 1605. (by Marcus Gheeraerts 1561-1635/36, Flemish, oil on canvas, 1610 © National Galleries of Scotland)

(Fig 5) Lady Margaret Hay, Countess of Dunfermline; later Lady Callendar. This portrait was painted when she was twenty three, eight years after she had married Alexander Seton. (by Marcus Gheeraerts 1561-1635/36, Flemish, oil on canvas, 1615 © Collection of Dunedin Public Art Gallery, New Zealand)

(Fig 6) ALEXANDER SETONIUS, FERMELINODUNI COMES, SCOTIAE CANCELLARIUS, OBIIT 66 ANNO AETATIS SUAE, 16 JULY 1622. (Alexander Seton, Earl of Dunfermline, and Chancellor of Scotland, died 16th July 1622, aged 66 years.) (© reproduced by permission Historic Environment Scotland)

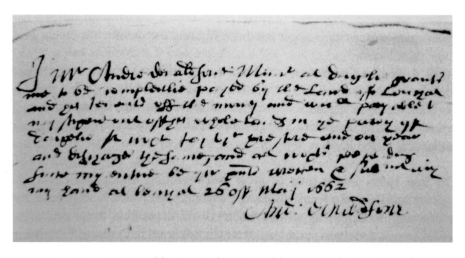

(Fig 7) Receipt signed by Mr Andrew Donaldson on 26th May 1662, for payment of his stipend out of the lands of Leuchat. Henderson Muniments (GD172/1531/2); (reproduced by permission of the National Records of Scotland)

(Fig 8) The Parish of Dalgety, with a distribution of elders' quarters, or districts, as they might have been around 1645–1650. The elder for each quarter would have been responsible for about twelve households.

(Fig 9) Detail from John Ainslie's map of the County of Fife, 1775, shows the position of the Manse to the west of Dalgety Kirk. Dalgety House and Donibristle (Dinnybirrsal) House are clearly marked, as is Cockairnie House, Fordell Castle and Fordell Mill. (Reproduced by permission of the National Library of Scotland)

(Fig 10) Children would be required to work on farms such as this at various times throughout the year. This shows a farmstead in the Dunfermline area c. 1690. (John Slezer, Theatrum Scotiae, c. 1690; Reproduced by permission of the National Library of Scotland)

Bell in.cot West Gable   Detail of Lettering 8ᶜ on Bell   Scale of   Feet

(Fig 11) O Mater Dei, Memento Mei; inscription round the
base of the bell that once hung in Dalgety Kirk and now
hangs in the bell-cote of St Fillan's Church, Aberdour.

(Fig 12) Oldest surviving Communion token from Dalgety Kirk.
On the obverse is 'D' for Dalgety, with the reverse showing the date
of 1700. (© National Museums of Scotland A-1944.88)

(Fig 13) The communion table was 'fenced off' and guarded by elders
to prevent those without a communion token sharing in the sacrament.
(by kind permission of the Church of Scotland, Life and Work magazine)

(Fig 14) The Communion cup, a mazer by design, was illustrated by Rev Thomas Burns in his Old Scottish Communion Plate (Large page edition)

(Fig 15) Edward Cleghorn's mark as the maker of the cup (L) and James Fairbairne's mark (R), as Deacon of the Incorporation of Goldsmiths of Einburgh were inscribed on the base.

(Fig 16) Penitents' seat, Holy Trinity Church, St Andrews, seventeenth century. (reproduced by permission, Library, University of St Andrews)

(Fig 17) Extract from Kirk Session records, 1st July 1649 – "Given out off the boxe for Issobell Kelloch's charges, in procuring ane comissione for her tryall, and in things that concerned her burning, 24lib. 4s. 4d.". (Dalgety Old Parish Register, reproduced by permission of the National Records of Scotland)

(Fig 18) Pitreavie Castle, as it would have been at the time of the Battle of Inverkeithing in 1651. (drawn by McGibbon and Ross, prior to their extensive alterations in 1885)

(Fig 19) Construction of Pitreavie Castle started in 1615. It was originally built to a U-shaped plan, with a symmetrical layout, the only entrance being on the inner side of the west wing. The old entrance is a fine Renaissance doorway, in the pediment of which are the initials S.H.W. (Sir Henry Wardlaw).

(Fig 20) A Memorial Cairn, erected by the Clan McLean Society in 2001, stands near to Pitreavie Castle. It bears an inscription in Gaelic commemorating those who died in the Battle of Inverkeithing.

(Fig 21) HIC.IACET.CORPUS. IONAIS.CORSAUR. PASTOR.LINUS.PAROCTIAE.
QUI.OBIIT. 20.DIE.MENSIS [M]AID.ANNO.DOM [168]0.AETATIS.38
"Here lies the body of John Corsair, minister of this
parish, who died 20th May [168]0, aged 38."

(Fig 22) Remains of Fordell Mill photographed in 1930; little now
remains except some overgrown fragments of the base of a wall. Fordell
Mill was noted on James Gordon's map of 'Fyfe Shire' published in 1642.
(© reproduced by permission of Historic Environment Scotland)

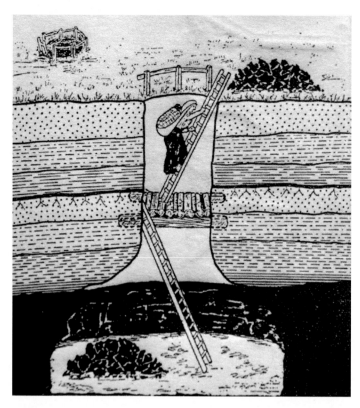

(Fig 23) Typical 'bell-pit', of a kind which used to dot the landscape in the northern part of Dalgety Parish. (© Coal Authority, reproduced by permission)

(Fig 24) Coal putting – miners employed their wives and children to pull sledges from the coal face to the pit shaft and then to carry the coal up the ladders to the pit head. (Illustration is from Great Britain Commissioners for Inquiring into the Employment and Condition of Children in Mines and Manufactories, 1842; used by permission of the British Library B20142-20a)

(Fig 25) Looking north towards Dalgety Kirk, the end of a pier showing laid stones with transverse footings, indicating a pier-head about 9m (30ft.) wide. (See Notes – Chap. 15 (8))

(Fig 26) The remains of jetties, west of Dalgety Kirk, can be seen at low tide from the Fife Coastal Path – what is thought to be the 'humel stone' is at the end of the jetty on the bottom right. The manse and the school were located approximately where the houses now stand. (© Air Images Ltd; reproduced by permission)

(Fig 27) At one time, salt pans were in evidence along the Fife coast. The foundations of pan-houses at St Monans are now all that remain of a once-thriving industry. Similar pan-houses would have existed at St David's.

(Fig 28) Salt pans in operation. (from The Art of Making Common Salt, William Brownrigg, 1748; Reproduced by permission of the National Library of Scotland)

(Fig 29) "Fordell's Lodgings" was the town house of Sir John Henderson of Fordell. In the upper hall is a plaque showing the Royal Arms of Scotland, commemorating Charles II's visit in February 1651, when he inspected the Scottish Army garrisons at Inchgarvie and North Queensferry. (Royal Arms photograph, taken c.1920 – photographer unknown)

(Fig 30) Linlithgow, showing the Tolbooth, with spire (centre) and Linlithgow Kirk and Royal Palace on the hill. (From John Slezer, The Town and Prospect of Linlithgow, Theatrum Scotiae, 1693; Reproduced by permission of the National Library of Scotland)

(Fig 31) There is no clear evidence as to where Andrew Donaldson is buried but a defaced gravestone at the east end of St Bridget's Kirk may belong to him. The open book at the top would indicate a man of learning.

(Fig 32) Memorials to Mr Archibald Campbell (R) and Mr William Henderson (L), his son-in-law who followed him as minister of Dalgety. Now both badly weathered.

Chapter 12

Battles and Protestations

Battle of Inverkeithing

As 1649 drew to a close, Scotland was, politically and ecclesiastically, at a crossroads, with its views diverging from those of England. After the execution of Charles I, the Parliament of Scotland recognised his son as King Charles II but refused to allow him to come to Scotland unless he accepted Presbyterianism and recognised the authority of the General Assembly of the Church of Scotland. Charles agreed, even to the extent of signing the Solemn League and Covenant, an act which the Scots regarded as a promise to have Presbyterianism installed in England, but which Charles regarded as a political necessity.

On 1st January 1651, six months after he had returned from exile in the Netherlands, Charles was crowned King of Scots at Scone, inheriting a country in a state of flux. Despite all Charles' promises, what had started as a joint venture between the Scottish and English parliaments to establish Presbyterianism had been usurped by a strict English Puritan regime which wanted neither monarchy nor Presbyterianism. Consequently, Scotland found itself changing sides and backing the king. The Scottish army's attention was no longer directed against Royalist forces but against those of Oliver Cromwell, the now undisputed leader of the Puritan faction of the English Parliament.

Cromwell's New Model Army was intent on destroying all remaining Royalist opposition which meant he had to gain control of Scotland. In a move to achieve this, Cromwell marched his forces north towards Edinburgh, meeting Lt. General David Leslie's forces at Dunbar on 3rd September 1650. As a result of poor tactics and the fact that the Act of Classes[1] had reduced the fighting strength of the army, it was a rout and Leslie was soundly beaten. After the Battle of Dunbar, the Scottish army had to regroup and by the following year Leslie's forces were based near Stirling. From there he felt there was a possibility of drawing Cromwell's forces into a position which would provide an opportunity for him to outflank Cromwell and leave the route to Edinburgh open. Leslie saw the gateway to Fife at Queensferry as a place to entice Cromwell's forces over the River Forth.

In July, Cromwell learned that the Scottish army had set-up a position at Castlandhill, outside Inverkeithing, and instructed Major-General John Lambert to cross the river, a difficult task given the treacherous currents and the barrage from the cannons mounted on Inchgarvie, a small island mid-way across. For the Scots, Major-General Sir John Brown, of Fordell, had dug in on the hillside and was waiting for reinforcements from Dunfermline under the command of Major-General James Holbourne. Lambert, however, had intelligence that troops in support of Brown were coming from Stirling and he decided to attack before they arrived.

The Battle of Inverkeithing was a bloody affair. It started on Thursday 17th July 1651 when "a pairtie of the English armie invaded the shyre of Fyfe. They landed att Enderkethen, and did intrenche themselfs ther. The 20 July, being Sunday, they fell upon a pairtie of our armie that came from Stirling, betuixt Dunfermling and Enderkethen, at which place seuerall of that pairtie were killed, suerall taken, and the rest fled."[2]

Sir John Brown was mortally wounded, and in August, "he depairted out of this life att Leith, whille he was prisoner with the English garesone ther. His corps were brought ouer to Rossee in Fyfe [Rossie House]. In Apr. following, his estate was sequestrat by the English, and a fyft pairt of it alloted to his lady yearlie".[3]

A number of reports of the battle exist, all with slightly different perspectives. One version indicates that, "The invaders left their tents and huts standing, and on the 17th, 18th, and 19th of July crossed to Inverkeithing. When this was made known in the royal camp, 'Our airmy come bak to Sterling, and marched neir to Dunfermling; and haiffing halted thair,

Holburne was employed with sum hors to marche, and ane great number of fute, to go on upone the enymie. McClayne of Dowart went on curagiouslie, and luiking that Holburne sould haif assisted thame with thair hors, they were deceavit, for the hors never went on for thair help; and so the Englisches wan that day'."[4]

For some reason, Major-General James Holborne delayed joining the battle (which is why Lambert thought Sir John Brown was in command) and when he did, his horse was routed by Lambert, and he fled the scene. The suggestion is that had he engaged Cromwell's forces, the Scottish army would have defeated the English, a fact later acknowledged by Cromwell. After the battle he was charged as a traitor but a trial in Stirling acquitted him. Nevertheless, for his cowardly and dishonourable action he was cashiered and prevented from holding any military or public office at any time in the future.

Retreat to Pitreavie Castle

Included in the Scottish army that day were eight hundred Highlanders from Clan McLean, under the leadership of Sir Hector Roy McLean of Duart. They fought a strong rear-guard action and were driven inland to Pitreavie Castle[5] *(Fig 18)* where, in spite of their desperate situation, and pleas for safety, the Wardlaw family elected not to help *(Fig 19)* and denying them access, stoned them from the roof. As tradition has it, in retreat they fought courageously in defence of their chief, calling out, as they were killed, "*Fear eile airson Eachuinn!*" [Another for Hector!] as their Clan chief, already mortally wounded, died from a musket shot. According to clan history, Sir Hector is supposed to have said, "What would you have me do? Would you have me fly like that cowardly old horseman, Holburn, and be for ever the scorn of honest men? Our honour and our loyalty demand that we do our best."

Only thirty to forty Highlanders are said to have survived, among them Sir Hector McLean's piper who, on returning to Mull, composed a lament in his honour. Translated from the Gaelic, it finishes, in true lament form:

> ... The tree of choicest apples
> Has been stripped at the moment
> Alas! O Mary! my ruin,
> The bloom has faded from the garden.

Lambert, in his report from the North Ferry on 22nd July, highlighted what he saw as the one-sidedness of the battle, "by a truly short dispute put them to an absolute rout. We killed upon the place (as most judge) 2000 and took 1400 prisoners, and amongst the rest, Sir John Brown, Major General of their Horse, and commander in chief of their Forces, Col. Buchanan and divers other officers were taken and slain. The reason why the slain exceeded the number of prisoners was because divers of them were Highlanders and had very ill quarter, and indeed I am persuaded few of them escaped without a knock. *(Fig 20)* I think we lost about 8 men; thus easy hath the Lord given us his mercy."[6]

Aftermath of the Battle

Cromwell, who had not been present at the battle, preferring to watch it from the woodlands of Barnbougle on the other side of the Forth, wrote to William Lenthall, the Speaker of the House of Commons on 21st July, basing his victory on his faith in God.

The battle was a decisive encounter, ending a long strategic deadlock between Cromwell's forces and the Royalists. Loss of the battle was a disaster, not only for the Scottish army but for the country as a whole. After the battle, Cromwell's forces went on the rampage and plundered the area. The town of Inverkeithing, under the control of General Monck, was "reduced to a poverty-stricken condition", the castle at Rosyth was badly damaged and Spencerfield House[7] was raided and a great quantity of "silver plate, arras, hingings, carpets, and other household plenishings" was stolen.

Cromwell and Lambert then "advanced with their troops to Perth and lay one night at Fordell and drove in their horses among General Brown's standing corn".[8] Legend also has it that during their plundering of the area at Fordell Mill, some of his troops invaded the miller's home and after repeated sexual violation of the miller's wife and daughter, the miller poisoned them. The miller and his family escaped but his assistant was hanged on a nearby tree.

Following the battle, Burntisland was also taken, giving Cromwell control of the Fife coast. The main garrison was billeted there with a small force stationed in Aberdour where they tried to make the best of their situation. Many of the men were not professional soldiers but drafted in by virtue of a landowner's obligations, a release from a prison sentence or a desire to escape a humdrum existence in search of fame and fortune. With the fighting over and men starting to think about returning home and settling down it was not surprising that relationships developed with local girls and human emotions came to the fore.

At some point, the Aberdour Kirk Session was posed a problem by an English soldier who presented himself to the Session seeking permission to marry a young woman of the town. The "grave question was started whether such a thing was lawful, and the minister was instructed to get the advice of the Presbytery on a matter of such importance." After deliberation, Presbytery's advice was that "she marie not the Englishman, by reasone of the unlawfulnesse of their invasione."[9]

Advice had also to be sought when widows, whose husbands had died in battle or were missing, wished to remarry and in September 1645, the Synod of Fife noted that "ministers suld not proceed to marie wemen in that cais without production of clear evidence of thair husband's death, or the sentence of the civile judge competent in such caissis."

The county of Fife paid a heavy price for opposing Cromwell, with nearly 8,000 men out of a total population of less than 100,000 enlisted in the army. Dalgety would have borne its fair share.

Andrew Donaldson Absent from Dalgety

On the weekend of the Battle of Inverkeithing Andrew Donaldson was attending the General Assembly of the Church of Scotland which had started meeting in St Andrews on 16th July 1651. "The 20 of Jul. being Sunday, the Ass meet at night (upon the defeate Cromuell had given our people about Dunfermling), and did adjourn this Ass till the 22, to Dundie. The forsaid night, att St Androus, subscribed with 21 or 22 seuerall hands of ministers, protesting against the lawfulness of this Ass; alleadging it was corrupt, ill constiute, and not friee. The names of some of the protestors were... Mr An[drew] Donaldson [Dalgety]."[10]

The dispute had arisen towards the end of the previous year when it had become clear that the General Assembly was divided with a group remonstrating, or protesting, as they believed that the Act of Classes had not gone far enough and that further purging was required. Against them stood the 'resolutioners', a more moderate group, "in favour of permitting all persons to fight who were not excommunicated, forfeited, notoriously wicked or obstinate enemies of the covenant. The 'resolutioners' were prepared to co-operate with the committee of estates, which on 25th November [1650] condemned the remonstrance."[11]

When the General Assembly reconvened in Dundee some ministers were deposed or suspended for "publicly preaching and speaking against the proceedings of both Church and State" and for being "ring-leaders in the matter of the Remonstrance". Feelings were running high on both sides and the Assembly was split, with "the moderate and royalist party of resolutioners claiming the support of about 750 out of some 900 ministers. The remonstrants, undaunted by lack of numbers, protested (so earning the name of 'Protestors') against the General Assembly of 1651…"[12] Donaldson, in making his position clear as one of the protesting minority, appeared to be walking a very narrow line.

Theft and Disruption

During Donaldson's absence the Kirk at Dalgety suffered under Cromwell's men. The Kirk Session record for 14th September 1651 noted that minutes since the previous meeting had been lost "by reasone off the insolencie and plunder off the enemie. Its declared by the deacones that kept the box that the englishes did breake up the box and take away the money, only some licht money that wes not in the box is yet to the fore".

Loss of church money was only one aspect in the disruption caused by Cromwell's soldiers. Local people were not slow to take advantage of the confusion and James Peacock in Letham entered James Paterson's house, during his absence, to help himself to a quantity of oatmeal. Janet Wilson and Isobel Williamson were caught stealing and Alexander Brown decided that rustling sheep was a more profitable source of funds. The Kirk Session was made aware of these misdemeanours and brought the culprits to book. James Peacock was already a familiar figure before the Session, but it is not known what punishment he, and the others, suffered. There would certainly have been the humiliation of the repentance stool and likely an appearance before the Civil Magistrate and probably a fine or imprisonment (or both).

Also stolen was the church hand-bell. The hand-bell (sometimes referred to as the mort or 'deid' bell) was rung by the beadle as he went round the parish to let people know about deaths and the time of funerals and, as such, it was an important item of parish life. The beadle at the time was Saunders Thomson, whose father, James, had been beadle before him. He had succeeded to the post after his mother's plea to the Session on the death of her husband: 27th April 1645 "This day the Sessione having receaved ane petition from Elspeth Muirhead, relict of unquhile James Thomsone, bellman, desyring that her sone might succeed to his unquhile father, in regard she was left poore with many children, and that this wold be a mean to help both her and them. The Sessione grants her petition, on thir termes, that the young man sall be received to serve for a while, and that, thereafter, if he be found qualified, he sall be continued and have the benefite that his father had befoir him; if not they sall remove him and make choyce of a fitter."

The hand-bell was worth money, and we can only assume that Cromwell's soldiers were more interested in the cash rather than the object and sold the bell on. Six months after it had disappeared, it was discovered in Kirkliston and the Session despatched Saunders Thomson to bring it back, providing him with an allowance of 24s to cover his expenses. He was successful in his quest as, "he has brought back the hand-bell, as he wes appointed; and that he behoved to give for it half ane croune, which is paid back to him out of the box."

English Civil War Ends

After his victory at Inverkeithing, Cromwell had to entice Charles II into the open. As Leslie was still in control of the Stirling area, Cromwell's troops moved up through Fife and into Aberdeenshire, ostensibly leaving a route open for Charles to march on London. Cromwell, on hearing of Charles' intention to do so, appointed General Monck to ensure that Scotland was kept in check while he moved south to counter that threat. En route Charles and the 16,000 strong Royalist army camped at Worcester where, on 3rd September 1651, they met Cromwell's forces in what turned out to be the final battle of the English Civil War. The Royalist forces were heavily defeated. Charles managed to escape and accompanied by some of his retinue, including Charles Seton, 2nd Earl of Dunfermline, fled to France.

With Charles II in exile, the government of Scotland was largely carried out from England, with a Scottish Council of State. Cromwell had made no attempt to impose any religious restrictions in Scotland and Presbyterianism carried on much as before. In fact, he left no discernible legacy in Scotland and, apart from a few uprisings, mainly in the Highlands, and a forcible dissolution of the General Assembly in 1653 (which would not meet again until 1690), there were no serious disturbances or political upheavals.

In 1653 Cromwell was appointed head of state as Lord Protector and governed with the help of his Council and the 'Protectorate' English Parliament, rejecting its offer in 1657 to be crowned as King of England. In September 1658, after his death in London at the age of 59, he was succeeded by his son Richard who, lacking any political or military support, was forced to resign in May 1659, leaving a power vacuum. With no clear leader emerging, General George Monck, who had been governing Scotland on Cromwell's behalf, marched his army[13] to London to restore some measure of control, in effect a *coup d'état*; the outcome of which enabled the 'Long' Parliament to reconvene. It concluded that Charles should be invited back from exile and the monarchy restored.

Chapter 13

Donaldson Deposed

Restoration of the Monarchy

Ten years after his coronation as King of Scotland, Charles, in April 1661, was crowned King of England. One of his first acts was to call a new parliament, the composition of which became mainly Royalist and Anglican. The Restoration of the monarchy in England (technically, the monarch had never been deposed in Scotland) had been generally welcomed but the new Parliament saw the Presbyterians losing ground and episcopal rule becoming dominant in England.

In Scotland, most people rejected episcopacy and embraced Presbyterianism, although only a minority now retained adherence to strict Covenanting ideals. The Protestors regarded Charles II's return as "the mother sin of the land"[1] and while many people thought that the interests of the Presbyterians were secure, the Protestors, of whom Andrew Donaldson was one, were not convinced. They saw Charles' re-establishment of Episcopacy in England and his leanings towards Roman Catholicism as a repudiation of the Covenants. They firmly believed that the Covenants were binding on him and on the Scottish people.

The Protestors' position was further weakened when the Parliament of Scotland, in January 1661, passed an act which framed an Oath of

Allegiance. This required people to testify and acknowledge Charles as the supreme governor of the kingdom "… over all persones and in all causes, and that… no person civill or ecclesiastick hath any jurisdiction, power or superiority over the same."

Episcopacy Restored

Two months later, in March 1661, the Scottish parliament passed the Rescissory Act which annulled the legislation of all parliaments since 1633. This effectively removed presbyteries and left in force the Acts establishing Episcopacy. Acts subsequently passed the following year formally restored episcopal government, revived lay patronage, declared the Covenants unlawful and, significantly, forbade private meetings or conventicles. Presbyteries and Synods were forbidden to meet.

To the Protestors this was a betrayal of all that had been fought for as Charles had reneged on his promises. "History records few examples of a more flagrant ingratitude and more scandalous breach of faith, than the re-establishment of Prelacy in Scotland. The persistent loyalty of Churchmen… deserved a better return… the conduct of Charles must be stigmatised as highly discreditable."[2]

Andrew Donaldson Continues to Protest

Episcopacy was once again in the ascendant and the establishment lost little time in exercising its prerogative. At the Parliament of Scotland held in May, the Estates made their position clear by repealing "the Magna Charta of the Presbyterian establishment, the 8th Act of the Parliament of 1592"[3] and restoring all episcopal functions. The Estates of Parliament went further in an "Act concerning such benefices and stipends as have been possessed without presentations from the lawful patrons: … therefore, his majesty, does statute and ordain that all those ministers who entered to the cure of any parish, in or since the year 1649… have no right to, nor shall receive, uplift nor possess the rents of any benefice, modified stipend, manse or glebe for this present crop of 1662 or any year following, but their places, benefices and kirks are by law vacant." The Act offered a lifeline to "every such minister who shall obtain a presentation from the lawful patron and have [support] from the Bishop between now and 20 September next to come, [he] shall from thenceforth have right to and enjoy his church, benefice, manse and glebe as fully and freely."

Donaldson, as he had been ordained prior to 1649 was, for the moment, spared, but his freedom to conduct worship was curtailed. There was to be no expounding of Scripture before the sermon, lecturing and explanation of texts were forbidden and only the reading of Scriptures was permitted. "The Archbishop of St Andrews, [James Sharp] at his Synod in October 1662, declared it to be the King's will 'that ministers do use the Lord's Prayer in Divin worship, and that when children are baptisd, their parents be required to give a publick account of the confession of their faith as formerly: also, that in singing of Psalms, use be made of the Doxologie so anciently and universally practised in the Church of Christ'."

The Estates permitted the bishops to make new admissions to the churches vacant since 1637. They further instructed that 29th May should be kept as a day of Thanksgiving for the King's Birth and Restoration and threatened such ministers as failed to observe it with deprivation. Tension was increased when they declared, "that all ministers who should be absent from… the Diocesan Assembly, without lawful excuse accepted by the Bishop, should, for the first offence, be suspended from their office and benefice till the next Diocesan meeting, and for the second, be deprived of their cure."

As if sanctions against ministers were not enough, the Estates turned their attention to those parishioners who refused to accept episcopal clergy and attended Presbyterian services. They declared that "all persons ordinarily and wilfully absenting themselves from the public worship of their [own] parish church" would be guilty of sedition; furthermore, landed proprietors would be fined one quarter of their rental for each year they transgressed and tenants, the loss of part of their 'free moveables' and for burgesses, the loss of burghal privileges, as well as a quarter part of their moveables.

Reintroduction of Bishops

With the reintroduction of bishops, it was not just the style of worship that was different, the governance and reporting structure of the Church of

Scotland changed. The power of Presbyteries was limited, and four levels of Episcopal Courts were implemented:

1. The Kirk Session remained as a parochial court consisting of the parish minister as Moderator, and of a number of elders and deacons. Their function was to manage local affairs, supervise the religious condition of the parish, exercise discipline, and attend to the poor.

2. The Presbytery, or Exercise, was composed of the ministers of a group of Kirk Sessions. Their business was to Exercise; act as a court of appeal from the Kirk Session; deal with persons refractory to the Kirk Session, and with cases of grave delinquency...

3. The Diocesan Synod – where the Bishop was present and is a court constituted... of all the ministers of the Diocese...

4. The National Synod[4] was established by Act of Parliament in 1663. It was composed of the Archbishops and Bishops, the Deans, the Archdeacons, the Moderator and a Presbyter of each Exercise, and representatives of the Universities and Colleges. The Archbishop of St Andrews was constituted President. They were empowered to determine upon such ecclesiastical matters as should be submitted to their consideration...[5]

Dalgety Kirk was placed in the Diocese of Dunkeld, in which it had been pre-Reformation, with Andrew Donaldson reporting to Bishop George Haliburton[6] who had graduated from King's College, Aberdeen in 1636. He was a Presbyterian who had been admitted as minister of Perth but had supported the Engagement and spoken in favour of Charles II. He became a Resolutioner and found himself at odds with his Kirk Session and the town council of Perth. He preached against the Solemn League and Covenant which enraged his Presbyterian colleagues and when he saw which way the wind was blowing, he embraced the Episcopalian revival. In May 1662, he was consecrated to the bishopric by James Sharp.

Restricted in his activities and having to report to a bishop was too much for Andrew Donaldson. Where was the religious freedom he thought had been won, at great cost? Where was the progressive society that had been envisaged by the Covenanters? Where, for that matter, was the better life for the parishioners that education and sound religious teaching were going to bring? Donaldson stuck to his beliefs and continued to protest in favour of what he regarded as the 'true faith'. His position and that of other protesting or nonconformist ministers was fast becoming untenable as the Presbytery accepted the 'Acts and Constitutiones' issued by Haliburton and approved by the Diocesan Synod on 14th April 1663.

Donaldson Deposed

Donaldson did his best to ignore Haliburton's fifteen 'Acts and Constitutiones' as he felt they were designed to inhibit the activities of ministers. Three of them focused on the penalties that would be imposed on 'the brethren' who failed to attend Presbytery or Synod meetings without seeking prior permission. Absence without due cause carried severe consequences, as in the 10th Act: "In regaird brethren doe much slight meetings of the Presbetrie at the ordinarie dyets thereof, to the disheartning of orderlie and observing brethren and causing thereby a scandle in the countrey, therefor it is ordained that evrie minister shall keep their Presbetrie meetings at their ordinary dyets; and each that shall be found absent, for the first fault, without ane lawful excuse of sickness, shall be rebuked, for the 2d suspended and for the 3d fault deposed."[7]

To make sure that he acknowledged the new order and the 'Acts and Constitutiones' now in force, Donaldson was summoned by Archbishop Sharp to a meeting of Presbytery. He elected not to attend. The Synod of Dunkeld then met on 29th October 1663, the outcome of which was that "The Prelate of Dunkeld, at his court, suspended four or five ministers, [including] Mr Andrew Donaldson".

Donaldson ignored the suspension and continued much as before. This did not meet with favour and Archbishop Sharp urged the Privy Council to eject him. It ruled that there were severall ministers within the diocese of Dunkeld who were "in manifest contempt thereof... doe persist in their wicked practises, still labouring to keip the hearts of the people from the present government of Church and State by their pernicious doctrin; and more particularly that Messrs ... Andro Donaldson at Dalgety... are chieff instruments in carying on that wicked course..." Donaldson and other protesting ministers were to be ejected from their parishes along with "... their wyves, bairnes, families, servants, goods and geir furth and frae their respective duelling places and manses".

This was harsh treatment meted out to those who did not favour the Episcopalian approach but, again, Andrew Donaldson ignored the ruling of the Synod. At a meeting of the Diocese of Dunkeld held on 5th October 1664, a year after his suspension, his fate was sealed when, "the Bishop of Dunkeld deposed all Nonconform ministers in his diocese, except for Mr Thomas Black, for whom the Countess of Rothes interceded". The following week, on 10th October 1664, Donaldson received a confirmatory letter from Bishop Haliburton in which he stated, "I now do declare, you Mr. Andrew Donaldson, sometime minister at Dalgety, deposed from all charge, not only there, but from all the parts of ministerial function within any diocese, or the Kirk of Scotland: assuring you, if you shall insist on that charge, either at Dalgety, or elsewhere, after you shall be acquaint with this sentence, that immediately, with the consent of my Synod, we will proceed against you with the highest censures of this Kirk." *(Appendix 3)*

Eviction

To ensure that Donaldson vacated his pulpit, Haliburton had been directed by Archbishop Sharp to send a party of soldiers to forcibly remove him and they arrived "on a Lord's day, when the people were gathered to hear him. It was Mr Donaldson's prudence which prevented a scuffle; and upon the government their orders to remove, he compromised the matter with the soldiers, and got leave to preach that day, upon his promise to leave that place".[8]

According to Charles Seton, 2nd Earl of Dunfermline and a good friend to Andrew Donaldson, who had served with him in the army in 1645, Donaldson's deposition was an outrage. As he was a lord of the Privy Council, he exercised some influence at court and persuaded Charles II to issue a warrant "re-instating him to Dalgety for life". That lifeline was short-lived as his negotiating skills clearly lacked the subtlety and deviousness of those of Archbishop Sharp, who managed to obtain a further warrant from the king which prohibited any minister, not just Donaldson, who had been deposed from his charge from returning to it. Donaldson was left with no choice but to leave his church and manse, with his wife and family. He, along with around 270 dissenting minsters throughout Scotland, was now homeless and forbidden to preach or hold private meetings. He was dependent on the

Christian charity and goodwill of his friends and members of his former congregation.

It has to be recognised that less than one third of ministers were evicted from their churches while the others remained in post and carried out their pastoral duties much as they had done before. The style of worship did not vary greatly between Presbyterian and Episcopalian services; it was the style of Church government that was the sticking point – ministers and elders on an equal footing through presbyteries or in a hierarchy through prelates. Donaldson and other like-minded ministers were in no doubt what 'the true faith' demanded, although by now they were a remnant of the covenanting group which had set out with so much zeal all those years ago.

Mr John Corsair, Minister

Five years after Donaldson was ejected from his pulpit Mr John Corsair was installed as minister in Dalgety Kirk. It might have been expected that an incoming Episcopalian priest would have had nothing to do with Donaldson. In fact, he might even have been warned by his Bishop[9] (and if not by him, certainly by Archbishop Sharp) against having any dealings with Donaldson just in case he, too, became corrupted.

As it turned out, John Corsair was, like Donaldson, a graduate of St Andrews University and was no doubt aware of his reputation as it is likely that it would have spread along the coast to that august seat of learning. For whatever reason, Corsair took a benevolent view of Andrew Donaldson and apparently allowed him to live in the laird's loft at the west end of the church where he had possibly been living since his removal, supported by the generosity of his parishioners. Whether this incurred the displeasure of his bishop, or not, is unknown but it indicated that at least some Episcopalian priests had a degree of compassion towards their Presbyterian brethren. They were probably only too well aware that their positions could be easily reversed.

John Corsair was born in 1643 and educated at St Leonard's College, St Andrews, graduating a Master of Arts on 27th July 1661. Transferring from South Leith, he was admitted to Dalgety on 27th January 1669. Little is known of his life, but he was married to Anna Carmichael, with whom he had one son. After her husband's early death, at the age of thirty-eight in 1680, she remarried and returned to Edinburgh.[10]

Within Dalgety Kirk itself, about halfway down the floor of the nave, is to be found a simple flagstone in his memory. *(Fig 21)* It is now, like many of the memorials very badly worn and sadly virtually illegible.

HIC.IACET.CORPUS. IONAIS.CORSAUR.
PASTOR.LINUS.PAROCTIAE.QUI.OBIIT.
20.DIE.MENSIS [M]AID.ANNO.DOM [168]0.AETATIS.38[11]

Following John Corsair was John Lumsdain, who arrived in July 1680 and transferred to the Second Charge, Canongate, Edinburgh in 1682. The church was vacant until early 1686 when John Row, son of John Row, the Principal of King's College, Aberdeen and grandson of the former minister in Carnock, was admitted. The congregation must have been wearied at the constant change of minister but John Row provided them with enough scandal to keep them talking for many a year, as at Lammas-tide 1686 he deserted the church, renounced the Protestant faith and converted to Roman Catholicism. On 30th July that year, he was granted a pension of £50 sterling by Charles II and an Act of the Court of Session confirmed that he was entitled to withdraw that pension until Whitsunday 1687, even though a successor, George Gray, had already been appointed. Gray, a graduate of Marischal College, Aberdeen, was admitted as the final Episcopalian minister, at some point before January 1687. He transferred to South Leith two years later.

The spiritual welfare of the parishioners was suffering from the neglect of the episcopal priests and their bishop but, unofficially, Donaldson remained active in Dalgety and the surrounding area. Many of his former congregation, even though it was against the law, continued to hear him preach, receive the sacraments, be married and have their children baptised by him.

Chapter 14

Life in
the Parish

Dwellings

Despite Donaldson's deposition and Corsair's arrival, life in the parish continued much as before. Work had to be attended to; children had to be schooled and the poor and sick of the parish had to be cared for; discipline had to be exercised; food grown to feed hungry families and homes had to be maintained.

Nothing now remains of any 'homes' or domestic buildings from the Dalgety of Donaldson's time.[1] Dwellings at that time would have been of poor quality, possibly of wattle and daub construction, and located in fermtouns or cottouns throughout the parish. "In the rural area [unlike burghs] stone building was rare, with lime mortar largely unused and the houses could quite accurately be described as hovels. They were thatched [with straw or turf] and ceilingless, the [timber-framed] walls frequently built with turf or clay, dirt floors were normal, there were no chimneys and interior lighting was provided by small glassless apertures which may also have had shutters."[2]

An English traveller, around the turn of the seventeenth/eighteenth centuries, described the houses of the 'Commonalty' in Scotland as "very mean, mud-wall and thatch at best; but the poorer sort live in such miserable huts as never eye beheld".[3] The dwellings in Dalgety were unlikely to have been different.

Food

Each 'house' would have had a kale-yard beside it, although vegetables were not widely eaten, as the view at that time was that they were nutritionally worthless and potentially harmful. Potatoes would not have been grown as it was not until the mid-eighteenth century that they were established in Scotland.

At breakfast they would have "a kind of hasty pudding of oatmeal, or peasemeal eaten with milk. They have commonly pottage to dinner [the main mid-day meal] composed of cale, leeks, barley or big [a form of barley] and butter and this is reinforced with bread and cheese and ale. At night they sup on sowens flummery of oatmeal [with milk or beer]."[4] Bread was often supplemented by oatcakes and the cheese was made locally by farmers' wives from skimmed milk, with the cream being used to make butter. From all accounts, the cheese they made was hard with little colour and a rather insipid taste.

Meat was expensive and, with the exception of the landed proprietors and men of substance, a luxury infrequently enjoyed. Hens were sometimes eaten, although they were more valuable for their eggs. The larger houses would have had a doo'cot for keeping pigeons as a source of meat and eggs. As the water was unsafe, most people drank ale, made from malted barley. Ale, with its fairly low alcoholic content, was cheap, as, unlike beer, it was made without hops. Among the well-to-do, claret and Rhenish, imported to Leith and Burntisland, were regular drinks.

In the large houses in the parish, a more varied diet was enjoyed. In 1692, Robert Alison, a miller in Dunfermline, was supplying Alison Kinnear, housekeeper to the Tweeddale family in Dalgety House, with malt, meal, pigs, ducks, a large quantity of chickens and capons and by 1695 had added veal and lamb to his deliveries.[5] Around the same time, May 1694, the Donibristle books record, "Account by Henry Oat [Stirling] with order by earl of Moray to James Stewart, Ardvorlich for kids, salmon, trout etc". The account books also record, on a regular basis, the purchase of veal, blackcock, pike and fresh butter; as well as 'groceries', sack, sugar, spices, claret, French wine, Palma wine and sherry.[6]

Bowls and plates were generally wooden, or perhaps pewter in the better-off households, and only knives and spoons would be used, as forks did not make an introduction until towards the end of the seventeenth century.

Winter could be particularly hard for people. It was difficult to feed animals during the winter and while some hardier ones would be kept for stock, in the autumn most of them would be sold, with some sent for slaughter and the meat dried or salted. Fish was similarly preserved and, additionally, may have been smoked. Famine was not unknown. Scotland had had a 'year of dearth' in 1674 and following a period of plenty the country was badly hit by a series of famines in 1695, 1696 and 1697–98, colloquially known as the 'seven lean years', when three failed harvests had a devastating effect, killing, it is estimated, somewhere between 5% and 15% of the population.[7]

Memento Mori

In the mid-late seventeenth century, the focus for people in Dalgety was survival. If they lived through birth and childhood, they were susceptible to death from hunger or various diseases (smallpox was endemic in Scotland in the 1680s). Life expectancy at birth was around thirty-five years but people who reached the age of thirty could expect to live for another twenty to thirty years.

Most people were buried in unmarked graves, as only those with some standing could afford a gravestone, and many families were commemorated by initials on simple, plain memorials, with no indication of a date, gender or age. For burial, people would hire a mortcloth as on 16th February 1698 "Given in by the Laird of Leuchate to the poor for use of the mortcloth" or on 31st October 1699 "Given in by John Kemptie for the use of the best mortcloth".

The gravestone of Bessie Steivson records that she was the wife of William Liddell, gardener to the Earl of Dunfermline at Dalgety House. Also on the grave slab is the death of (presumably) their son, George, who was a gardener to the Earl of Moray at Donibristle. Given the dates, it is possible that Bessie died as a result of childbirth:

Heir lyes the corps of Bessie Steivson spous to William Liddell
gardner to the Earle of Dunfermelyne at Dalgati 1644; Heire
lyes the corps of George Liddell gardner at dunnibirsle who
departed this lyff the 29 day of July 1690 and of his age 45.

Some of the gravestones carry the words "Memento Mori" (Remember you must die), and symbols of mortality – an hourglass, representing the passing of time, and the skull and crossed bones, a reminder that death comes to everyone; or a winged soul, a sign of immortality that was intended to represent the soul leaving the body at the time of death and ascending to wait until the Day of Judgement, when the body would rise to join it. *(Fig 3)*

Sometimes, as with George Liddell, we catch a glimpse of people born after Andrew Donaldson had arrived at Dalgety and to whom he would have ministered, whether he was installed in the parish or not, some of whom he would have baptised and possibly married. Another parishioner was Helen Mathieson, wife of James Hay, a farmer in Little Fordell, who died in 1713, aged 55. Their son, John, and grandchildren, John and Jane, are buried alongside.

One of the finest mural tablets to survive, in memory of Janet Inglis, Lady Menstrie, *(Fig 2)* is on the south wall inside the Kirk:

"In memory of the Lady Menstrie, snatched away by death on November 30th [1681] Here lies the body of one known to many as the devoted daughter of the Laird of Cramond and wife of the Laird of Menstrie. During her life upon earth she followed wisdom. Now too, on high where she is free from worldly cares, her goodness has won her the friendship of Christ, and glory without spot has been given her by Eternal Justice. Henceforward she will sing her Hallelujah in the Heavens."

and in a second epitaph:

"Lest this lady should win honour too great for a mortal, God Almighty has taken her to his bosom."[8]

Janet Inglis was the daughter of John Inglis of Cramond, and in 1670 she had married James Holborne, laird of Menstrie, the son of Major-General Sir James Holborne, the Scottish army commander disgraced after the Battle of Inverkeithing. The Holbornes owned a town house in Inverkeithing, next to the parish church, and after the death of his wife, James Holborne married his cousin Jean, the daughter of Alexander Spittal of Leuchat and Elizabeth Holborne, in August 1692. In turn, his daughter Janet, born in 1672, married her cousin, James Spittal[9] in 1695. On the floor within Dalgety Kirk, a graveslab records the death of a Charles Holborne on 20th November 1681, ten days prior to (presumably) his mother, who probably died as a result of childbirth.

Enjoyment and Overindulgence

Life, which was described at the time by the English philosopher Thomas Hobbes as "poor, nasty, brutish and short",[10] had its lighter moments. Weddings, or 'penny bridals', were always a time for joy and celebration, although in the eyes of the Church there was often too much joy and too much celebration, particularly as they were generally held on Sundays – the Lord's Day. People attending the wedding would pay one penny towards the cost of the entertainment which often involved pipers or fiddlers, who frequently over-enjoyed their ale, and as a result the merriment sometimes became overexuberant. Penny weddings had been riotous affairs in the area for many years and "began to be very 'uproris in Dunfermling' where 'Sandie Dempster, the wading fidler' took an active part at them with 'playin' and kickin' up and dancing'."[11]

Intemperance was a sin. The Synod of Fife, meeting in Dunfermline in May 1645, "considering the great abuse that still is amongst the most pairte of the commones, by gathereing of multitudes to Pennybridles" restricted the number of people that could attend the celebrations to no more than twenty. The Synod took a firm line and "appointed that ministers shall be peremptor in prosecuting the tenor of the Act of Justice of Peace. As also, ordaines that the hostleres who make such feasts shal be censured by the Sessiones." Not only were the celebrants under stricture but the innkeepers were liable to feel the wrath of the Church, as indeed were ministers and elders not doing their utmost to curb enjoyment.

With the passage of time, that injunction had either been forgotten or ignored, for the Synod in April 1650 had to remind elders about behaviour at 'brydales' and overindulgence and swearing generally, "that the elderis of the quarter quhair the brydale is, tak notice of personis transgressing and rebuik them for the first, and gif thet be fund againe, to advyse with the Presbiterie anent the censure". Swearing, blaspheming and overindulging were constantly in the sights of the Synod, as was the "unseasonable haunting of aill houses and long sitting thair". Men should be working and if it was vagrants who were drinking was this at the expense of the Church's 'poor box'? The Session was also reminded by the Synod, "that selleris of aill to these quho are drunk, or excessive in drinking, sall fall under the same censure with the drinkeris". The Church was always able to find an excuse to clamp down.

Donaldson Remarries

At some point Andrew Donaldson was engaged in another marriage. His first wife, Helen, had died, probably in the mid-1650s, leaving a son, Alexander, who had been baptised in 1649 and a daughter, Elizabeth, born in 1652. His second wife was Beatrix Chalmers and she bore three children. Helen, named after his first wife, who in 1682 married Henry Mackie, Chamberlain to Sir Peter Halkett of Pitfirrane. After his death, she subsequently married Sir William Henderson, the Laird of Fordell, to become Lady Henderson. His second daughter, Beatrice, married Mr Alexander Stedman, minister at Beath, in August 1693 and his son, Andrew, later became a property owner and baillie in Inverkeithing. Beatrix died in Inverkeithing on 10th October 1743, nearly fifty years after the death of her husband. Given their circumstances and beliefs, and the circles they were moving in, it is hard to imagine Andrew Donaldson indulging in anything as frivolous as a 'penny wedding' or having "an uproris time".

Poor Relief

Apart from the nobility and landed gentry, few people in the parish had money or even a settled existence behind them and for some, cash distributed from the church box was their main source of income. The *First Book of Discipline* had proposed that, "the children of the poore must be supported and sustained of the charge of the Kirk". That proposition never materialised but the intention was clear – helping the poor had to be a continual part of the work of the Church.

Every parish was expected to have a list of its own poor, the 'ordinarie poore', and to give them tokens, or seals, as evidence of their status.

Dunfermline Presbytery, in 1631, ordered all its parishes to have lead seals made to be given to the poor living in each parish and only those with seals were entitled to receive money from the church box.[12] Kirk Sessions were quite willing to help their own poor but not so keen to help the 'sturdy and idle beggars' (the able-bodied but work-shy) who roamed the countryside. A seal was evidence of entitlement to money from the parish poor box and without it, beggars were likely to be sent on their way.

There was no set rate for poor relief. When Andrew Donaldson became minister 12s distributed to the ordinary poor, on the first Sunday of the month, was the custom and practice. Kirk Sessions, however, were dependent on collections in the box at the church door to provide whatever level of subsistence they felt was needed. Elders would know which individual or families required help, although accepting the charity of the Session was regarded as a personal disgrace. On occasion, people had no option but to request assistance. In October 1644, William Wilson "ane pure man" appealed to the Session to be "receaved as an ordinarie poore, in regard of his age and infirmitie". His supplication was granted.

Another case, in April the following year, saw the Kirk Session consider the "great miserie of Christian Purson, one of the ordinarie poore, quho is lying sick, ready to die, and hes nothing but that which she gets out of the boxe, once in the month, ordains that 12s be sent her every Lord's day, so long as it sall pleas God that she live heir; and, if she die shortly, that John Stennous caus get ane kist [coffin] and other such things that sall be needful for her buriall, quhilk the Sessione sall caus to pay."

War tended to increase the number of people requiring help and the Kirk Session was mindful of families where men had been drafted into the army. With little income, there was a need for support. 10th May 1650, "The Sessione taking into consideration the mony poor, indigent bodies in the parish, forby the ordinar poor and the present necessitie that they are into, appoints some present supplie for them, viz. to Marjorie Cupar and Marjorie Patersone, there, everie one of them 40s. Item to Thomas Lillie's bairns, 4lib; to Agnes Fairlie's bairnes, 4lib; to Elspeth Muirhead's bairns, 55s..."

The 'poor' was not just a blanket term for those in need as the Kirk Session, as often as not, directed its support to specific individuals, often not residents of the parish, such as "Jeane Jamfrey, ane poore godlie woman in the Queinsferrie" who received 3lib, as hers was a "necessitous caise". The disabled were not neglected. In October 1654, the Session "considering the necessitous caise of Allane Mitchell, in the Ferrie [North Queensferry] ane pious man y^t has laitlie fallen and broken his leg, appoynts him to get 10 merks for his present need". Veteran soldiers were also assisted. In July 1655 6*lib* was "given to one Leutenant John Mure, having testimonialls from Glasgow and Paisley, bearing his godlie and sober carriage and his present want". Those who had suffered a calamity were helped, as the Kirk Session in December 1656 "receaving ane letter from the Kirk-sessione off Aberdour, desiring some help to James Tailzor, who laitlie haid all his horses smoored by the fall off his hous, recomends to the deacons to collect something for him".

Special collections for the poor started the month after Andrew Donaldson arrived in Dalgety and continued throughout his ministry. On 1st September 1644 "This day collected throw the Kirk [in addition to 51*s*. 4*d*. raised the same day for the ordinary poor] after sermon, for some poor people recommended to the Presbytries and congregationes of Fyfe, by the General Assemblie, the soume of 23*lib*. 8*s*". Such was his concern for the poor that all the Kirk Session minutes of that time have as their opening statement, "Collected for the poor..."

While donations placed in the church box were 'free-will offerings' the Kirk Session nevertheless took a keen interest to ensure people were giving enough. In January 1653, the Session "considering the meanness off the present collections and that there be mony who are able that give either little or nothing, appoynts the minister to reprove uncharitables the next Lord's day and to stirre up people to their dutie heir." One can only imagine what the 'uncharitables' felt when they listened to the minister's sermon.

Trades and Occupations

Those who could work were expected to do so. From symbols on some gravestones in Dalgety kirkyard, there is evidence of blacksmiths (Robert Roneld, who died in 1707 was one), a maltster and a flesher (butcher). Given the need for items for daily living, it is likely there would have been trades such as carpenters, wrights, spinners, weavers and dyers; tailors and cordiners. Coalmining and saltmaking were also sources of employment, and we know from some of the gravestones that farming was a major activity. Other trades such as saddlers, stonemasons or coppersmiths and lead workers would likely only have been found in the burghs.

The larger houses would have employed a range of people, probably with a chamberlain overseeing the management of the household, a housekeeper and servants looking after personal needs, kitchen and household activities and grooms and stable boys to care for the horses and keep the stable and yard clean. It is highly likely that Andrew Donaldson would have employed a servant girl to help his wife with chores in the manse and a man to work on the glebe.

There are no records indicating whether medical doctors were working in the parish and attending patients during Donaldson's time. Towards the end of the century, it is known that an apothecary was active in Inverkeithing, and it is likely people would have walked there to seek out his services. Dalgety had charmers and healers, often accused of being witches, but most of them performed useful functions, from offering remedies for headaches to acting as midwives. It was often the case that ministers would have had rudimentary medical training during their studies and landed gentry involved in warfare would have a knowledge of how to treat certain conditions. Edinburgh was fast becoming a centre for medical skills and knowledge, and it is not beyond the bounds of possibility that recourse would have been made to the expertise available there.

There may well have been local fishermen. "The common people along the [west] coast of Fife… according to the seasons of the year, are either seamen or landmen; they make nets and in smaller boats, fish all the year for cod and ling and other white fish; and have larger boats for taking herring and macharel in the time of the drove."[13] It is unlikely that Dalgety would have had a fishing industry as such and any fish caught would have been for family consumption or for selling or bartering at the markets.

Brewers and Ale Houses

Kirk Session records indicate that there was at least one alehouse in the parish and, consequently, there would have been innkeepers and brewers, although it is difficult to speculate where inns or alehouses might have been in Donaldson's time. There may well have been a number of small brewhouses, scattered throughout the parish, making ale for consumption in the immediate locality. An indication that there were many alehouses appears to be contained in the Kirk Session minutes for 29th June 1645. The

Earl of Moray is recorded as regretting the "abuse of drunkenness" in the part of the parish where he lives and "desyres that some cair be had for the curbing of it: and withal shew what he has done himself, in his own bounds, concerning the aill-houses; to wit, that all under him that sell aill are discharged under ane penaltie to sell aill to any they exceed moderation." The Session approved this course of action and "appointed everie heritor and elder in his quarter to do the lyke."

Brewing, where malting of the grain may have taken place, had been carried out in the parish for centuries. It was known to have been underway in the parish by October 1421 as it was recorded that the Abbot of Inchcolm had to replenish his supplies on the island and he sent the cellarer with servants to fill up casks with beer brewed at Barnhill, the home farm of the abbey. With grain for milling or brewing requiring a low moisture content, there may have been grain-drying kilns in the parish.

Gardeners

Gardening was another significant occupation. Donibristle, which had been refurbished by the 4th Earl using English craftsmen, was described in 1677 as "a fine house, built square and regular with the windows proportionable. In the middle of the eastern court is a fountain, in the middle whereof stands a Mercury, with one foot on the back of a tortoise, which turns up its neck and spouts water up to a great height and washes the Black's skin. Here are many good gardens, walks and groves and a very fine bowling green."[14] When the 4th Earl died in 1653, his widow continued to live in the property, maintaining the garden and planting many trees. We know from the records that gardens were maintained at Fordell Castle, Dalgety House and Leuchat.

Gardening was a hard physical life, and the gardener was expected to keep the grounds tidy, maintain the paths and scythe the grass, cut hedges, plant and prune trees, maintain an orchard, sow vegetable seeds and harvest the produce for the household. In addition, he might have been expected to train an apprentice, maintain flower beds, manage beehives, make cider from the apples as well as building seed boxes, preparing compost heaps and repairing his tools.

A gardener had a position of authority and standing in the household and when Robert Meikle died in September 1685, a fine mural memorial was erected on the west gable of the Seton loft. The original text is no longer there but partly translated, read, "… a most faithful servant to the earl of Dunfermline, who died at the age of 45… in him honesty, wisdom, virtue, candour and a snow-like [unsullied] simplicity were combined."[15]

As befitted his status, the post was well-recompensed. We learn from an account rendered in 1643 by James Cuthbertson, gardener at Donibristle, that he was owed one hundred and twenty-eight pounds Scots as a year's wages for him and his man.[16] As the under-gardener would have received little more than half of the gardener's wage, Cuthbertson would have been paid around ninety pounds Scots per year, equivalent to between £7 and £8 sterling. He also received "for the space of three yeirs for three suits of clothes at 20s sterling the piece". George Liddell was a successor to Cuthbertson, and he was followed by, possibly, his son, as a contract was drawn up with the Earl of Moray and an Alexander Liddell on 10th December 1697 "for the keeping of the earl's gardens at Donibristle".[17]

Millers

With a mill in the parish there would have been millers and baxters (bakers) and probably smaller bakehouses for making oatcakes or bannocks, as they provided a cheaper alternative to bread and were affordable by the poor. Bread was a staple food and millers were key in converting the various grains into flour for the bakers. As oats were plentiful, bread was often oatmeal bread but the ordinary gray bread was made from a flour mixture of rye, barley and wheat, often with ground dried peas added. White bread, made from wheat flour, although nutritionally less beneficial, was more expensive because the additional process of sieving the grain to remove all the bran added to the cost, to the extent that only the wealthier families could afford it. The grain was milled at Fordell and Pitadro Mills, both close to each other but on opposite sides of the Fordell burn, just south of Fordell Castle. At some point the latter mill fell into disuse, probably when the lands of Fordell and Pitadro came together under the laird of Fordell's ownership.

The mill at Fordell (Fig 22) is first mentioned in a charter of King James IV, dated at Edinburgh, 1st May 1511, although all that remains today are overgrown fragments of the base of a wall. Originally, it was a two-storey building with the principal entrance in the south gable through an arched doorway. A stone panel, apparently taken from some older building, was inserted above the main entrance. It bore the date 1585 and had the initials I H, for John Henderson of Fordell, and, separated by a crescent, the initials I M, for Jean Murray, his wife.[18]

The Hendersons did not make their fortune from milling grain but from letting out land to tenant farmers and working the minerals that lay beneath the soil. Exploiting the coal, and the colliers, provided a more than comfortable living for them.

Chapter 15

———

Colliers
and Salters

Coal and Colliers

By the latter half of the seventeenth century, coalmining was playing a significant part in the life of the parish, generating great wealth for the Henderson family. Coal was first discovered in the lands of Fordell and surrounding areas in the fourteenth century, with the Augustinian canons from Inchcolm Abbey involved in its extraction up to the time their monastic way of life came to an end. Evidence of their digging coal was documented in 1533, when George Henderson of Fordell accused the Abbey of mining coal on his land and the Abbot of Inchcolm was summoned by King James V to answer for their actions.

Around that time coal mines were, literally, pits, usually shaped like a bell – broad at the base with a narrow funnel to the top. *(Fig 23)* The name 'pit' has become synonymous with a deep coal mine and people still talk, even in the twenty-first century, of 'going down the pit'.

Depending on the depth, access would be gained by a series of ladders. It was dangerous work, as ladders and shafts could give way, the 'bell' could collapse or the pit could flood, often with fatal results. Coalmining was unregulated and the landowners were intent on gaining as much profit as they could – even at the expense of their workers.

Miners were paid by the amount of coal delivered at the pithead and they often employed their wives and older children to carry the coal they had dug to the surface. *(Fig 24)* Wages varied, depending on the mine owner and the work that was carried out. In 1670, David, Earl of Wemyss wrote, "I am still working the level... with two men in it day and night (except on Sunday). I give them 10s Scots a day, their bearers 4s Scots a day, the windles men get 6s Scots a day or night. I sharp their picks and furnish them with all the candles they burn..."[1] In Dunfermline the lowest pay in 1671 was 6s 8d a day. By 1680 a colliery owner could expect to sell his coal for 1 pound 4s Scots per ton although Scotch, or 'great', coal might realise a further 30% and 'small' coal less by a similar amount.[2]

Servitude of Miners

Miners were not free men. According to an Act of Parliament of 1605, colliers and salters could only leave their employment with permission and with a testimonial from their employer. In practice, this meant that colliers and salters were enslaved by the landowners. Where miners were unlawfully engaged by other employers, a challenge had to be lodged within one year and a day when, if the challenge was upheld, the 'new' employer had to return them within twenty-four hours or face a fine of £100 for each day they failed to comply. The act permitted physical punishment for wayward colliers and also authorised coal owners to apprehend "all vagabonds and sturdy beggars and put them to labour."

Many of the landowners were members of the Privy Council, responsible for drawing up the legislation, and with their own fortunes at stake ignored any conflicts of interest. If workers had had mobility, shortage of labour would have driven up wages and reduced the mine owners' profits. Salters were similarly treated, as saltpans depended on a regular supply of coal and most of the pans belonged to the colliery owners.

An Act of 1641 reinforced the 1605 Act and drew other categories of workers into the fold, such as "watermen who bale and draw water in the coal mine... windsmen and gatemen". This later Act also further restricted their freedom, "because the said coal miners and salters do lie from their work at Easter, Yule, Whitsunday and certain other times, which times they employ in drinking and debauchery to the great offence of God and prejudice of their master, it is therefore statute and ordained that the said coal miners and salters and other workmen of coal mines in this kingdom work all the six days of the week under the pains following, that is to say: that every coal miner or salter who lies idle shall pay 20s [i.e. 3 days' pay] for every day…". This was a harsh penalty, particularly as 'lying idle' could be the result of illness, or injury sustained in the mine.

Theoretically, men became 'slaves' by choice by working for a year and a day under one master, or by the custom of 'arling'. "The 'arles' consisted of a present given to the collier and his wife at the time of their baby's baptism in return for a promise that the child would be brought up as a miner. The vow was not legally binding but in practice, it made serfdom hereditary, for no miner would suppose that such a vow was legally fraudulent."[3] In practice, it became impossible for a man who had once laboured in a colliery or a salt work to avoid enslaving himself, together with his wife and children, who frequently worked with him. "As a result of the enforcement of these Acts, the number of labourers who remained free declined rapidly until, by the end of Charles II's reign, nearly every collier and salter found himself and his family bound to one employer for the rest of his life."[4]

At the beginning of the seventeenth century around seventy to eighty families in the parish were involved in mining; as the century progressed, that increased significantly. Miners were relatively well-paid and, despite the working conditions, employment as a miner had its attractions. Agricultural labourers found themselves drawn into mining, as much of the work on land was seasonal and men had to earn money all year round to feed and clothe their families. The lure of higher wages meant many workers never returned to the land, and, given the legislation, found they were ensnared for life.

Condemnation of the working conditions or the status of miners, or salters, did not come from the Church. Their social standing was low, and the Church had an ambivalent attitude towards them and because of that, and the nature of the work they were doing (they were digging towards hell and towards the devil, was one view) the Church was sometimes reluctant to let them attend worship on a Sunday. To emphasise their lowly status, the Church did not permit them to be buried in consecrated ground.

Quality of the Coal

The coalfields of Fordell were amongst the oldest and best in the country, producing different types of coal for a variety of purposes. "In Fiffe ar won blak stanis, quhilk hes sa intollerable heit, quhen thay ar kendillit, that thay resolve and meltis irne, and ar thairfore richt proffitable for operatitm of smithis."[5] Fordell coal was much sought after as it produced a high heat with little ash, good for use by blacksmiths and, in much later generations, for the boilers of steam ships. The Hendersons of Fordell were keen to capitalise on this mineral wealth.

Initially, coal would have been 'picked' from the ground, probably at points closer to the coast where the coal seams were nearer the surface, but as the seams moved inland, they became deeper, necessitating the digging of deeper shafts and 'roads' through which to extract the coal. In Andrew Donaldson's time the landscape would have been littered with pits, most of them concentrated in the area north of Fordell Castle, around Clinkhill, near to what was recently the Muirdean open-cast mining site.

As mine owners, the Hendersons of Fordell were among the more responsible and enlightened in the country. Sir John Henderson, who had been created a baronet by Charles II in 1664, developed one of the first adits, or day levels, in a mine, which greatly helped with drainage and safety. In much later years several Fordell pits were linked together and created a common day level which drained water into the Fordell burn.[6]

With the introduction of iron fire baskets and better-designed chimneys, Scotch coal was much prized by the landed gentry in Scotland and London, where it had become fashionable to heat houses with coal. Donaldson, given his status, may have had a coal fire in the manse and it is likely that the schoolhouse would have had one. The fireplace in the Seton loft in the Kirk indicates that coal was burned there.

Transporting Coal

Moving coal from the Fordell pits to boats at the coast was a slow process as it was brought down to the bay at Dalgety by horse in "deep bulky panniers". The horses, small, sturdy pack-horses, "typically carried about 4 cwts. [just over 200kg] and a pony 2 cwts. Only one journey per day was normally involved: the round trip was approximately five miles with the first part to the coast under heavy effort".[7]

Carts were not in regular use at this time, except in the larger burghs, as the roads, in spite of legislation forcing those in authority "to keep the highways in good repair", were inadequate. By law, every man aged between fifteen and sixty was supposed to carry out three days' work (unpaid) in the summer and another three in the autumn working on maintaining the roads.[8] Men could commute their labour by paying a small sum of money, but this was of little benefit to the road authorities who had to hire workmen at greater cost. This 'voluntary' labour, which was generally given by the poorer members of the community who could not afford the commutation fee, appeared to be highly inefficient and, given the state of the roads, equally ineffective.

The main road from Inverkeithing to Beath and on to Perth, the 'Great North Road', formed, for part of its length, the Dalgety Parish boundary but "from the old records it is clear that horses with panniers did not use this road. Instead, various pathways were used to take the coal to the boats. One led past Letham to the small coastal estate of Seafield and an important route led to the shores of Dalgety Bay which were the property of the Earl of Moray. The Fordell Hendersons had some ancient right of usage on a small pier not far from the old kirk[9] (Fig 25) and also used the shore somewhat to the west of this."[10]

The bay at Dalgety is shallow with mud flats exposed at low tide and, certainly now and probably then, unsuitable for any large boats. In Donaldson's time, coal was loaded on to flat-bottomed boats or barges, probably holding no more than 10 to 15 tons, and taken to burghs such as Inverkeithing or Kirkcaldy, where it was transferred to larger boats and shipped to various locations, including London. There is a suggestion that, "coal as late as 1680 was brought from Fordell in panniers, on horseback, by the beach, and was shipped chiefly to Holland."[11] Whether the boats that could berth at Dalgety were large enough to sail to Holland is a moot point.[12]

Coal Disputes

Coal was money and disputes between landowners were not uncommon. The Registers of the Privy Council for Scotland record that in May 1644 a complaint was lodged by Charles Seton, Earl of Dunfermline, against Sir

John Henderson of Fordell for "detaining a collier belonging to the said Earl". The argument was that "John Henderson of Fordell received Andrew Adamson, 'fied coilyear' to the said earl of Dunfermline 'who had served in his coale of the Crocegates of the Mures of Dunfermline tuo yeeres bygane or thereby and who did remove himselfe away and is interteanned and keeped be the said Johne without testimoniall'." Dunfermline claimed that although Adamson was Henderson's tacksman, he was not Henderson's 'fied' servant but his. "The Lords, after hearing and advising, ordain the said Laird to deliver back the said Andro to the Earl and pay him £100 for each of the times [days] he was requisitioned and refused, extending in all to £2,000."[13]

There is a declaration[14] which confirms that coal was shipped out from the bay at Dalgety during Andrew Donaldson's time. It contains the substance of an argument between Sir Robert Henderson of Fordell and the Earl of Moray regarding the building of dykes by the latter which obstructed a right of way and prevented Henderson shipping coals from the bay.

In giving evidence, "Robert Adamson and James Stanhous say that they both remember the coals being shipt along by the humbel stone[15] for more than fifty years without interruption at the places which is right oposite to the mance... They also afirm that the long bots some time load at the kirk and other places on Dalgety ground and also that the coals horse befor the minister's yard was built went down throw betwixt the mance and scoole. *(Fig 26)* Old John Bevreg in park hall agrees... The above wer all coal carriers and knew everything that past. Mr William Thomson hath shipt coals more than fortie years. John Balingal and William Finlayson remember of the coals being at the Humel Ston and along ther about without interuption. The customhous in Kircaldies books is a sufficient wittness that Dalgety was always a publick crick for shiping Fordel coals and that the barques and boats allways ancared in any pairt of the bay without interuption...". The Declaration further noted that Andrew Donaldson and his successors supplemented their income as "The ministers of Dalgety have been in the consistent use of selling the sea wreak that comes in upon the ground."[16]

Salt and Salt-Making

As much as coal miners and their families were part of Andrew Donaldson's parish and fell within the church's oversight so too did salters, a group very much in the same position as colliers and included in the same servitude legislation.

Salt was a prized item as an essential element of the diet; it not only brought out the flavour of food but helped to preserve meat and fish for export or domestic use through the long, cold Scottish winters. Salt-making had been recorded in Dysart as far back as 1483[17] and had spread along the Fife coast: "There are known to have been saltpans at Culross, Kirkcaldy, Dysart and Fordell[18] in 1574."

When salt-making began at St David's and whether pans were operational during the seventeenth century "is hard to say. [It is possible] that salt manufacturing *would* have gone on at, or near, St David's – as Scottish salt-makers were protected in the later seventeenth century, making it a lucrative trade to be in. There were certainly pans at Inverkeithing. Also, many Forth-side collieries depended on saltpans as a user of the 'small' coal which in many cases made coal-working profitable."[19]

At St David's, pans would have been located close to the sea to take advantage of incoming tides. *(Fig 27)* Filling the pans by hand was preferred, as seaweed and other debris could more easily be kept out, but it had the disadvantage of taking longer and time not spent heating the pan was money lost. Latterly, separate ponds were kept in which seawater was collected and allowed to settle, with impurities dropping to the bottom. The 'clean' seawater was then transferred to the saltpans for boiling. The pans would have been in a pan-house with a roof or cover, enough to let the smoke and steam out and prevent the rain from diluting the saline solution.

Salt-making was dependent on technology and having a market for the product. The process was simple and straightforward, although it required great skill to produce reasonable quality salt without damaging the pans. In the seventeenth century, saltpans (originally made from lead) were manufactured from rivetted wrought-iron sheets which were easily corroded by the brine, discolouring the salt in the process.

Pan were built over a furnace *(Fig 28)* and varied in size but were about 14½ feet long by 11½ feet wide by 18 inches deep and they were filled with water to a depth of 15 inches, holding about 1,300 gallons of seawater. "A strong fire [using panwood or 'small' coal] is lighted in the furnace and then the salt boiler takes the white of three eggs (or blood from the butcher, either sheep or black cattle) and incorporates them into the saltpans while the water is lukewarm. As the water grows hot the whites of egg separates from it a black frothy scum which rises to the surface and covers it all over. As soon as the pan begins to boil this scum is all risen and it is time to skim it off... After the water is skimmed it appears perfectly clear and transparent. They continue boiling briskly till so much of the aqueous part is evaporated, leaving a strong brine almost fully saturated with salt."[20] The pans were then refilled with seawater three, four or more times to enhance the density and quality of the salt – the slower the evaporation, the better the quality. Depending on the number of fillings, the ratio of coal to manufactured salt was around 6-8:1 (i.e. 6 to 8 tons of coal to produce 1 ton of salt; 8 tons being considered the economic limit) and it would take between twenty-two and twenty-eight hours. As always, it became a matter of economics – time and cost versus profit.

Salt Taxes

The bulk of Scottish sea salt was low-grade – most of it was slightly damp, had impurities and its preservation qualities were limited. Bay salt, originating from the French town of La Baie, near La Rochelle, and made by sun-evaporation of seawater, was of higher quality and much preferred for preserving meat, although much Scottish salt was adequate, but not ideal, for gutted herring that was packed and exported. As an example of how French salt was prized over Scottish salt the Privy Council in March 1678 requisitioned supplies for the army and set the price they were willing to pay for various commodities, among them "French gray salt at ten shillings per peck", while Scottish salt only commanded "five shillings per peck".

At various times, the Scottish salt trade benefited from taxes that were imposed on imported salt or from wars in Europe which interrupted trade. As a consequence, both domestic demand and export opportunities to Baltic countries grew and in the seventeenth century, after wool and fish, salt became Scotland's third largest export. Controlling the salt market, both at home and abroad, became a political tool and a means of raising state revenue. In May 1670 Charles II banned the import of salt by anybody who had not purchased a licence and the following year, Parliament complained that by importing foreign salt "the ancient and usefull manufactory of salt is lyk to be ruined and many thousands of poor people brought to extrem povertie, and finding also that by the unlimited importattion of forrain salt wee are frequently defrauded of our customs and excyse..."[21] Salt has been described as "that important and necessary article"[22] and is at one and the same time, an essential commodity for life, a source of revenue and the cause of international conflict.

Work or Worship?

Salt-making was labour-intensive and once the process had started it had to continue until it finished. The salt pans depended on a high tide and if that happened to come at the wrong time on a Saturday or Sunday the salters were faced with a dilemma – miss work or miss church.

The Synod of Fife kept up a stream of complaints about salt-making on the Sabbath. In April 1629 it refused to grant "any such toleration" to a request from a salt-pan owner to allow half his workforce to attend church in the morning and the other half in the afternoon, and stressed "salt pans not to gang at al upon the Saboth". In April 1641 the Synod referred matters to the Presbyteries of St Andrews, Kirkcaldy and Dunfermline "to deale with the masteris of the salt pannes not to require the sext draught, that the whole Sabbath may be keiped unprofaned." The following year, Synod had mellowed slightly as it had agreed the "Salt pannes to be put owt twixt 12 hours on Satterday night, till midnight of Sonday" but it was not budging on people attending church.

In October the following year the Synod lost patience, as it found itself unable to prevent people working on the Sabbath, "The quhilk day considering the multiplied relapse of salteris in Sabboth breaking and how frequentlie thei have mocked God... doe thairfour ordain, that efter intimatione heirof, the salteris that shall persist in Sabbath breaking, being lawfullie convict of thair sinne, shall make thair repentance in the publick place and to double thair dayes of apeiring befor the congregatione... and that they be heirby expresslie suspendit from the Sacrament of the Lord's Supper, till such tyme as thei give proof of their reall reformatione."

So, how did the Church offer pastoral care to these people and help them in their situation? Did Donaldson, and those who followed him, not see serfdom as a problem? Perhaps they resorted to the fact that, 'that was the law' or they knew that Parliament was obsessed by the need to put the poor to work; or was it the case that the influence of the landowners on them was just too great and the Church would have lost more than it gained? For Donaldson and all that was happening around him, maybe it was just not a high priority or perhaps he just chose to ignore it?

The Church, for that matter, may have felt that this was the natural order of things and people had to know their place in society. From our twenty-first-century perspective, it is certainly a condemnation that the Church did not speak out against the employers and stand up for those who had no voice. As a result of the Church's inaction, "serfdom thus fell about the necks of the colliers [and salters] when a group of their employers in a privileged position in the state saw it as a possible means of securing sufficient cheap labour. Seventeenth-century society did not protest either...; church and state alike saw it as a simple and admirable way out of an economic dilemma. ... In what senses can the civil wars, the covenants and the revolutions of the seventeenth century be held to be about the basic liberties of man when all the contenders paused in the struggle to confirm, as a matter of automatic common-sense, the serfdom of the least privileged?"[23]

Chapter 16

Donaldson Imprisoned

After he was deposed in 1664, pastoral care remained a concern for Donaldson, and he continued to preach and minister to members of his former congregation. His links with families such as Henderson of Fordell, Spittal of Leuchat, Mowbray of Cockairnie and the Earls of Moray and Dunfermline meant he had friends in high places with homes to provide a degree of shelter. In 1666, Sir John Henderson of Fordell purchased a building opposite Inverkeithing parish church. It became known as Fordell's Lodgings *(Fig 29)* and Donaldson was reputed to have stayed there for a time.

Mr Robert Blair

The Henderson homes were frequently used for conventicles and illegal meetings and Donaldson would regularly hold services in them. Also a known visitor was Mr Robert Blair, who, at the age of twenty-three, had been appointed Professor of Moral Philosophy at the University of Glasgow. He had been a negotiator for the Treaty of Ripon, after the 2nd Bishops' War, and one of the Scottish Commissioners to confirm the Solemn League and Covenant. Highly regarded, he had been appointed a chaplain to King Charles I in Scotland. In 1646, he had been elected Moderator of the General Assembly of the Church of Scotland.

His position as a Presbyterian minister in St Andrews became intolerable as soon as James Sharp was elevated to the archbishopric, and in 1662 he was called before the Privy Council. Subsequently ejected, he was denied a permanent home in Kirkcaldy and took up residence in Couston Castle, overlooking Otterston loch. There, he was visited by many people from the surrounding area, including ministers such as Donaldson, who were debarred from preaching 'the Word'. It was more than likely that he would have accompanied Donaldson to Fordell's Lodgings and Fordell Castle where Sir John Henderson, the laird, was an elder in Dalgety Church. Blair, "a most faithful preacher of the Gospel", died at Couston Castle in 1666 and as it lay within Aberdour parish he was buried in St Fillan's kirkyard.

Hill of Beath Conventicle

Remaining a Presbyterian was becoming a challenge, as Charles II was proving to be almost as intransigent as his father in insisting that Episcopalianism was to be the established form of Church government and worship. In an effort to provide an olive branch to rebels, Charles granted an Indulgence in 1669 to all 'well-behaved' deposed ministers to allow them to return to their former churches with a manse, glebe and small stipend, with penalties to be applied if they strayed beyond their allotted parish. Failure to observe the terms of the Indulgence resulted in punishment "according to law and the degree of the offence."

This left little leeway for strict Presbyterian ministers. Donaldson and most other non-conformists did not accept the Indulgence, and many continued their 'illegal' preaching in houses and fields. Word of mouth was an effective method in disseminating information about these meetings, on one occasion powerful enough to persuade one thousand people to attend the conventicle on Sunday 19th June 1670 at the Cloich,[1] near the summit of the Hill of Beath.

It was more than likely that Andrew Donaldson would have climbed the Hill of Beath that Sunday, given that the preachers were none other than Mr John Dickson, former minister at Rutherglen, and the celebrated Mr John Blackadder, deposed minister from Troqueer, near Dumfries. People were so keen to hear them that they had begun to assemble on the hill on the Saturday afternoon. "Many lay on the hillside all night, some stayed in a constable's house near the middle of the hill, others were lodged near about. Mr Blackadder came privately from Edinburgh on Saturday night, with a single gentleman in his company. At Inverkeithing, he slept all night in his clothes and got up very early."[2]

The service started about eight o'clock. Mr Dickson, "having lectured for a considerable space" then preached on the text, "For he must reign, till he hath put all enemies under his feet" *(1 Corinthians Ch.15 v.25, KJV)* and finished his sermon around eleven o'clock. Mr Blackadder, after a period of private meditation, started the afternoon service with prayer and preached from *1 Corinthians Ch.9 v.16*, "For though I preach the gospel, I have nothing to glory of: for necessity is laid upon me: yea, woe is unto me, if I preach not the gospel"*(KJV)*. Among those attending the conventicle was "James Lamb, Dumfermling, who raised the psalme".

The Hill of Beath conventicle passed off with little incident. The horse of the lieutenant of the militia was restrained by the crowd but Mr Blackadder intervened, saying, "We came here to offer violence to no man but to preach the gospel of peace; and, sir, if you be pleased to stay in peace, you shall be as welcome as any here; but if you will not, you may go; we shall compel no man"[3]

Mr John Blackadder

John Blackadder[4] was a noted Covenanter and an inspiring preacher. He had been born at Inzievar, near Oakley, and attended the University of Glasgow, where he graduated Master of Arts in 1650. He was called to the parish of Troqueer and admitted in 1652. Like Donaldson, he protested against the imposition of prelacy and following the restoration of episcopacy in 1662 he was deprived of his charge. Ignoring warrants for his arrest, Blackadder travelled the country as an itinerant preacher and was widely regarded as one of "the boldest and most successful in collecting, at these places, the scattered followers of Christ".

On the Monday morning, after leaving David Sterk's lodging house at Fordell, he, his servant and Mr Dickson rode to North Queensferry with the intention of catching a boat across the river. They found that the authorities were intending to arrest them, and an embargo had been placed on all boats. They faced a long ride to the bridge at Stirling to cross the Forth there and make good their escape.

The Privy Council was in no mood to give quarter and in August 1670 it accused Blackadder of "seduc[ing] the subjects from their obedience to his Majesties lawes and to perswad them to withdraw and separate from the publick worship of God in their paroch kirks, and in a seditious and tumultuary manner".[5] The Privy Council "ordaines letteres to be direct to messengers at armes to denunce the saids persons his Majesties rebell, and putt them to the horn, and to escheit etc." In 1678 Blackadder fled for his life to the Protestant community in Rotterdam. When he returned in 1681, he was captured and imprisoned on the Bass Rock, where he died five years later.

Action Against Conventiclers

Strict action was taken by the authorities to clamp down on conventicles and the Privy Council acted swiftly in apprehending and questioning people who had been on the Hill of Beath. "Robert Walwood of Touch in the paroch of Dunfermline being examined anent the conventicle keeped at the Hill of Beeth upon the Sunday, being 19 day of Junij instant, [and] ... declares he was present, declares the occasion of his knowing off that conventicle was that one Saturday morning a widow woman in Dunfermlin, called Agnes Parson, spous to [...] Blak, a tayleour, told him thereof...".[6] He continued his testimony when he declared that, "he heard that the tuo ministers after they left preaching went that night to David Sterks house, a tenant under Fordell that keepes a change house; and 'depones there were severall of the persons present had swords and pistolls'." Walwood was fined 500 merks, imprisoned until he paid it and bound over for 2,000 merks, on pain of attending any more conventicles.[7]

A great number of other Covenanters were interviewed but selective amnesia was present, and none could recall, apart from the odd name, who else had been there. "David Mather... knew not the ministers preached nor no persons were there except some of his oune neighboures, whose names he refuses to tell." Mather, even under oath, divulged nothing and was found by the Privy Council to be "guilty of contumac". He, and others, were fined 500 merks and sent to prison "to lie in irons during the council's pleasure".

John Vernor, another who had been present at the conventicle and who "refused to betray his honest neighbours and acquaintances, 'to the fury of persecutors' was most barbarously dealt with. He was fed on bread and water and put so close in the irons that his leg gangrened, which within a little cost him his life". A Robert Orr from Milnbank, who had had a child baptised, was found guilty and banished "out of the king's dominions". He was transported to the plantations.[8]

Attempts at Toleration

With the upsurge in conventicles, it was clear, even to Charles II, that his policy of indulging non-conforming ministers and trying to bring about a measure of reconciliation had had only limited success. Factions had been at work in government over the past few years attempting to find a settlement to the ecclesiastical problems and "conciliation could have taken either of two courses, 'comprehension' of the presbyterians in the establishment by means of modifications which would have made the structure of the Church acceptable to all but the most intransigent; or 'accommodation', tolerance of presbyterians outside the national Church".[9] In the event, Charles did neither of those. Given Donaldson's views, it is highly likely that he would have been classed as one of the "most intransigent" and not amenable to anything except Presbyterianism throughout both kingdoms. In September 1672, Charles issued a second Indulgence to ministers outed since the year 1661.[10] For staunch Presbyterians, like Donaldson, the struggle continued, and he again refused to be indulged.

Privy Council Increases the Pressure

In June 1674 Charles II issued a Proclamation[11] which obliged Heritors and Masters to keep themselves, their families and servants from attending conventicles. They were expected to sign a Bond in agreement. The punishment for attending a house conventicle was set at "twenty-five pounds Scots for each tenant labouring land, twelve pounds for each cottar and for each servant man, a fourth part of his year's fee and the husband the half of these fines for such of their wives or children as shall be at any house conventicle, and the double of the respective fines for each of the said persons that shall be at any field conventicle".[12]

Some of Donaldson's parishioners found themselves facing the court. A meeting of the Privy Council on 25th June 1674 records that "the keiping or being present at conventicles is expresly prohibitd… the persons underwrytten have keeped or bein present at severall conventicles, and particularly at field conventicles… the Laird of Fordell, and William Henderson his brother, who are knowne to be inciters of the people at Dunfermlin to field conventicles". And if that was not enough, "the fornamit persons have directly contraveened the tenour of the said act of Parliament and thereby incurred the paines and penalties therein conteanit, which ought to be inflicted on them… Henderson of Fordell".[13]

The Laird was summoned to appear before the Privy Council but opted not to attend. Non-appearance was a serious offence, and, on the 21st July, he was summoned again. The Lords clearly felt Sir John Henderson had a case to answer and he was bound over to appear again on the "first Thursday of September nixt… he finding sufficient caution under the paine of ten thousand merks to appear personally at the forsaid dyet".

With friends like the Hendersons, and using places like Fordell Castle, or Fordell's Lodgings, Donaldson continued his pastoral and ministerial duties. None of these activities escaped the attention of the authorities and on 9th July 1674 the Privy Council met again and increased the pressure on people found to have been present at conventicles, indicating that "they shall be fyned in the soumes following and imprisoned untill they pay their fynes".[14]

The Privy Council went further and laid strict punishment on those aiding and abetting traitors and rebels. "All persons who doe harbour, resett, supply or intercommon or doe anywayes correspond or keip company with any persons that are declared traitours or rebells or who are sentenced, adjudged and found guilty of hie treason, or who are aiding, abateing or assisting to the saids traitours ought to be severely punished".

Among those listed as usurping authority was George Spence in Fordell, who "have keeped and bein present at house or field conventicles near the places afterspecifeit, viz. Dalgatie"; and a Robert Gedd of Baldridge [a locality to the north-west of Dunfermline] who "did acknowledge that he had bein at tuo conventicles in houses, one in Fordell Hendersons house". Gedd was found guilty "of being at four field conventicles and fynes him in the half of his yearly valued rent for each of these conventicles and ordaines him to be committed instantly to prison to remain thereintill he make payment of his fyne". The following month, the Lords of the Privy Council receive a petition from Robert Gedd, who had been forced to sell some of his land in order to raise the money to pay his fine and "... doe ordain him to be sett at liberty, he first paying to his Majesties cashkeiper his fyne... extending to one thousand fyve hundreth and threttie thrie *lib.* 6*s.* 8*d.* Scotts".

Donaldson "Put to the Horn" and Intercommuned

Time was not on Andrew Donaldson's side and he was summoned to appear before the Privy Council on 16th July 1674.[15] The Privy Council pointed out that only ministers who had been "authorised or tolerat by the bishop of the dioces" could hold church services and lawfully preach; the only exception was that non-conformists could preach "in their owne houses and to these of thir owne family" – even inviting a neighbour or a friend was to be found guilty of holding a conventicle.

Donaldson ignored the summons. The Privy Council then recorded that he was "in oppen and manifest contempt of our authority and lawes" for holding public meetings and conventicles. "Being oftymes called and not compeared, the Privy Council ordaines letters to be direct to messengers at armes to denunce them his Majesties rebells". This was no barrier to Andrew Donaldson and less than one week later a further complaint was made to the Privy Council that he had been holding conventicles. By the end of the month the rebels, including "Mr Andro Donaldson, somtym minister in Dalgetty" were duly "put to the horn... by vertue of letters of denunciation" and proclaimed as such at the market crosses in Edinburgh, Dunfermline and Linlithgow amongst others.

As he was a man of strong convictions, this did not curtail his activities and in July 1676 his name again appeared before the Privy Council, as it did the following month. On 6th August Donaldson, along with others, was accused of continuing to preach illegally and was said "to continow in their rebellion by the resett, supply and intercommoning which they have with severall of their friends to the high contempt of his Majesties authority and lawes". This time Donaldson found himself intercommuned and the punishment meted out by the Privy Council was extremely severe. People were forbidden to have any contact with him or offer him food or shelter, on pain of imprisonment.[16] Donaldson was not to be deterred and he continued his preaching and another complaint was lodged in August 1677, of a conventicle that had been held in 'Dalgatie'.

Donaldson Arrested and Imprisoned

The level of support he was receiving must have been a great comfort and encouragement to Donaldson, but his problems remained and one evening, [probably] in the spring of 1678, he was arrested. "Mr Andrew Donaldson, now an old infirm man, came with his family to live in Inverkeithing, where Mr David Lauder, was episcopal minister. This worthy old man was so cautious, that he would never preach, either in his own house or any other, in the time of public worship. But sometimes on the Sabbath evening, he preached to his own family, and some others in the town did come in. For no other cause than this, a party of soldiers came one night and carried him out of his bed, old and infirm as he was, straight away prisoner to Linlithgow Tolbooth,[17] *(Fig 30)* where he continued more than a year, without any thing being laid to his charge."[18]

Parishioners Fined

The authorities were keen not just to prevent the activities of rebels such as Donaldson but to keep the population under their thumb and stop the spread of seditious Presbyterian material. Throughout the country men were brought to book for not signing the bond against conventicles. In January 1678 the Privy Council noted a "List of Noblemen and heretours in the shyres of Fyiff and Kinrois that have as yit not signed the bond for the publique peace": in "Dumfermeling Presbitrie: The Laird of Fordell, James Holborne of Menstrie, John Moubray of Cowcarnie, Earle of Murray" are named; and in "Dalgatie Paroch: Sir John Airskine, Robert Mowbray, Lewchate, Earle of Dumfermline and Alexander Thomsone",[19] are noted as heritors who have not signed the Bond against conventicles and "disorderly walking".

For those arrested at conventicles the punishment was "fyning or closs imprisonment or banishment by sending them to the plantationes in the Indies or elsewher as the Councill shall think fitt". The fate of those who were transported to the plantations was no deterrence to people in the parish and in November 1678 the Privy Council again records the name of Dalgety, "in contravention of the acts against conventicles, withdrawing from parish churches, entertaining and corresponding with traitors etc.".

Donaldson would have taken hope from men in the parish who were willing to make a stand and from families who were prepared to assist him. Many paid dearly for the cost of their loyalty as "seven families were fined in £300 each for what were termed disorderly baptisms" – that is their children had been baptised by other than a lawfully authorised minister, in this case by Andrew Donaldson. Robert Adamson, Clinkhill and Elspeth Mitchell were fined £300 for a disorderly marriage and others were "fined in the sums set over against their names for house-conventicles at which Andrew Donaldson or some other ejected minister preached the word of life".[20] Twenty-three families, probably around 12%-15% of the number in the parish, suffered as a result of their stand for the Presbyterian cause. In total, £8,400 was extracted from them, money which they could probably ill afford. In addition, Alexander Spittall, Laird of Leuchat, a noted conventicler, was fined £1,200 by Middleton's Parliament.

Chapter 17

———

Death of Donaldson;
the Century Comes to a Close

The Killing Time

Donaldson's plight was similar to many others and with a tightening of the restrictions on holding conventicles and the government's decision to station militia at various places to 'keep a lid on things', resistance began to strengthen. Matters came to a head in May 1679 when Archbishop Sharp, as he returned home to St Andrews, was murdered on Magus Moor by a group of Covenanters. A pamphlet, published in London the following year, purported to be "A True Relation of what is Discovered concerning the MURTHER of the Archb^p of St Andrews". It laid the blame on John Balfour of Kinloch and his brother-in-law, David Hackston of Rathillet, a "vile person [who] had nothing of good in him".

Coming from the episcopal stronghold of Aberdeen, Sharp was widely regarded as someone who had favoured the episcopal cause for the sake of personal gain. His death galvanised the Covenanters who raised an armed conventicle and defeated a force under the command of John Graham of Claverhouse, 1st Viscount Dundee, 'Bonnie Dundee', at Drumclog, in June 1679. Their victory was short-lived as later that same month their forces were crushed by the Duke of Monmouth, Charles II's illegitimate son, at Bothwell Bridge. Over eleven hundred prisoners were captured and sent to "The Covenanters' Prison", an area now within Greyfriars kirkyard. It began a period known as 'the Killing Time'.

Government attitudes hardened and a few radical rebels elected to fight on under the leadership of Richard Cameron. He had been born in Falkland in 1648 and raised as an Episcopalian but, after consideration, he embraced Covenanting ideals and committed himself fully to the Presbyterian struggle. With his small band of followers, known as "the Cameronians",[1] he engaged government forces on Airds Moss, on 22nd July 1680, where he and his brother were killed. Hackston of Rathillet was captured and taken to Edinburgh, where he was later executed. The Covenanting mantle was picked up by James Renwick who continued a Covenanting ministry until his capture and execution in 1688.

Cameron and his devotees were extreme in their views, and the small following they had demonstrated the general mood in the country which, unlike fifty years previously, had moved away from strong support of the Covenants. Times were changing; the national psyche was scarred by the atrocities and bloodshed, and remembrance lay deep in people's souls. The Martyrs' Memorial in Greyfriars kirkyard is a present reminder of the sacrifices made by Renwick and others to establish freedom of religious expression and install Presbyterianism as the preferred Scottish approach.

Donaldson Released from Prison

After the battle of Bothwell Bridge, which was pivotal in signalling the reduced influence of the Covenanters, a degree of leniency was introduced which granted indemnity to Covenanters and authorised house conventicles. Andrew Donaldson found himself released from prison. "The Lords of his Majesties Privy Councill do hereby give order to the magistrats of Linlithgow to sett at liberty Mr Andrew Donaldsone, minister... they finding caution, ilk ane of them, under the paine of ten thousand merks for their appearance when called, conforme to kings letter, at the sight and to the satisfaction of the Lords Register".[2]

The heritors in the parish lost little time before lodging a petition with the Privy Council, "from Sir John Henderson of Fordell, James Holburne of Menstrie, Alexander Spitell of Leuquhat, Robert Mowbray of Cowcairny for themselves and in name and behalfe of the remanent heritours and parochiners of the paroch of Dalgetie, Mr Andrew Donaldsone be allowed to preach in termes of the act, in reguard he hath found sufficient caution acted in the books of Privy Councill conforme to the bond under the penalty of six thousand merks Scots money".[3]

Donaldson accepted the indulgence to be released and restrict his activities to within Dalgety Parish. It was a freedom that could have been easily curtailed, as shortly afterwards "the Privy Councill doe ordaine... the shireff of Fife and his deputy to suppress a meeting house in the paroch of Dalgetie, it being unwarrantably set up".[4] On this occasion, Donaldson escaped censure.

He was known as a staunch Presbyterian, a protesting minister, and a man dedicated to the Covenants. He had been deposed, put to the horn, intercommuned and imprisoned. He had had fifteen years of hardship and privation – maybe not to some the signs of good fortune but he was still in his parish (although not as the incumbent minister) and he had not been executed or banished to the plantations. Good fortune, or faith that his God would not let him down?

Death of Charles II

Charles II had shared similar views to his father about the divine right of kings but had never followed his father's zealous approach. As 'The Merry Monarch', he had preferred a hedonistic lifestyle and while he had a number of illegitimate children his wife, Catherine of Braganza, failed to produce any legitimate heirs. Charles, mindful that he would be succeeded by his brother James, who had converted to Roman Catholicism around 1668–69, opted for a judicious course and arranged for his niece, Mary, James's daughter by his first wife, Ann Hyde, to marry the Dutch protestant Prince William of Orange.

After he had been restored to the throne of England in 1660, Charles had had to deal with the aftermath of Cromwell. He had had to contend with the second and third Anglo-Dutch wars, the Great Plague in London in 1665 and the Great Fire of London the following year, as well as trying to find a solution to the Presbyterian and Covenanting problem in Scotland.

Closer to home, the English Parliament was continuing to assert its right to be the pre-eminent authority of government, but Charles retaliated, latterly dissolving parliament for the last six years of his reign. The country survived the 'popish plot', a fictitious scheme dreamt up by Titus Oates, although the incident had stirred up anti-Roman Catholic feeling. Charles' wife was Catholic and he had himself flirted with Roman Catholicism; and to the anger of many, converted to it on his deathbed in February 1685. He was succeeded by his brother, James, Duke of York, as King James VII & II.

Accession of James VII & II

Andrew Donaldson now found himself in a difficult position. James' first parliament declared it treason to own the National Covenant 'as explained in the year 1638' and made attendance at a conventicle punishable by death. Against the wishes of the English Parliament James issued a proclamation which granted toleration to Roman Catholics and published a letter inveighing against "those enemies of Christianity… the field conventiclers, whom we recommend you to root out with all the severities of our laws".[5] By 1686 James' views had moderated and the following year (June 1687) a proclamation stated that the king's subjects were allowed "to meet and serve God after their own way, be it in private houses, chapels or places purposely hired or built for that use".

The grant of toleration "transformed the ecclesiastical situation. Before this point, the hopes of a restoration of the presbyterian system had seemed remote, and the many Scots who had a preference for presbyterianism, without being fanatical, had become conformers, acquiescing in the existing regime and attending the parish churches. Now it was all different. In any parish a presbyterian preacher could open a meeting house, in free competition with the parish minister who was apt to find his congregation dwindling. The presbyterians grew in strength, refugees returned from Holland and there was once again an active presbyterian party which began to develop a regional organisation which would provide a possible alternative to the establishment. Presbyterianism had again become a cause with a future."[6]

James Seton, 4ᵗʰ Earl of Dunfermline

James Seton had become the 4ᵗʰ Earl of Dunfermline in 1677, on the untimely death of his brother, Alexander, at the age of thirty-five. Despite the earldom, he was in need of money, as his father, Charles, the 2nd Earl, had gambled away much of the family fortune. In August 1683 he petitioned the Privy Council to allocate him half of the land and estates, and half the estate's rental income which had, at one time, belonged to his grandmother, Lady Margaret Hay (Lady Callendar), and now belonged to Alexander Livingston, 2nd Earl of Callendar. The Privy Council was not impressed by Callendar's arguments and awarded Seton a "yeares aliment of fyve hundred pounds sterling" and if the Earl of Callendar failed to pay, then letters of horning would be issued against all his "tennents, tacksmen, factors, chamberlaines and others".[7]

In his younger days, Seton had served under Prince William of Orange but had changed sides in support of James VII & II and became a proponent of episcopal worship. Following James' relaxation of worship, the Scots Presbyterians, unlike the Episcopalians, were now feeling more secure, but as a staunch Roman Catholic James did nothing to hide his own beliefs. His supporters, the Jacobites,[8] felt that military success was key to recovering their position and mounted a brief but ultimately unsuccessful rebellion and, in spite of a stunning victory against Protestant forces at the Battle of Killiecrankie in July 1689, the Jacobite leader, Graham of Claverhouse, 'Bonnie Dundee', was fatally wounded. The Jacobite cause was lost at the Battle of Dunkeld, in August, where the Cameronians formed the backbone of the army. Commanding a troop of Jacobite horse in these battles, was James Seton.

After Dunkeld, King James fled to France, accompanied by James Seton. As a result, Seton was declared an outlaw and his estates were forfeited, but in recognition of his loyalty, James bestowed on him the Order of the Thistle, an honour created by James in 1687 to reward his key supporters. Seton had married Lady Jean Gordon, daughter of the Marquis of Huntly, in 1682 but they had no children and when he died in 1694 the earldom died with him.

Another founding member of the Order of the Thistle was Alexander Stuart, 5th Earl of Moray. His elder brother having died young, he had succeeded to the title in 1653. He had been a political figure for many years but, following the murder of Archbishop Sharp (May 1679), he had been nominated as Secretary of State by his uncle by marriage, the Duke of Lauderdale, a post that James VII & II insisted that he share with Charles, 2nd Earl of Middleton. An opponent of Presbyterianism, he was an antagonist during 'the Killing Time' in helping to suppress Presbyterian uprisings.

In 1686 he was appointed Lord High Commissioner to the Parliament of Scotland, the same year in which he converted to Roman Catholicism. After William ascended the throne, he was deprived of office and imprisoned as a suspected Jacobite. He died at Donibristle in 1701.

James VII & II Exiled

In spite of showing toleration, King James successfully managed to alienate those who might have been his supporters and when his second wife, Mary of Modena, gave birth to a son[9] this prompted the English Parliament in 1688 to invite Prince William, and his wife Mary, James' daughter, to take the throne to prevent a Roman Catholic succession. William's invading army landed in southwest England in November 1688 and to prevent him becoming a martyr to the Roman Catholic cause James was allowed to flee to exile in France.

From his base in France James continued his campaign to regain the throne. His forces were beaten in battle at Cromdale in May 1690, bringing to an end Jacobite resistance in Scotland. He turned his concentration to Ireland, aware that William was planning to invade to consolidate his power. He subsequently met William's army at the River Boyne, near Drogheda, in July 1690, where he was soundly defeated.

William and Mary Assume the Throne

William and Mary were welcomed by most people, although the Scottish Episcopalians and Roman Catholics, by and large, remained faithful to the Stuarts and the Jacobite cause. When William asked the Scottish Bishops for their allegiance, they were non-committal in their support, reputedly answering, "so far as law, reason, or conscience would allow".

With a Protestant monarch on the throne, Presbyterianism in Scotland was assured, although England retained the episcopal system of Church government. In England, the supremacy of parliament over monarchy was complete. In Scotland, suggestions which had been aired previously about a political and economic union with England resurfaced and within a few years Scotland would not only be united through the crowns but share a common parliament with their 'auld enemy'.

King William paved the way for an atmosphere of toleration and in October 1690, the General Assembly of the Church of Scotland met for the first time since 1653. Deposed ministers, including Donaldson, were restored to their churches; the *Westminster Confession of Faith* was confirmed, and the concept of divine rule was repudiated. At that Assembly, Lord Carmichael, the King's Commissioner, addressed the Brethren: "... we never could be of the mind that violence was suited to the advancing of true religion. Moderation is what religion requires, neighbouring Churches expect from and we recommend to you."[10]

John Locke, the influential English philosopher, whose ideas influenced the Bill of Rights,[11] summed it up when he wrote in 1689, "Absolute liberty, just and true liberty, is the thing we stand in need of. No man is hurt because his neighbour is of a different religion from his own, and no civil society is hurt because its members are of different religions from one another".[12] Words which we would do well to heed today.

Death of Andrew Donaldson

For Andrew Donaldson, the so-called 'Glorious Revolution' of 1688 and the General Assembly of 1690 turned everything full circle. He was back in his manse and his pulpit and in 1690 he was elected Moderator of the Presbytery of Dunfermline. In August 1690, he is recorded in the notes of the Privy Council as presiding over the installation of the minister at Culross, "Mr James Fraser... as ane testificat under the hands of Mr Andrew Donaldsone, moderator and James Lamb,[13] clerk to the presbytrie of Dumfermling... having deprived Mr Robert Wright and Mr Alexander Young, the incumbents, of their benefices for ther disobedience and not praying for their Majesties."[14]

Towards the end of his life, Andrew Donaldson suffered from paralysis and dementia and died, it is thought, in 1694 or 1695, around the age of seventy-five. *(Fig 31)* Thirty years later, "and many yet alive have a most savoury remembrance of this worthy person". Mr Samuel Charters, minister of Inverkeithing, in a letter to Robert Wodrow, wrote, "He was singular for a heavenly and spiritual temper and very much of a holy tenderness and ardent love to Jesus Christ at all times, discovered themselves in every thing he did; that many religious persons, since the revolution, in that country, at their death, owned, that Mr Donaldson was the mean of their conversion and edification. In a word, he was not only eminent in holiness, and the faithful discharge of his office, but likewise a person of a very solid judgement, and great wisdom and prudence".[15]

His estate took some time to be wound up as his son, Andrew, is recorded as taking steps in December 1696 and October 1697 to reclaim a portion of stipend due to his father. "Discharge by Andrew Donaldson, lawful son of the deceased Mr Andrew Donaldson, late minister at Dalgety, to John Baxter, tenant in Barnhill, in name of Alexander, Earl of Moray for 13 bolls victual of the stipend due to his deceased father – 14 October 1697".[16]

Mr Archibald Campbell

The people in the parish needed a period of stability to come to terms with all that had happened during the previous thirty or so years. Their next minister, Archibald Campbell, attempted to provide it. It is likely that Campbell, born in 1667, was native to the area as he was educated at the University of Edinburgh, graduating a Master of Arts on 18th July 1692. He was admitted to the ministry at Dalgety on 27th August 1696 and the following year, in May 1697, he married Isobel Baird, the daughter of Robert Baird, a bailie of Inverkeithing, and Margaret Wellwood, eldest daughter of William Wellwood, the younger, portioner of Touch (now part of Dunfermline). Archibald and Isobel had three sons; Charles, Archibald and Robert, a merchant in Edinburgh, and two daughters; Margaret and Susanna, the younger of whom married a relation of her mother's, Robert Wellwood of Touch and Garvock. Margaret married twice – firstly James Harrower, a merchant and shipmaster, and latterly Mr William Henderson, who, in September 1717, followed her father as the minister of Dalgety parish.

Archibald Campbell had come to a parish that had suffered greatly in the cause of Presbyterianism but his endeavour to steady it was made more difficult by the economic collapse of trade throughout the country. The problem was compounded by four years of failed harvests and a disastrous enterprise by Scotland to establish a colony on the Gulf of Darien on the Panama isthmus in Central America.

The Darien Scheme

The Company of Scotland for Trading to Africa and the Indies had been established by William Paterson, who had co-founded the Bank of England in 1694 and founded the Bank of Scotland in 1695. It was the organisation which, in the mid-late 1690s, masterminded the scheme to establish the colony of 'New Caledonia' in Panama with a view to developing trade in the Americas and establishing a trade route between the Atlantic and Pacific – not in itself a bad concept.

The Darien Scheme was seen as a threat to European ambitions and which the Dutch East India Company did its utmost to wreck. It was an enterprise which the English Parliament condemned as a danger to English commerce and obstructed in every possible way and which King William spoke out against and subsequently elected not to support. Consequently, potential English backers withdrew, leaving the financial risk almost entirely within Scotland. The Scheme was crippled by corruption, was inadequately prepared, incompetently managed and the colony, once it was set up, was unable to resist disease, starvation, or marauding Spaniards. It failed so spectacularly as to nearly bankrupt the country. The Scheme's demise left much of Scotland, but particularly the Lowland area, "almost completely ruined".

Subscribers to the Company, and there were over 200,000, included lords and earls, ministers, surgeons, apothecaries, widows, guilds and societies, and whole towns, such as Inverkeithing. Every level and sector of society was involved. In Dalgety, several people had subscribed – Cap[t.] William Henderson of Fordell had contributed £200; James Holborne of Menstrie, £400; James Henderson, Pitadro, £100; James Spittal, Leuchat, £200; Alexander Kirkwood, servitor to the Earl of Moray, £100 and Lady Callendar's nephew, John, Marquis of Tweeddale, £1,000 and his son, Lord Alexander Hay, £400; John Hay, servant to the Marquis of Tweeddale, £200.[17]

Within the locality tragedy also struck. Hugh Litster, the third son of a former minister in Aberdour, and a sailor on board *The Rising Sun* of the second Darien expedition, perished, at the age of twenty-two. His ship, which had been dismasted in a storm, was sunk by a hurricane off the harbour bar at Charleston, South Carolina in August 1700. All on board were lost.[18]

The Century Comes to a Close

Instead of a settled parish, Campbell was faced with an impoverished one, a parish in sore need of ministry, healing, and pastoral care. As the tumultuous seventeenth century ended, Campbell and his fellow ministers were left with an admonition from the Church of Scotland's Commission of Assembly in an effort to heal differences in the Church [and by implication the country] and move forward as a united body: "We do believe and own, that Jesus Christ is the only Head and King of his Church; and that He hath instituted in His Church, officers and ordinances, order and government, and not left it to the will of man, magistrate or church, to alter at their pleasure. And we believe that this government is neither prelatical nor congregational, but Presbyterian, which through the mercy of God, is established among us; and we believe we have a better foundation for this our church government than the inclination of the people or the laws of men."[19]

Archibald Campbell served the parish until his death. His badly worn memorial, and that of his son-in-law, William Henderson, are located on the outside of the south wall at the eastern end of St Bridget's Kirk. *(Fig 32)* Translated it reads:

Isaiah 26.19 'Their own dead shall live...' Here are hidden the remains of Archibald Campbell, a man truly a wise and saintly minister, diligent towards his flock, preacher of the Holy Gospel at Dalgety – he died July 21st, 1714 at the age of 47. This memorial was erected here to her– dear husband by his widow Isabella Baird who now lies buried in the same place, died [ ] October 1727.

He lived under the shadow of Andrew Donaldson, and it would be a generation or so before Covenanting struggles and ideals faded from memory. Time was needed to heal the wounds, but the future of the parish was stabilising, and life was beginning to return to a degree of normality. Prosperity was beckoning and there was no need for Archibald Campbell to have to keep looking over his shoulder – the spectres of religious persecution had been vanquished.

Envoi

A literary critic in the 1950s, reviewing a book by G D Henderson, was of the opinion that, "for Scottish churchmen, the seventeenth century was a century seething with excitement". For churchmen on the ecclesiastical swing between Presbyterianism and Episcopalianism it was more likely a century of uncertainty and despair. For Andrew Donaldson, being deposed, 'put to the horn', intercommuned, imprisoned, and fined may have seen him seethe but unlikely with excitement. Donaldson's approach had been one of dogged and stubborn resistance to anything other than what he regarded as the 'true' faith. Excitement there may have been in some quarters but for ordinary people, for the farmers, the gardeners, the labourers, the colliers and salters, the cottars, the women and children, any excitement was always compromised by the brutality of the times.

Brutality had many guises. It was clearly evident during the wars that raged during much of the century, not least at the Battle of Inverkeithing, where no quarter was shown by Cromwell's men to Hector McLean and his Highlanders. Brutality was also evident in the lack of compassion and assistance coming from those in Pitreavie Castle, who not only denied them entry but actively prevented them from reaching a safe haven.

Subtle forms of brutality made themselves evident in the attitude and actions of early ministers in the parish. Mr Paton, seemingly abandoning Christian principles to deny his fellow cleric from Aberdour his rightful salary, and Mr Robert Bruce, three years after Dalgety had become a church in its own right, claiming he had been deprived of income as a result and for the next twenty-one years receiving stipend that might rightly have been judged to belong to Andrew Donaldson. These actions beg the question as to what these men thought ministry in a reformed church was about. Paton was unsubtle in his desire for a comfortable life for little effort, Bruce less so. Robert Bruce was a turncoat. He had originally embraced Episcopalianism before joining the Covenanters and, when faced with deposition, reverted to his original faith. Principles were of little concern to him.

The early days in the parish were exciting from the point of view that the Reformation was still 'new'. Only forty years had passed since the religious revolution had thrown off centuries-worth of unreformed Christian dogma and people, never mind Protestant ministers, were still trying to understand the full implications of what had taken place. What was the truth of it all? It is remarkable, that a movement protesting against the corruption of the Roman Catholic Church had become so dominant in such a short space of time. Perhaps Paton had a residual pre-Reformation element in his background that inclined him towards the actions he took and perhaps he did not see the acceptance of a bribe or helping himself to parish funds as anything out of the ordinary – was this not the way some priests had always behaved?

Change, however, was coming and underlying life in the parish in the first part of the century was the inexorable move to overcome medieval feudalism in favour of a more modern society. Another factor was the transfer of the Scottish court to London when James VI assumed the English throne on the death of Elizabeth. Men go where the power is located and in 1603 there was an exodus of some of Scotland's brightest talent; a similar exodus occurring when William assumed the throne in 1688. In some senses, with nobility and lairds often absent, the lack of authoritative voices in the community enabled men like Paton and Bruce to flourish.

Throwing off the shackles of medieval feudalism was not without pain. There was a tradition at court of James encouraging music and poetry but with the court now in London there was little opportunity for musicians or writers in Scotland. The artistic life of Scotland stultified to a degree, and it was not helped by the early Church of Scotland, which discouraged poetry and music that was not devotional in nature. Scotland had not yet reached the point of progressive impetus, unlike England where such as Isaac

Newton, Christopher Wren and Henry Purcell were towering figures and where the sciences, medicine and the arts were making great strides.

In the villages and burghs, divorced from access to literature (apart from the Bible), many people suffered from poverty of the mind and as most people were unable to read and write the consequences were that many still held to a belief in the power of charms and spells. Poverty of the mind was an intellectual deprivation, while poverty of the spirit, so evident before Donaldson's time, was addressed through his preaching. No less of an issue was the tangible poverty of everyday living – lack of money, food or employment and the inability to lead a dignified life without recourse to charity.

Andrew Donaldson appeared to recognise that for some people, poverty was a natural state and, no matter their actions, they were unable to break free from its bonds; for others, poverty was something they had fallen into through unforeseen circumstances and for some, old age and illness prevented them from earning and cast them into the ranks of the poor. His compassion for the poor was without question and evidence of his strong Christian faith. Every Sunday, money was collected for the poor and Communion Sundays were no exception. There was an expectation on his part, although probably not always realised, that the congregation would increase its giving for the poor due to the nature of the occasion.

Communion was a solemn sacramental feast and for Donaldson, not one to be entered into lightly. People had to be worthy of receiving a token to allow them to share in communion. Receiving a token was not a matter of course, as it depended on an examination of not only a person's faith but the way they lived their life. In a sense, Donaldson was placing his reputation on the line – were his sermons meaningful and pertinent such that people would be set on a godly path, were his teaching and catechising of a high enough standard to educate the congregation, to the point they could be regarded as worthy?

People were human, and in many cases, they failed to live up to the mark and suffered the ignominy of being barred from communion. For those who qualified, did their 'worthiness' rub off on others? Communion could be seen as a means of division and each communion season there may well have been dissident voices regarding the selection of 'the worthy' and comments expressed about those who received a visit from an elder for failing to attend. But no matter, Donaldson saw his contribution as keeping God at the forefront of peoples' lives.

The Church's insistence on driving people towards a 'godly society' was seen by later writers as 'religious terrorism'. It was clear that the image of the biblical shepherd as one who led his flock was lost on them. In driving the community towards God, there was little option for people but to acquiesce. The Church worked closely with the State and its actions often found themselves enshrined in law – baptism legislation was indicative of their indivisibility. There was no option but to have your children baptised. There was no option but to attend the examination on faith and doctrine prior to communion and little option of avoiding the repentance stool if you misbehaved.

By the second half of the century there had dawned the realisation that education was the key to developing a mature nation and that with that maturity came a freedom from the religious absolutism of the Church. Arguably, Andrew Donaldson's greatest contribution was the founding of a school and the employment of properly qualified schoolmasters. The focus on education, replicated throughout the country, without doubt, helped lay the foundations for a Scotland to blossom and flourish by the middle of the next century.

It is in education that Donaldson is ahead of his contemporaries. The heritors prevaricated over the location of a school, the building of it and the paying of a schoolmaster. Was this through lassitude or parsimony, or did they not understand the value that education could bring? Perhaps they felt threatened by a more educated populace? To Donaldson, none of these arguments was of any import; he knew the value of education from his university days. The ability to read the Bible and thus be brought closer to God was a factor in his decision to found a school but he would not have been unaware of what was happening in England, and on the continent, and he knew that progress could only come about by everyone receiving an education – old as well as young. His abiding legacy would have to be in setting up a school and educating the Dalgety youngsters.

Education of the older people in the community was more of a problem, as most of them were illiterate. They were more set in their ways, unlikely to understand the full value of what education meant and, therefore, more susceptible to superstitious practices. How many Christians still 'touch wood', throw spilt salt over their left shoulder or only pick up a fallen glove with their left hand? Such practices die hard, even today, and more so in Donaldson's time. But, at what point do superstitious practices become malevolent witchcraft? At what point does the offering of relief for a headache or an unexplained pain become witchcraft?

The medieval mind had been conditioned by the Church to accept that anything that went against God must have been by the actions of the devil. The arrival of the plague, a famine or a storm meant that people had forsaken God and had to suffer due punishment. Scientific understanding was not sufficiently advanced to know that death could be caused by such as appendicitis or the drinking of unclean water. Chanting some words of comfort or offering a remedy in the form of a natural herbal concoction and having that person die, when there would have been little chance of survival, brought suspicion on the 'healer'.

There were thirteen cases of witchcraft in Dalgety, in a short-lived witch-hunt. In Donaldson's favour was the relatively small number that were convicted and the shortness of the persecution. It is supposition to suggest that Donaldson actively spoke out against witch-hunting, but with the evidence from the rest of Dunfermline Presbytery it is clear that Dalgety had few cases. Donaldson probably recognised that regular preaching of the 'Word of God', keeping God at the forefront of people's minds, and education were the keys to removing superstitions.

Preaching and probably an intellectual drive to adhere to the 'true' faith of Presbyterianism drove Donaldson to becoming a Protestor against the General Assembly decisions. That not all his colleagues shared his views mattered little to him. He was concerned with sticking to his beliefs and was not to be deflected by bribes or offers to live a more comfortable life.

Donaldson was one of around 25% of ministers who protested and were ejected from the parishes as a result. The majority, one suspects, were reluctant to lose their income. What were principles in the face of not receiving a regular stipend? The question is probably answered by the fact that when Presbyterianism was finally restored in 1690 most of the ministers continued as though nothing had happened, although, in many quarters, there must have been difficult conversations to be had.

Donaldson had suffered grievously from maintaining a hard line but then, so had many of his heritors and parishioners. It is clear, that it took a great deal of courage on their part to stand with Donaldson and support his beliefs, but it is unlikely this would have happened if Donaldson had not been a well-liked and respected minister. His basic human compassion for people and his underlying concern, whether it was for the poor or the uneducated, had endeared itself to the hearts of his parishioners. The dividend was being paid.

Life generally, during the seventeenth century, certainly at the beginning, was hard for Dalgety parishioners. Living in hovels, with a restricted and monotonous diet, most of them would never have moved from where they were born, although some men might have seen service in the Covenanting armies. Roads were no more than tracks and people, if they wanted to attend markets in Inverkeithing, would have had to walk. Market days always had an attraction for country dwellers with ale houses to visit, friends to chat to, information about the state of affairs to be gathered, as well as the business of selling and buying. Everybody knew everybody else, there were no secrets. Inequality was evident, diseases still ravaged the country, and a long life was not generally expected.

Were the parish and country better off at the end of the century? Probably, although the century had ended with a Scotland, and some of Dalgety's parishioners, impoverished, as a result of the Darien Scheme. There was a settled monarchy, a stable national Church and in the parish, a thriving school and employment. The people of Dalgety had yet to realise the full scale of the forthcoming effects of political and economic union with England. They did not know that more Jacobite rebellions were looming; that by the middle of the next century agricultural improvements, the Scottish Enlightenment and the Industrial Revolution would change lives and working practices.

The reforming of the Church, which had started with Martin Luther in Germany and spread to Scotland by 1560, had endured wars and revolutions and was now, nearly one hundred and fifty years later, complete – a reformed system of Presbyterian Church government and worship was firmly in place. The Men of the Covenant had endured, and Dalgety was on the cusp of becoming an industrial powerhouse through the extraction and sale of its coal.

Appendix 1

Dalgety Kirk, also known as St Bridget's Kirk

The origin of the church in Dalgety is uncertain although the remains of the building that are standing today are the result of works spanning four centuries. When a church was first established is unknown but from the Bull issued by Pope Alexander III in 1178, we know that a church was in existence by that date. The evidence indicates that the first stonework of the remains of the current building were not erected until the mid-thirteenth century.

The early church was a single-chambered structure with an earthen floor. The masonry of the nave is rubble, latterly harled and the windows and doors have exposed dressings. There is a buttress at the south-east angle, the only buttress on the structure, which may be thirteenth-century work. The south door, towards the western end, which has an arched head formed in two stones, resembles sixteenth-century work, although precise dating is impossible. The other doors and windows are of seventeenth-century origin, but most of the older features have gone, and all the windows have been altered to admit more light. The only pre-Reformation feature left is a piscina, which is placed at the east end of the south wall, close to where the altar would have been positioned.[1]

The church building remained very much unaltered for three hundred years or so until after the Reformation, when the following century saw the addition, at the west end, of the Seton family burial vault, and a laird's loft and retiring room on the first floor. The walls are built of ashlar, and it was recorded as being a fine piece of architecture with proportion and detail being exceptionally good and a panel above the vault door bearing traces of a painted inscription. The laird's loft is a handsome and well-proportioned chamber, having a wide opening to the interior of the kirk; the walls are panelled in stone between the windows and a moulded stone cornice returns at wall-head level. The ceiling was reported to be elliptical in form, constructed of lath and plaster.[2]

The Inglis Aisle (Inglis of Otterston) was completed in the first part of the seventeenth century and originally had five panels set in niches in its west wall. The earliest of the panels apparently recorded the death of Elizabeth Heriot in 1621, who was "the spouse to Williame Ingls (sic) of Otterstoune".[3] The next panel was to be that of her husband. The niches are still there but no trace of the panels now remains.

Post-Reformation, a pulpit was built in the centre of the south wall and galleries were added on the east and west walls. A stone floor was laid in 1645.

A fragment, thought to be of a medieval monument slab, probably thirteenth-century, is built into the entrance jamb of a small watch-house set into the west wall of the kirkyard.

The church itself fell into disuse in 1830, when a new parish church was built nearer the main Inverkeithing-Aberdour road. St Bridget's Kirk was later unroofed by the then Earl of Moray. It is now in the care of Historic Environment Scotland.

St Bridget

It is unclear as to why Dalgety Church was dedicated to St Bridget. As far as is known St Bridget (c.452 – 524) never visited Scotland. Consecrated in Ireland as a bishop she founded a monastery at Kildare, that catered for both monks and nuns, and became a very revered figure within the religious community.[4]

The *Charters of the Abbey of Inchcolm* which survive were published by the Scottish History Society in 1938 (editors D. Easson and A. MacDonald) but throw little light on St Bridget or her connection with Dalgety. It appears that the monastery at Kildare had a relationship with Abernethy, in its heyday the principal royal and episcopal seat of the Kingdom of the Picts, and that a Lawrence of Abernethy, Lord Saltoun, was described in the charters as the "last lay abbot of Abernethy".[5] A member of this same Abernethy family had a charter to land in Dalgety, believed to be around the 1460s, and one hypothesis is that it was not unknown for lairds to introduce saints' dedications to the main church of their land-holdings.

A pre-Reformation memorial tablet (1540) to "ane Honorabil Man callit William Abernethie" is located inside the kirk, at the east end of the north wall. On the floor of the nave, a memorial slab, now badly weathered and illegible, commemorates another William Abernethie, possibly his grandson, with a date of 1612.

Most early documents, particularly seventeenth-century Kirk Session, Presbytery and Synod records, generally just refer to "Dalgety Kirk". Perhaps this was done for clarity as "Dalgety" is recognisable and identifiable, whereas "St Bridget's" would always have to be further qualified; or, perhaps, the Presbyterian Church did not wish to be seen to adhering to anything which might be regarded as Roman Catholic. In any event, there is no evidence to support any claim as to the origin of the connection of St Bridget and Dalgety and it cannot be stated with any degree of certainty why or when the name of the saint was applied to the church.

It is worth noting that Taylor with Márkus suggests that St Bridget may be linked to the name of Donibristle – one meaning of which he records as "Fortification of Breasal or the Ui Bresail". He provides an alternative meaning which suggests the name may derive from "dun", a hill or fortification, qualified by the kin-name "Ui Bresail". Taylor with Márkus goes on to say, "According to Bridget's genealogy, she belonged to the kin of Ui Bresail. In early medieval history we know that members of a saint's kin were closely involved with the promotion of his or her cult over a wide geographical area, so this juxtaposition of a St Bridget dedication [for the church] and place-name containing her kin name may not be coincidental".[6]

Appendix 2

————

Scottish Weights, Measures and Currency

Weights and measures during most of the seventeenth century were not generally standardised but it would appear as though:

Weights:

16oz. (ounces)	= 1lb (pound)
14lbs	= 1 stone
20 stone	= 1cwt (hundredweight)
20cwts	= 1 ton
5 tons	= 1 chalder (Depending where you lived in the country, the amount in a chalder varied – in some places it was as little as 2 tons, in others 5 tons.

Dry measures:

1 chalder	= 16 bolls
1 boll	= 6 imperial bushels (48 dry gallons); 140lbs imperial measure

1 bushel	= 8 [dry] gallons
1 firlot	= ¼ boll (i.e. 4 firlots to the boll)
1 peck	= ¼ firlot (i.e. 16 pecks to the boll)
1 lippie	= ¼ peck (i.e. 4 lippie to the peck)

Wet measures:

4 gills	= 1 pint (= approx. 0.56 litre)
2 pints	= 1 quart
4 quarts	= 1 gallon (= approx. 4.5 litres)
mutchkine	= A Scottish measure equal to an English pint (or ¾ of an imperial pint, ¼ of a Scottish pint)
chopin	= a Scottish measure, about an English quart

The Guildry in the Burgh of Inverkeithing[1]

In an attempt to standardise measures, ensure fair prices were charged and reduce the likelihood of customers being 'sold short' Inverkeithing, in 1688, defined each measure as:

meal firlote is to hold 21 pynts and ane mutchkine

the peck 5 pynts and ane mutchkine and the fourth part of a mutchkine...

the half peck 5 chopins and half a mutchkine and the 3rd part of a mutchkine.

the Leipie to hold 5 mutchkines and 4th part of ane mutchkine and ane 16 part of a mutchkine.

ane half Leipie to hold ane chopine, half a mutchkine and the 32 part of a mutchkine.

Item the bear and oats firlot 31 pynts. The peck 7 pynts and 3 mutchkines. The half peck 4 pynts Laiking half a mutchkine.

The Leipie ane Quart Laiking a Gill. The half Leipie ane pynt laiking half a gill.

Currency:

Money was counted in pounds, shillings and pence:

1 doyt	= 1/12th of a penny
2 doyts	= 1 bodle
2 bod	= 1 plack or groat (1 groat = 1/3 of a penny)
3 placks	= 1 bawbee
2 bawbees	= 1 penny *(d.)*
12 pennies	= 1 shilling *(s.)*
20 shillings	= 1 pound *(lib)*
21 shillings	= 1 guinea
2 shillings & six pence	= half-a-crown
5 shillings	= 1 crown

A Scottish pound was generally calculated as being worth one twelfth of a pound sterling.

A merk, or mark, was a Scottish silver coin which, in the seventeenth century, was valued at 13s 4d or 2/3 of a Scottish pound, about 1 English shilling.

An 'angel' was so-called as on the face it had an image of the Archangel Michael slaying a dragon. In value, during James VI's reign, it was worth around 11s, just over £7 Scots. It was replaced by the guinea.

A guinea was so-called as it was originally made from gold mined in the West African country of Guinea. It was first minted in 1663 and contained ¼ ounce of gold.

Appendix 3

Letter from Bishop George Haliburton, deposing Andrew Donaldson

"Sir, – These five Synods past, your brethren of the Synod of Dunkeld have waited upon your presence to have concurred with them in all ministerial duties that relate to discipline, according to the strict Acts of Parliament and Council enjoining the same, and the Acts of your Synod requiring your presence, and enjoining your keeping of session, Presbytery, and Synod. Notwithstanding, you have still seditiously contemned the laws of the State, in not keeping your Synod, though you knew the ordinary diets as well as others: and against the law and practice of the Church, and your peaceable brethren, has still schismatically divided yourself from your brethren, in session, Presbytery, and Synod: and well considering their own patience and slowness to proceed against you, having formerly suspended you, and yet unwilling even to intimate that, causing it only come to your ear, hoping that their kindly forbearance should in end gain your submission to an union with them; yet still meeting with nothing from you but obstinate and ungrate continuance in your seditious and schismatic way, they unanimously, at the last meeting of the Synod, holden at Dunkeld, the 4th day of October, 1664, did think and vote you worthy of deposition from your ministerial function. Likeas, I did in the name, and by the authority of Jesus Christ, and in the name, and with the consent of all my brethren, actually at that time depose you: which I now do declare, you Mr. Andrew Donaldson, sometime minister at Dalgety, deposed from all charge, not only there, but from all the parts of ministerial function within any diocese, or the Kirk of Scotland: assuring you, if you shall insist on that charge, either at Dalgety, or elsewhere, after you shall be acquaint with this sentence, that immediately, with the consent of my Synod, we will proceed against you with the highest censures of this Kirk. In verification of all the premises, I have subscribed them, and sent them express to you for your warning, that you may not pretend ignorance, but may yield obedience, and not contravene.

Perth, 10ᵗʰ October 1664. George Dunkeld."

Cited by Robert Wodrow, *The History and Sufferings of the Church of Scotland* pp. 409ff 1842

Glossary of Words and Terms

Some words and terms, and some ecclesiastical terms, in common use during the seventeenth century are unfamiliar to us now. The *Etymological Dictionary of the Scottish Language,* John Jamieson, 1808, and the abridged version of 1846 provides some information about word meanings and usage. Two excellent resources for the Scots language are to be found in the *Dictionary of the Older Scottish Tongue* (Scots up to 1700) and the *Scottish National Dictionary* (1700 onwards); both are available online at dsl@ac.uk.

Seventeenth-century terms

Ad pios usus	for pious or charitable uses
Adit (or day-level)	a means of draining water from a pit by gravity into the open air or 'day'
Anent	concerning
Arras	chamber-hangings of the kind woven in Arras, France; also attributed to bed clothes, coverlets etc.
Beir, bere or sometimes bear	barley
Bigget	built
Blotted	accused of being

Branks	a scold's bridle; an instrument of punishment for those guilty of defamation
By and attoure	over and above
Calumniate	slander, spread evil reports
Candlemas	2nd February, a Scottish quarter day; known within Roman Catholicism as the Feast of the Purification of the Blessed Virgin Mary
Change house	An inn or lodging house
Compear or compeir	to present oneself, in a court, in consequence of a summons
Contumac	contumacy – obstinate disobedience
Cordiner	archaic Scots word for a shoemaker
Cottar	a farm worker occupying a cottage in return for labour. In the seventeenth century, cottars accounted for a quarter to a third of the population; occupied small amounts of land from lease-holding farming tenants; many were engaged in trades, such as weaving, or blacksmithing
Courche	covering for the head
Delate or dilate	to charge with a crime
Depone	to testify on oath
Deprehendit	apprehended
Escheat or escheit	to confiscate property etc.
Fermetoun(s)	farming townships. where a small number of families share arable land and common grazing – pre-agricultural improvement of mid-eighteenth century
Firmance	state of confinement
Flyeting	brawling or scolding in public (with swearing, name-calling etc)
Fyes	fees
Hird	one who tends cattle
Hodden-grey	applied to homespun cloth which has the natural colour of wool
Intercommune	to have dealings with a rebel or outlaw; a person who was intercommuned was forbidden to have contact with others

Interteanned	supported, maintained
Knock beir	thresh barley
Lammas	1st August, a Scottish quarter day. 'Lammas' is a corruption of the Loaf Mass, a Roman Catholic rite to celebrate the first harvests
Langsumness	tediousness
Leited	listed
Lett	hindrance
Licit	lawful
Lowne (or loon)	a rogue or worthless fellow
Maleson or malisone	a curse
Meanit	mentioned
Mutch	a head-dress for a female
Oxgate or oxgang	nominally the amount of land tillable by one ox in one season, around 12-13 Scottish acres or 1/8th of a ploughgate
Ploughgate or ploughland	an area of land of 8 oxgangs, regarded as being around 100 Scots acres
Poind	Scottish legal term – to seize and sell the goods of a debtor
Portioner	the owner of a small portion of a larger piece of land; a laird of a small estate
Pro secundo	for the second time
Promoveing	improving
Propone	propose
Quhilk	which
Rayiotte	riot
Relict	widow
Sea wreak	coal washed up on the beach
Sclandour	slander
Smoored	smothered, suffocated
Snood	a headband with which the hair of a young woman's head is bound up
Sourlie	surely
Sow-back	a head-dress worn by an old woman (probably from

	its curved shape)
Sowens	flummery, made of the dust of oatmeal remaining among the seeds, steeped and soured
Streaking	striking
Tacksman	holder of a tack (or lease) usually for substantial rent or teinds
Thairanent	concerning that
Tippet	a long, narrow strip of cloth forming part of a hood; a preaching scarf
Toties quoties	as often as
Tried out	sought out
Trewker	someone involved in bartering
Umquhile or unquhile	deceased
Voyis	decide by vote
Wading	wedding
Wants	lacks

Ecclesiastical terms

Beadle	A minor church official, whose chief duty is to attend to the minister but who may also officiate as gravedigger and church bellman.
Books of Discipline	The 1st book (1560) adopted by the General Assembly defined the constitution and polity of the Church. A 2nd book approved in 1579 was ratified by Parliament in 1592 and recognised in 1690 as the Presbyterian basis of the Church of Scotland
Deacon	A layman appointed by the Kirk Session with responsibility for the money gathered in the church box. He attended Session meetings
Doxology/doxologie	A short hymn of praise to God, often added to the end of a psalm
Elder	A layman ordained by the Church and set apart, as a member of a Kirk Session, to assist in the conduct of Church affairs and to assist the minister in supervising

	the spiritual affairs of the parish
Exhorter	A layman appointed to give a religious discourse
General Assembly	The supreme court of the Church of Scotland, with an equal number of ministers and elders elected as their representatives by the presbyteries. A Moderator presided over the annual meeting
Glebe	A portion of arable land adjoining the manse, which allowed the minister to grow vegetables and maintain a horse and possibly a cow. The glebe was part of the minister's living
Heritors	The land-owners in a parish – i.e. proprietors of heritable property with land subject to payment of taxation. They were obliged to maintain the church building, surrounding land, the manse and the glebe. Responsible for paying the minister's stipend
Kirk Session	The lowest court of the Church of Scotland. It consisted of the minister and a number of elders. The Kirk Session met weekly, or oftener if required, and oversaw the spiritual welfare and discipline of the parish
Manse	The house of a Scottish minister of religion which belonged to the Church
Mortcloth	The pall, the velvet covering draped over the coffin at a funeral
Patronage	The right of an individual, the patron, to present a minister to a parish. Lay patronage in the Church of Scotland was abolished in 1649 but reimposed between 1669 and 1690, during the Restoration Episcopacy, after which it was again abolished
Prelate/prelacy	a bishop or other high ecclesiastical dignitary (from the Latin meaning 'one set over others'); the government of the Christian Church by clerics of high social rank and power
Presbytery	A court of the Church of Scotland consisting of the ministers from a group of neighbouring parishes and an elder from each Kirk Session. In the seventeenth century it met as required but, at least, monthly

Reader   At the Reformation there were not enough Protestant ministers to serve the parish churches and the office of Reader was created as a practical solution. In parishes where no minister was available, Readers were appointed to read the Scriptures and lead the congregation in prayer. They were not licenced to preach. The office had died out by the mid-seventeenth century

Synod   A court of the Church of Scotland, ranking above Presbytery but below the General Assembly. It comprised three or more adjoining presbyteries and consisted of all clerical and lay members of the presbyteries within its bounds. It met every six months

Teinds   A tithe, or tenth part of the revenues of the land originally set apart (pre-Reformation) to support the priest, the church and its services, and the poor of the parish. The parish of Dalgety had been appropriated to Inchcolm Abbey which gathered the teinds. These had to be paid irrespective of who owned the land. After the Reformation teinds had become alienated and a large proportion were seized by the crown and granted to laymen, to the financial detriment of the Church of Scotland. See *The Books of Assumption of the Thirds of Benefices* ed. James Kirk 1995 p. 63.

Notes

Preface

1. Easson, D and MacDonald, A (eds): *Charters of the Abbey of Inchcolm* , Scottish History Society, 1938 pp. 1-4.
2. Ibid, pp. 168-170.
3. Dalgety Kirk had some Kirk Session minutes stolen by Cromwell's troops in 1651 and tragically minutes, including most of the second half of the seventeenth century, were lost in a fire that burned down Dalgety manse on 16th July 1897. The loss of these records has made it more difficult to fully understand what was happening in the parish during the seventeenth century. *Note:* Since writing this book, Kirk Session records are now available online through the *Scotland's People* website (National Records of Scotland).

Chapter 1 Introduction Dalgety and the National Context

1. Many aspects of Roman Catholic teaching were condemned by Martin Luther in his 95 Theses, including the selling of Indulgences for the remission of sins, which were supposed to lessen the time a person spent in purgatory before entering heaven. Purgatory had been introduced into Roman Catholic teaching around the twelfth century, although with little Scriptural basis. It was regarded as a halfway house between heaven and hell. Paying for masses to be sung by a priest for a dead relative was another way of lessening the time spent in purgatory, as well as lining the pockets of the priesthood. Luther also objected to the fact that money raised by the sale of Indulgences was applied to the rebuilding of St Peter's Basilica in Rome.
2. Ryrie, Alec: *Protestants*, Wm Collins, 2017, pp. 85-86. "Western Christendom [around the tenth century], developed its concept of heresy, a word that literally means 'choice'. A doctrinal error is not heresy. Heresy is an act of the will: asserting your own judgement

rather than submitting obediently to the mind of the Church, guided by the Holy Spirit. An error only becomes heretical when someone consciously and deliberately defies the Church's ruling. Orthodoxy versus heresy is more about obedience versus wilfulness than truth versus error. Heresy is a moral offence, not an intellectual one. Heresy was treated as a crime, which ultimately could mean death by burning, although the ideal outcome of a heresy trial was always repentance." There was a fine dividing line between being executed for heresy and dying as a martyr to the faith. Ryrie also wrote: "Martyrs are literally *witnesses* – believers who bear witness to their faith in the most vivid and unanswerable way, by choosing to die rather than renounce it. Because martyrdom was the highest honour for which any Christian might hope, to be persecuted was, paradoxically, proof of God's love." On that basis, depending on your point of view, George Wishart was either a heretic or a martyr.

3. Reid, Harry: *Reformation*, The Saint Andrew Press, 2009 p. 320.
4. Divine Right of Kings – The belief that kings derived their authority from God, a position that could be traced to the biblical story found in 1 Samuel, where the prophet Samuel anointed Saul, and then David, as king over Israel.
5. Burntisland Parish Church (St Columba's) was one of the first post-Reformation churches built in Scotland (1595). It was designed on a unique square plan which had people sitting on all four sides of the church, with the pulpit and communion table in the centre. It reflected the Reformers' belief that the preaching of 'the Word', baptism and the Lord's Supper were all to be celebrated in the midst of the people of God.
6. Hetherington, William Maxwell: *History of the Church of Scotland... to 1841*, John Johnstone, 1842 p. 205.
7. Ibid, p. 206.
8. *The Diary of Mr James Melville*, the Bannatyne Club, 1829.
9. Reid, Harry: *Reformation*, The Saint Andrew Press, 2009 p. xxx.
10. Black, George F: *A Calendar of Cases of Witchcraft in Scotland 1510–1725* (The New York Public Library, reprint 1971) p. 18 citing Lecky's *History of the rise and influence of the spirit of rationalism in Europe, Vol. 1*, D. Appleton & Co., 1919 pp. 143-144.
11. Puritans were English Protestants who sought to 'purify' the Church of England of Roman Catholic liturgy, ceremony or practices, maintaining that the Church of England had not been fully reformed under Henry VIII. Originally used as a term of derision, Puritans were generally regarded as being more intensely protestant than other protestants.

Chapter 2 Early Days in Dalgety Parish

1. Ross, William: *Aberdour and Inchcolme*, David Douglas, 1885 p. 222.
2. Hetherington, William Maxwell: *History of the Church of Scotland... to 1841*, John Johnstone, 1842. (As with many of Hetherington's comments, a prejudicial point of view, perhaps not wholly objective).
3. Spottiswoode, John: *The History of the Church of Scotland*, London, 1685 p. 513.
4. Row, John: *The History of the Kirk of Scotland*, The Wodrow Society, 1842 p. 165.
5. Harris, Tim: *Rebellion*, Oxford UP, 2014 p. 171 – citing the Earl of Clarendon's *History of the Rebellion* (1648).
6. Row, John: *The History of the Kirk of Scotland*, The Wodrow Society, 1842 p. 311.

7. Seton, George: *Memoir of Alexander Seton*, Wm Blackwood, 1882 p. 114.

8. Ibid, p. 153.

9. Ibid, pp. 197-198.

10. Ibid, p. 155.

11. Jacobus Arminius (1560–1609) was a Dutch theologian who rejected key Calvinist teachings such as predestination and believed that God's grace was potentially available to all penitent, true believers who were free to accept or reject God's grace as they saw fit – in other words, salvation could be achieved through free will. To Calvinists this seemed no different from the Roman Catholic Church's doctrine of universal redemption. Harris, Tim: *Rebellion,* Oxford UP, 2014 p. 302.

12. Lumsden, John: *The Covenants of Scotland*, Paisley, 1914 pp. 214-225.

13. Makey, Walter: *The Church of the Covenant 1637–1651*, John Donald, 1979 p. 19. "To be put to the horn" was an old legal term in Scots law; it was a warrant issued by the sovereign charging the person named with whatever misdemeanour was noted. Whatever the crime, the culprit was proclaimed at the Market Cross in Edinburgh and other burghs, together with three blasts of a horn. Letters of Horning were issued to the person charged and were often accompanied by a poinding of a person's assets.

14. GASHE project by John O'Brien, Glasgow University Archive Services, 13 August 2002.

15. Pamphlet, printed for Samuel Gellibrand: *The Mystery of Iniquity yet working in the Kingdomes of England, Scotland and Ireland for the destruction of Religion truly Protestant,* London, 1643 p. 16.

Chapter 3 Covenants and Wars

1. Donaldson, Gordon: *The Making of the Scottish Prayer Book of 1637*, Edinburgh University Press, 1954 p. 7.

2. Ibid, p. 60.

3. Row, John: *The History of the Kirk of Scotland*, The Wodrow Society,1842 p. 408.

4. Thomson, D P: *Women of the Scottish Church*, privately published, 1975 pp. 60-65.

5. Makey, Walter: *The Church of the Covenant 1637-1651*, John Donald, 1979 p. 20.

6. Ibid, p. 19.

7. The National Covenant was in three parts, the first was an updated version of the Negative Confession signed by James VI in 1581. This was, essentially, a strongly worded rejection of everything to do with Romanism and had been James' attempt to allay suspicion that he had leanings towards Rome. The second part, prepared by Archibald Johnston of Warriston, was a list of the numerous Acts of the Parliament of Scotland which confirmed Presbyterianism and condemned Romanism, and the third part, written by Alexander Henderson, was the actual Covenant which was to be sworn to. Alexander Henderson, minister at Leuchars, was reputedly related to the Hendersons of Fordell. He was Moderator of the General Assembly of the Church of Scotland in 1638 and one of the commissioners who negotiated the peace treaty at Berwick-upon-Tweed to bring the 1st Bishops' War to an end. He was a commissioner to the Westminster Assembly of Divines. He died in 1646 and is buried in Greyfriars' Kirkyard. *Oxford Dictionary of National Biography* pp. 288-293.

8. Lord High Commissioners were appointed to the Parliament of the Kingdom of Scotland

between 1603 and 1707 as the Sovereign's personal representative. The Act of Union 1707 made this function redundant, but a Lord High Commissioner to the General Assembly of the Church of Scotland has been appointed each year, since 1690, as the Sovereign's personal representative.

9. Pamphlet, printed for Samuel Gellibrand: *The Mystery of Iniquity yet working in the Kingdomes of England, Scotland and Ireland for the destruction of Religion truly Protestant,* London, 1643 p. 17.

10. The Parliament of Scotland, officially the Estates of Parliament, was the legislature of the Kingdom of Scotland. The parliament, like other such institutions, evolved during the Middle Ages from the king's council of bishops and earls. Consisting of the "three estates" of clergy, nobility and the burghs sitting in a single chamber, the parliament gave consent for the raising of taxation and played an important role in the administration of justice, foreign policy, war, and all manner of other legislation. The Committee of Estates governed Scotland during the Wars of the Three Kingdoms when the Parliament of Scotland was not sitting. It was dominated by Covenanters of which the most influential faction was that of the Earl of Argyll. The Committee derives its name from the "Estates of Scotland" which was an alternative name for the Parliament of Scotland.

11. Rushworth, J: *Historical Collections, Vol. 3,* 1692, pub. 1703 p. 428ff.

12. The five were John Hampden, Arthur Haselrig, Denzil Holles, John Pym and William Strode. William Lenthall was the Speaker of the Commons during the Long Parliament and, in response to Charles' question as to where the five men were, is reputed to have replied, "May it please your Majesty, I have neither eyes to see nor tongue to speak in this place but as the House is pleased to direct me, whose servant I am here".

13. Christensen, Paul: 'Charles Seton, the reluctant rebel?' Article in *History Scotland,* Vol. 17, Nos. 4-6, 2017 where the author discusses Charles Seton's difficult relationship with Charles I, and sheds light on the ambivalence Seton felt about the Covenanters.

Chapter 4 Donaldson's Training and Ordination

1. Foster, W R: *The Church before the Covenants,* Scottish Academic Press, 1975 pp. 93ff.

2. Ibid, p. 94, citing Edinburgh Presbytery minutes 24 October 1587.

3. Hunter, John: *The Diocese and Presbytery of Dunkeld 1660–89,* Hodder & Stoughton, 1917 p. 373.

4. Ross, William: *Glimpses of Pastoral Work in Covenanting Times,* James Nisbet & Co, 1877 p. 80.

5. Ibid, pp. 11-12.

6. Row, John: *The History of the Kirk of Scotland,* The Wodrow Society, 1842 p. 473.

7. Ecclesiastical Records, *Selections from the minutes of the Synod of Fife, 1611–1687,* Reprint, originally printed for the Abbotsford Club, 1837 p. 127.

8. Ross, William: *Glimpses of Pastoral Work in Covenanting Times,* James Nisbet & Co, 1877 p. 18.

9. Chambers, Robert: *Domestic Annals of Scotland, Vol. 2,* W & R Chambers, 1859 p. 154.

10. A true copy of the *Acts of the General Assemblies of the Church of Scotland:* printed in the Year 1682; Session XVIII, 12 February 1645 p. 270ff.

11. *Dalgety Kirk Session records*, 29 June 1645.

Chapter 5 Donaldson and War

1. Young, Andrew: *History of Burntisland*, Kirkcaldy, 1924, 2nd Edition p. 92.
2. Furgol, Edward M: *A Regimental History of the Covenanting Armies 1639–1651*, John Donald Ltd, 1990 pp. 137-138.
3. McRae, Alisdair: *How the Scots won the English Civil War*, The History Press, 2013 p. 110. "… not only was the want of religious teaching one of the causes of disorder which began to spread… but it favoured the growth of heresy in the ranks."
4. Ibid, p. 48.
5. Furgol, Edward M: *A Regimental History of the Covenanting Armies 1639–1651*, John Donald Ltd, 1990 pp. 88-93.
6. Ibid, p. 215.
7. Following the accession of Charles II, Montrose was restored to his previous position by the king. He returned to Scotland in 1650 with the intention of raising a Royalist army but had limited success and, latterly, suffered a crushing defeat in April 1650 at Carbisdale where he surrendered to Neil Macleod of Assynt at Ardvreck Castle, who promptly handed him over to the authorities. The following month he was tried and hanged in Edinburgh. After the Restoration, Charles II, in recognition of Montrose's service to the Royalist cause, had his memory officially rehabilitated and his body exhumed and re-buried in the High Kirk of St Giles.
8. Chambers, Robert: *Domestic Annals of Scotland, Vol. 2*, W & R Chambers, 1859 p. 156.
9. Papers lately delivered in to the Honourable Houses of Parliament by the Commissioners of the Kingdom of Scotland, concerning The Proceedings of the Scottish Army and their intentions 30 May 1646 signed by Lauderdale, A Johnston, Charles Erskine, Hugh Kennedy & Robert Barclay.
10. Donaldson, Gordon: *Scotland, James V–James VII*, Oliver & Boyd, 1971 pp. 336-339.
11. Ibid, p. 337.

Chapter 6 The Kirk Session

1. Parish of Dalgety, Rev Peter Primrose: *Statistical Account of Scotland, Vol. 2*, Sir John Sinclair (ed), William Creech, 1795 pp. 260ff
2. Stephen, William: *History of Inverkeithing and Rosyth*, G & W Fraser, 1921 p. 3-4.
3. Henderson, Alexander: *Government and Order of Church of Scotland, Sect V – Eldership*, 1641.
4. Stevenson, William: *The Presbiterie Book of Kirkcaldy*, James Burt, 1900 pp. 95-96.
5. Moray Muniments: NRAS/217/Box 5/1614.
6. After the Reformation and the closure of the monasteries, collection of tiends (tithes) for church use largely fell into abeyance with tiends appropriated by the crown or wealthy landowners. Dalgety, as a daughter church of Inchcolm Abbey, found that it was left with little or no income to maintain itself.
7. Maxwell, William: *A History of Worship in the Church of Scotland*, Oxford UP, 1955 p. 99.

8. Foster, W R: *Bishop and Presbytery*, SPCK, 1958 p. 112.
9. Rev Peter Primrose never moved, as it was to be another thirty-five years before a new manse was built (1830) on the brow of the hill near to Barns Farm. It is now a private residence, renamed "Ardmhor".
10. Ross, William: *Glimpses of Pastoral Work in Covenanting Times*, James Nisbet & Co, 1877 p. 34.

Chapter 7 Parish School

1. Beale, James M; Withrington, Donald (ed.) *A History of the Burgh and Parochial Schools of Fife*, Scottish Council for Research in Education, 1983 p. 35 – citing Dundonald Kirk Session minutes 19th Jan 1640.
2. Ibid, p. 15.
3. Ross, William: *Glimpses of Pastoral Work in Covenanting Times*, James Nisbet & Co, 1877 p. 49.
4. Beale, James M; Withrington, Donald (ed.): *A History of the Burgh and Parochial Schools of Fife*, Scottish Council for Research in Education, 1983 p. 82.

Chapter 8 Sunday Worship

1. Henderson G D: *Scots Confession, 1560*, Church of Scotland, 1937 p. 7.
2. Lindsay, Ian G: *The Scottish Parish Kirk*, The St Andrew Press, 1960 p. 46. After Dalgety Kirk fell into disuse in 1830, the bell continued to hang in the bell-cote until 1926 when it was relocated to St Fillan's Kirk, Aberdour at the time of its restoration, where it is still in use today.
3. After Anderson, there is no further record of a Reader being appointed in Dalgety. A Reader in the seventeenth century Church of Scotland (see Glossary) should not be confused with a Reader in today's Church of Scotland – the two offices are not the same. A Reader today undergoes a three-year period of training, following which they are licensed by Presbytery to conduct all aspects of public worship, with the exception of celebrating the sacraments.
4. The General Assembly of 1645, mindful of the Westminster Assembly that was underway, frowned upon this practice of bowing (i.e. of kneeling in private prayer): "It is the judgement of the committee, that the ministers bowing in the pulpit, though a lawful custome in this Kirk, be hereafter laid aside, for satisfaction of the desires of the reverend Divines in the Synod of England, and for uniformity with that Kirk."
5. Proclamation issued by King Charles I at Whitehall, 15 October 1633 and ratified by an Act of the Parliament of Scotland.
6. The pulpit was the most prominent item of 'furniture' in the church. Pews were not common and in the 1650s Communion Tables were not yet a permanent feature of churches. Donaldson's new pulpit remained in use until 1830 when it was recorded that the then minister fell through the floorboards, as they had become rotten.
7. The Reformed Church of Scotland declared that baptism and celebration of communion (the Lord's Supper) were to be its only two sacraments. The Roman Catholic Church had recognised seven: baptism, Eucharist [communion], penance [confession], confirmation, marriage, taking Holy Orders and extreme unction [anointing of the sick and dying].
8. Lindsay, Ian G: *The Scottish Parish Kirk*, The St Andrew Press, 1960 p. 47ff.

9. A gossip originated from Old English, 'godsibb', meaning a child's godparent or sponsor at a baptism. Over time this changed to 'a good friend, usually a woman' and to its current use as 'idle chatter and rumour'.

10. Burns, Thomas: *Old Scottish Communion Plate*, R & R Clark, 1892, Small paper edition p. 497.

11. Patrick, Millar: *Four Centuries of Scottish Psalmody*, Oxford UP, 1949 p. 3.

12. Ibid, p. 51.

13. In 1899, after the Rev. Stewart Rose was inducted into Dalgety Parish Church, he found a box in the church containing the names of psalm tunes. Amongst the cards, he found one for a tune called 'Dalgetie' which was unknown to him and of which there was no record. Mr Rose appealed through the *Dunfermline Press* for information. Three years later he received a copy of the tune, "Found among some old papers. Glasgow. J. S.". It is not known who wrote the tune, or when, although it is thought to date from the nineteenth century. The tune sent to Mr Rose was harmonised in 1985 by William Scott, then organist in Dalgety. It was originally sung to Psalm 91. See Arnott, Robin: *Of Monks and Ministers*, Dalgety Parish Church, 1992 pp. 54-55.

14. Jhone Angus was, according to Millar Patrick, "one of the conventual brethren of Dunfermline Abbey, and sometime precentor there, who accepted the Reformation". The tune appeared in the 1615 Scottish Psalter. See *"Jhone Angus – Monk of Dunfermline & Scottish Reformation Music"* by J Reid-Baxter, M Lynch & E P Dennison, Dunfermline Heritage Community Projects, 2011.

15. Ross, William: *Glimpses of Pastoral Work in Covenanting Times*, James Nisbet & Co, 1877 appears to have made an error, the pulpit recess is very clearly in the south wall.

16. Ibid, p. 94. Ross paints an idealistic picture of the gathered congregation, one which was more than likely to have been taken from his imagination.

Chapter 9 Communion

1. *Scottish Population Statistics*, James Gray Kyd (ed.) including Webster's Analysis of Population 1755, The Scottish History Society, 3rd Series, Vol. XLIII, 1952 p. 39. It is difficult to know just how many people lived in the parish during the seventeenth century. The Hearth Tax records for 1691-95 indicate that there were 198 hearths in the parish. Taking account of those in the 'big' houses, and such as blacksmiths' furnaces, kilns, bakeries and other workplaces requiring a fire, a rough estimate suggests there may have been around 100 or so habitable dwellings. In 1755 the Rev. Alexander Webster, an Edinburgh minister, published an analysis of Scotland's population and concluded that in Dalgety, "there were 761 persons…". When the first Statistical Account was published (1795), the population had increased to 869. It is unlikely that the population of Dalgety parish, in Donaldson's time, would have been any greater than 761.

2. Burns, Thomas: *Old Scottish Communion Plate*, R & R Clark, 1892 p. 60.

3. Burns, Thomas: *Old Scottish Communion Plate*, R & R Clark, 1892 p. 17.

4. The Kirk Session records of Auldhame, Tyninghame and Whitekirk in East Lothian for 1615–1850 noted that "as much as 'five gallons' [about 20 litres] is ordered at one time, but this had often to serve for many more than the usual congregation, as people

sometimes came from other parishes as well." (Communion in Dalgety today would use approximately 1 litre of port.)

5. Stevenson, Robert: *The Communion in Dunfermline in the 17th Century*, A. Romanes, 1900 p. 17.

6. Burns, Thomas: *Old Scottish Communion Plate*, R & R Clark, 1892 p.16 writes: "The wine in use was claret and not port as in our time. This is accounted for by the close relation then subsisting between Scotland and France, whence large importations of claret were made. The cheapness must also have been a strong recommendation, for the Church was extremely poor and poverty had been used as an excuse for non-observance of the sacred feast."

7. Young, Andrew: *History of Burntisland*, Kirkcaldy, 1924, 2nd Edition p. 80.

8. Burns, Thomas: 'An Old Communion Custom – Fencing the Tables', (*Life and Work*, December 1924) p. 27. "After the Reformation, every possible precaution was taken to preserve the sanctity of the Sacrament. Hence originated the 'fencing of the tables…' The phrase can be traced back to those times when it was found necessary to erect barricades or palings to prevent unwarranted or undesirable persons from invading hallowed ground. In some cases, the 'fence' is referred to as 'flakettis' such as are used by farmers in their fields for confining sheep or cattle to a restricted area. These fences… had two 'yettis' [gates] or 'durris' [doors] at each of which an elder was stationed… and whose duty was to prevent anyone passing through the gates who did not possess a token."

9. Ross, J M: *Four Centuries of Scottish Worship*, The St Andrew Press, 1972 p. 14.

10. A good example of a preaching tent, from Carnock, is held in the National Museum of Scotland. This was a wooden hut, something like a sentry box with a tent-like roof; the object was to give the preacher shelter from the wind and rain. Although the Carnock tent dates from the early 19th cent., it is representative of the "tents" that were in common use in earlier centuries.

11. Burns, Thomas: *Old Scottish Communion Plate*, R & R Clark, 1892 p. 57.

12. *Archives* of the Incorporation of Goldsmiths, Edinburgh.

13. Rev Thomas Burns in his *Old Scottish Communion Plate*, large page edition, R & R Clark, 1892 carries a description of the Dalgety Communion Cups. Tragically, along with some Kirk Session records from previous centuries, these were destroyed in a fire in Dalgety manse, on 16 July 1897. Their loss prompted Mr Burns, then minister at Insh, near Kingussie, to write to the *Scotsman*, 22 July 1897, regretting that congregations the length and breadth of the country did not take their heritage more into account by safeguarding what he regarded as national treasures. Writing of the Dalgety cups he said, "The vessels were perhaps the finest specimens of their antique type in Fifeshire. Historically, their value was priceless…".

Of the Church nationally he said, "Through fire and robbery, the Church today mourns a loss which money can never restore. It must be confessed that the Church has been very remiss in the past, and through carelessness Church records and vessels have disappeared beyond all recovery. Surely this lamentable fire at Dalgety manse should awaken an increased desire among my brethren to see that no such fate shall endanger theirs." His words did not entirely fall upon deaf ears as legislation was introduced which compelled churches to deposit records at Register House in Edinburgh. See also, *The Dunfermline Journal*, Sat. 24th July 1897.

Chapter 10 Discipline and Repentance

1. Ross, William: *Glimpses of Pastoral Work in Covenanting Times*, James Nisbet & Co, 1877 pp. 174-5.

2. Todd, Margo: *The Culture of Protestantism in Early Modern Scotland*, Yale University Press, 2002, devotes chapter 3 to discussing repentance in the Church of Scotland and, although not a sacrament in the reformed Church, argues that performing repentance followed a formula and ritual, not widely dissociated from Roman Catholic sacramental practices, to which [pre-Reformation] people had long been accustomed. It fulfilled a need to bring people who had transgressed to justice before God and, at the same time, allowed the 'righteous', or obedient, to observe the penitents' humiliation.

    In some churches, the repentance stools had varying levels; the more serious the sin or misdemeanour, the higher the level at which the penitent stood. Todd noted: [Bringing someone to the repentance stool to perform repentance] "would have provided a dramatic visual display just before the sermon, and it surely spoke to its observers in a way no sermon could about the meaning of sin and godliness, about the threatening presence of agents or dupes of Satan in the midst of God's people and especially about condemnation and (finally) forgiveness. It was, as medieval penitential processions had been, a complex theology brought to visible, tangible life." (p. 154). "It was genuinely humiliating, in a spiritual as well as social sense. The penitent was not merely embarrassed before his neighbours, he was humbled – a virtuous stance – before God." (p. 169).

3. Seton, George: *Memoir of Alexander Seton*, Wm Blackwood, 1882 p. 162.

4. Sibbald, Robert: *The History, Ancient and Modern, of the Sheriffdoms of Fife and Kinross*, R Tullis, 1710 p. 121. Forbes Robertson in his *Early Scottish Gardeners and their plants 1650-1750*, Tuckwell Press, 2000 p. 147 notes that the gardens at Dalgety House were "larger and well-known" and established by1677."

5. Kirk, Thomas & Thoresby, R; Hume Brown, P (ed.): *Tours in Scotland 1677 and 1681*, David Douglas, 1892 p. 15ff.

6. *Oxford National Dictionary of Biography*, James Livingstone, p. 60.

7. The records are incomplete and one can only presume that the 'admonishment' was a form of repentance. The well-off always had the option of resorting to buying their way out of the more humiliating aspects of the rite and a substantial financial donation to the church box would ensure that that happened. Perhaps Lady Callendar availed herself of this facility? See: Todd, Margo: *The Culture of Protestantism in Early Modern Scotland*, Yale University Press, 2002 pp. 175-176.

8. *The New Statistical Account of Scotland, Vol. 9, Fife*, William Blackwood, 1845 p. 191.

9. *Mr John Lamont's Diary*, James Clarke, 1830 p. 119.

Chapter 11 Witchcraft and Superstition

1. Larner, Christina: *Enemies of God*, Chatto & Windus, Vintage Publishing, The Random House Group 1981 p. 7.

2. Not all witches were female but with only around 12%-15% of males involved, it is generally assumed that witches are female and, unless specifically noted otherwise, are referred to accordingly.

3. Black, George F: *A Calendar of Cases of Witchcraft in Scotland 1510–1725*, The New York Public Library, reprint, 1971 pp. 18-19.
4. Hume Brown, P: *Registers of the Privy Council, 2ⁿᵈ Series, Vol. 8 1544–1660* p. 200.
5. Black, George F: *A Calendar of Cases of Witchcraft in Scotland 1510–1725*, The New York Public Library, reprint, 1971 p. 59.
6. Brown K M et al, eds.: *The Records of the Parliaments of Scotland to 1707*, 1877 p. 200ff. (St Andrews, 2007-2014); online at: www.rps.ac.uk/; A1649/5/29 – 12 July 1649: 'Supplication of the presbytery of Dunfermline for a commission for the trial of those suspected of witchcraft'.
7. Hume Brown, P: *Registers of the Privy Council, 2ⁿᵈ Series, Vol. 8 1544–1660* p. 195.
8. Ross, William: *Glimpses of Pastoral Work in Covenanting Times*, James Nisbet, 1877 p. 200ff.
9. Ibid, p. 205.
10. *Mr John Lamont's Diary*, James Clarke,1830 p. 12.
11. Dunfermline Presbytery records – 7ᵗʰ January 1650 and 30ᵗʰ January 1650.
12. Ross, William: *Glimpses of Pastoral Work in Covenanting Times*, James Nisbet, 1877 p. 195 refers to one of Andrew Donaldson's elders being buried at St Theriot's Chapel, Fordell, with the unfounded suggestion that superstitious practices may have been involved: "… consisted in carrying the dead body round the church in the direction of the sun, from east to west by south, which was an old Pagan custom." Perhaps this accounted for the reference to the laird of Fordell's burial? The superstitious practices could, of course, have been no more than saying a prayer or reading a portion of Scripture, both of which were frowned upon.
13. Ecclesiastical Records, *Selections from the minutes of the Synod of Fife, 1611–1687*, Reprint, originally printed for the Abbotsford Club, 1837 p. 170.

Chapter 12 Battles and Protestations

1. The Act of Classes, passed on 23ʳᵈ January 1649, was designed to establish the loyalty of public officials. Offenders were grouped into four classes and found liable for a graduated scheme of punishment. The first class consisted of officers and persons in public offices – plotters against the Covenant or promoters of the Engagement. They were debarred from public office and from serving in the army during their lifetime. The second class were opponents of the Engagement; the third class were 'lukewarm neutrals' and the fourth class were holders of positions of trust who had fallen below the standards expected of such persons.
2. *Mr John Lamont's Diary*, James Clarke,1830 p. 32.
3. Ibid, p. 34.
4. Stodart, Robert R: *Browns of Fordell*, privately printed, 1887 p. 40.
5. Pitreavie Castle was originally built by Sir Henry Wardlaw, 1st Baronet of Pitreavie. He had bought the estate in 1608 for 10,000 merks Scottish. Wardlaw was Chamberlain to Queen Anne, wife of James VI of Scotland, became a Baronet of Nova Scotia in 1631 and died in 1637. He was succeeded by Henry, his eldest son. Construction of the house started in 1615 and was originally built to a U-shaped plan, with a symmetrical layout, the only entrance was on the inner side of the west wing. The old entrance is a fine Renaissance doorway, in the pediment of which are the initials S.H.W. (Sir Henry Wardlaw).

Pitreavie is considered to be an important example of an early seventeenth-century symmetrically-planned house, in the style of Sir James Murray, the King's Master of Works, and is similar to his Baberton House of the 1620s. It was substantially remodelled in the nineteenth century. It was requisitioned in 1938 for use by the R.A.F. during World War II and remained a military establishment until 1996 when it was converted into private apartments.

6. Stephen, William: *The History of Inverkeithing and Rosyth*, G & W Fraser, 1921 p. 520.

7. Spencerfield House, lying between Inverkeithing and Dalgety, was built by Henry Scott (d.1616) probably shortly after his marriage in 1592 to Elizabeth Henderson of Fordell (d.1622). At the time of the battle, it was tenanted by Sir Robert Douglas of Blaikerstouns. *(British Listed Buildings)*.

8. Chalmers, Peter: *Historical and Statistical Account of Dunfermline, Vol. 2*, William Blackwood, 1859 p. 281.

9. Ross, William: *Glimpses of Pastoral Work in Covenanting Times*, James Nisbet, 1877 p. 220.

10. *Mr John Lamont's Diary*, James Clarke, 1830 p. 33.

11. Donaldson, Gordon: *Scotland, James V-James VII*, Oliver & Boyd, 1965 p. 342.

12. Ibid, p. 353.

13. Monck's army had been based at Coldstream in the Scottish borders and the troops that marched to London formed the basis of what became the Coldstream Guards, now one of the British army's foremost regiments.

Chapter 13 Donaldson Deposed

1. Hunter, John: *The Diocese and Presbytery of Dunkeld 1660–1689 Vol. 1*, Hodder & Stoughton, 1917 p. 3; citing Row's 'Life of Blair' p. 287.

2. Ibid, p. 10.

3. Ibid, p. 13.

4. Ibid, pp. 59-60.

5. Ibid, p. 60; The National Synod never met.

6. Haliburton's life; see *Oxford National Dictionary of Biography* p. 571.

7. Hunter, John: *The Diocese and Presbytery of Dunkeld 1660–1689 Vol. 1*, Hodder & Stoughton, 1917 pp. 126-130.

8. Wodrow, Robert: *The History of the Sufferings of the Church of Scotland*, 1721 p. 410.

9. By this time, Mr Henry Guthrie had succeeded George Haliburton and had been consecrated Bishop of Dunkeld on 24th August 1665.

10. Scott, Hew: *Fasti Ecclesiae Scoticanae, Vol. 5*, Oliver & Boyd, 1925.

11. An observation, from Erskine Beveridge, Dunfermline, a keen amateur historian, who, in 1896, recorded details of some memorials at Dalgety Kirk: "Obviously, the stonemason has made some mistakes although he seems to have been sufficiently familiar with the commoner gravestone formulae; one imagines the text was written (not dictated) in an unfamiliar, probably cursive hand. Presumably, the man's name was John (IOHANIS) Corsar. For the strange LINUS PAROCTIAE, I propose HUIUS.PAROCHIAE – Paroctiae does not exist; and I cannot explain the intrusive D in the word May which is usually abbreviated to MAI." A copy of Beveridge's manuscript research is held in the Reading Room, Dunfermline Carnegie Library.

Chapter 14 Life in the Parish

1. No trace is left of any dwellings from that period in the seaward part of the parish; although John M Leighton in his *History of Fife, Vol. 3*, Joseph Swan, 1840 p. 243 writes "An old village once existed at Dalgetty, which has been entirely removed" and Barbieri in his *Gazetteer of Fife*, Maclachlan & Stewart, 1857 p. 135 notes, "The old village of Dalgety is now only to be found in history", there is no evidence to support in fact that a village of Dalgety, as such, ever existed.

   Contemporary references suggest that the dwellings around Donibristle House were demolished and removed in the earlier half of the eighteenth century. The then Earl of Moray had built a new mansion between 1700 and 1720, to replace the previous one which had burned down, and was clearing ground to create a large open area and garden. Historic Environment Scotland's list of Designed Landscapes indicates, "By 1781 an informal parkland landscape, probably designed by Thomas White had been laid out on the Donibristle policies."

   Rev Peter Primrose, in his description of Dalgety Parish in Sir John Sinclair's *Statistical Account for Scotland*, William Creech, 1795, noted that there were about 190 houses in the parish, of which "only 12 are feus", the rest belonging to the proprietors. It would, therefore, have been relatively easy for proprietors to clear houses and allow for development.

   The historian, Dr Paula Martin, in a letter to the author in February 2015, wrote: "the fact that such settlements were able to be removed suggests they were not on a main thoroughfare, they did not hold markets and were really just a cluster of cottages belonging to the landowner. So they were almost certainly single-storey thatched cottages, perhaps not much more than a fermetoun."

   Apart from anything else, the coalfields were being developed in the north of the parish and the population was gradually moving inland to take advantage of employment opportunities. Demolition and clearance of houses near the coast, in the mid-1700s, would have been a result of this population shift. Shortly after the closure of Dalgety Kirk in 1830 it would appear as though all remaining houses near the coast had been demolished.

2. Corbet, Gordon ed.: The Nature of Fife, article – *Landscape and History*, Graeme Whittington & Chris Smout, Scottish Cultural Press, 1998 p31.

3. An extract from: *A Trip to Barbarous Scotland* by an English Gentleman (c.1708) cited by Scott A F: *Everyone a Witness: the Stuart Age*, Purnell Book Services, 1974 p. 48.

4. Gibson A J S and Smout T C: *Prices, food and wages in Scotland 1550–1780*, Cambridge UP, 1995 p. 231, citing Smollet, Tobias: *Works* p. 559.

5. Mowat, Sue: *Fire, Foe and Famine, Dunfermline 1600–1700*, Dunfermline Community Heritage Projects, 2014 p. 389. The Earl of Tweeddale was the brother of Lady Margaret Hay, a former occupier of Dalgety House, and he had gained control of the Regality of Dunfermline, including the mills, in 1652.

6. *Moray Muniments*: NRAS/217/Box19/752-753 & 759.

7. Cullen, K: *Famine in Scotland: The 'Ill Years' of the 1690s*, Edinburgh University Press, 2010 p. 2 & p. 124; Cullen notes (p. 14) that the "seven lean years", a reference to the seven years of famine in the Book of Genesis, "has largely been dismissed by historians as being inaccurate and based merely on religious belief that a lapse in moral standards was to blame for God's wrath in sending unseasonable weather to destroy the crops and punish the sins of the Scots."

8. The mural tablet inscription is in Latin. A full record of all the gravestones in St Bridget's kirkyard is contained in Arnott, R G K: *The Gravestones of St Bridget's Kirk, a photographic record*, 1989.

9. Stephen, William: *History of Inverkeithing and Rosyth*, G & W Fraser, 1921. James Spittal of Leuchat died in 1770, at the age of 98. He had been Provost of Inverkeithing and a Member of the Scottish Parliament for Inverkeithing burgh, from 1702–1707, following his father, Alexander, in that role. He was the last surviving member of that Parliament.

10. Hobbes, Thomas: *Leviathan*, 1651. In his book, he describes the natural state humankind would be in, were it not for political community. "… In such condition, there is no place for Industry; because the fruit thereof is uncertain; and consequently no Culture of the Earth; no Navigation, nor use of the commodities that may be imported by Sea; no commodious Building; no Instruments of moving, and removing such things as require much force; no Knowledge of the face of the Earth; no account of Time; no Arts; no Letters; no Society; and which is worst of all, continuall feare, and danger of violent death; And the life of man, solitary, poore, nasty, brutish, and short."

11. Henderson, Ebenezer: *Annals of Dunfermline*, John Tweed, 1879 p. 297.

12. Foster, Roland: *The Church before the Covenants*, Scottish Academic Press, 1975 p. 82 – citing *Culross Kirk Session records*, 20th November 1631.

13. Sibbald, Robert: *The History of Fife*, R Tullis, 1710 p. 121.

14. Kirk, Thomas and Thoresby, Ralph; Hume Brown P (ed.): *Tours in Scotland 1677 & 1681*, David Douglas, 1892 p. 16. The bronze statue of Mercury (artist unknown) is now in a private collection. It stands 1.5m high and was apparently purchased in London by the 4th Earl of Moray. Since Kirk's visit in 1677 Donibristle House has been burned down three times; after the last time in 1858 it was never rebuilt.

15. *Erskine Beveridge manuscript*, Carnegie Dunfermline Library.

16. *Moray Muniments:* NRAS/217/Box 5/1143, June 1646.

17. Ibid, NRAS/217/Box 20/2442, 10 December 1697.

18. Royal Commission for Ancient and Historical Monuments in Scotland (now Historic Environment Scotland).

Chapter 15 Colliers and Salters

1. Gemmell, John: *The Wemyss Coalfield*, Institute of Mining Engineers, 1909 pp. 556-557.

2. Hunter, Tom: *Mining in the Crossgates Area of West Fife (in particular Fordell colliery)*, privately published, 2001 p. 49.

3. Smout, T C: *A History of the Scottish People 1560–1830*, Collins, 1969 p. 181. Jameson's *Scottish Dictionary*, abridged version, William Tait, 1846 defines an "arle" as "an earnest of whatever kind, a pledge of full possession" or "a piece of money given for confirming a bargain". It should be noted that men were not slaves in the traditional sense as they were paid for the work they undertook, but conditions made it impossible for them to leave their employer, effectively placing them in servitude.

4. Nef, John U: *Rise of the British Coal Industry, Vol. 2*, Routledge, 1966 pp. 157, 161.

5. Boece, Hector: *The History and Chronicles of Scotland*, 1527 (in Latin); Trans. John Bellenden, 1536.

6. Hunter, Tom: *Mining in the Crossgates Area of West Fife (in particular Fordell colliery)*, privately published, 2001 p. 103.

7. Ibid, p. 65.

8. Foyster, E and Whatley, C: *A History of Everyday Life in Scotland*, Edinburgh University Press, 2010 p. 253.

9. Graham, Angus: *Proceedings of the Society of Antiquaries of Scotland 1968 Vol. 101* pp. 232-33, notes: "Dalgety, Fife NS 170837: The 6-in. O.S. map surveyed in 1855 marks "Old Pier" just W. of the old parish church of Dalgety, indicating no structure but only a strip of loose stones or boulders running down from the high-water mark across the tidal flats. The feature still exists and in its seaward portion there can be seen a row of large laid stones, evidently the footings of the E. face of a pier or jetty. About 120 yds. below the high-water mark these run into some transverse footings which suggest a pier-head about 30 ft. wide: but the remains are too scanty to reveal a definite plan and their explanation is made more difficult by some further transverse footings about 60 ft. further out. As nothing is marked on this site on an estate map of 1768, one must suppose that the pier was built after that date, and became ruinous or was demolished before 1855, or that it was a good deal older, and had already gone out of use by 1768." In a *Map of the counties of Fife and Kinross* (Sharp, Greenwood & Fowler, London, 1828) a pier is very clearly shown to be in existence.

10. Hunter, Tom: *Mining in the Crossgates Area of West Fife (in particular Fordell colliery)*, privately published, 2001 pp. 65-66.

11. Young, Andrew: *History of Burntisland*, · Kirkcaldy, 1924, 2nd Edition p. 81; citing a private document, written in the early part of the nineteenth century, by Provost James Speed, Burntisland.

12. Captain Iain Grant, formerly with Forth Ports Authority, in a letter to the author: "Sailing to Holland from Dalgety could have been a possibility as the boats would have been big enough. Boats would have a draft of no more than 1 metre and probably be flat-bottomed as it would be likely that they would sit on the bottom over low water whilst loading. Two or three experienced men, with good local knowledge of the area and the tides, would be able to handle a boat up to ten or twelve metres in length with 15 tons of cargo, by using a sail and oars; and be able to come and go probably three hours before and three hours after high water. The mean range at spring tides is 4.8 metres and at neap tides is 2.4 metres. These are mean ranges but on occasions the actual range can be just over 6 metres."

13. Hume Brown, P ed.: *Registers of the Privy Council for Scotland, 2nd Series, Vol. VIII 1544–1660* pp. 22-3.

14. National Records of Scotland: *Henderson of Fordell Muniments* – GD172/481: Memorial and depositions regarding Sir Robert Henderson's right to a road by the minister's house and to ship coal at Dalgety. The document is undated but thought to be around 1730–35.

15. While there is no indication on any map, it is thought that the "humbel" or "humel" stone (i.e. 'hummel', meaning without projections or prominences, presenting a flat, level appearance, smooth and bald (*Scottish National Dictionary*) is the one which is visible at low tide from the coastal path at Sealstrand, close to the remains of ruined jetties, and given that the document indicates it is "right opposite" the manse.

16. National Records of Scotland: *Henderson of Fordell Muniments* – GD172/481/2.

17. Sibbald, Robert: *The History of Fife*, R Tullis, 1803 p. 322.

18. Murdoch, R & Lewis J: *Excavations at the St Monans Saltpans 1990–96* p. 6. The authors, by suggesting Fordell probably meant St David's bay, where the saltpans were owned by the Hendersons of Fordell.

19. Whatley, Prof. Christopher: University of Dundee, in a letter to the author, March 2015.

20. Brownrigg, William: *The Art of Making Common Salt*, C. Davis et al, 1748 pp. 56-61.

21. Hume Brown, P ed.: *Registers of the Privy Council for Scotland, 3rd Series Vol. III 1669–1672* p. 311.

22. Whatley, Prof. Christopher: *That Important and Necessary Article, The Salt Industry and its trade in Fife and Tayside c. 1570–1850*, Abertay Historical Society, 1984.

23. Smout, T C: *A History of the Scottish People 1560–1830*, Collins, 1969 p. 183.

Chapter 16 Donaldson Imprisoned

1. Ordinance Survey maps note: "Cloich – a deep hollow or hiding place near the summit of the Hill of Beath".

2. Wodrow, Robert: *History of the Sufferings of the Church of Scotland*, 1721 p. 156.

3. Ibid, p. 157.

4. *Oxford National Dictionary of Biography* pp. 917-18.

5. Hume Brown, P ed. *Records of the Privy Council of Scotland, 3rd Series, Vol. III 1669–72* p. 205.

6. Ibid, p. 660.

7. Wodrow, Robert: *History of the Sufferings of the Church of Scotland*, 1721 p. 158.

8. Banishment to the plantations (America or West Indies) was not just a punishment, it was a means of resolving a shortage of indentured labour.

9. Dickinson, W & Donaldson, G eds. *Source Book of Scottish History, Vol. 3*, Thos. Nelson & Sons, 1954 p. 166.

10. Ibid, p. 168.

11. Ibid, pp. 172-173.

12. Sibbald, Robert: *The History of Fife*, R Tullis, 1803 p. 455.

13. Hume Brown, P ed. *Records of the Privy Council of Scotland, 3rd Series, Vol. IV 1673–76* pp. 206-208.

14. Ibid, pp. 228-230.

15. Ibid, pp. 237-239.

16. Hume Brown, P ed. *Records of the Privy Council of Scotland, 3rd Series, Vol. V 1676–78* pp. 18-19.

17. The tolbooth (now the Burgh Halls), was built in 1668–70 by John Smith, on the site of the previous one which had been demolished on the orders of Cromwell; it contained a debtors' prison. The building was entirely altered in 1807 and after a fire in 1847 restored with its current Renaissance-style façade. In 2011, during major renovations, the bars of a cell from the original building were discovered – perhaps where Donaldson was held.

18. Wodrow, Robert: *The History and Sufferings of the Church of Scotland, Vol. 2*, 1722. App. cxxviii.

19. Hume Brown, P ed. *Records of the Privy Council of Scotland, 3rd Series, Vol. V 1676–78* pp. 639-40.

20. Ross, William: *Glimpses of Pastoral Work in Covenanting* Times, James Nisbet & Co, 1877 pp. 231-32: citing Robert Wodrow in *The History and Sufferings of the Church of Scotland*, 1721.

Chapter 17 Death of Donaldson; the Century Comes to a Close

1. "The Cameronians", the origin of the Scottish army regiment formed in 1689, lay in the heartland of the area which Richard Cameron used for rallying covenanting support.
2. Hume Brown, P ed. *Records of the Privy Council of Scotland, 3rd Series, Vol. VI 1678–80* p. 315.
3. Ibid, p. 360.
4. Ibid, p. 341.
5. Donaldson, Gordon: *Scotland, James V – James VII*, Oliver & Boyd, 1971 p382 – citing Wodrow, Robert *The History and Sufferings of the Church of Scotland* 1721.
6. Donaldson, Gordon: *Scotland, James V – James VII*, Oliver & Boyd, 1971 pp382-83.
7. Hume Brown, P ed. *Records of the Privy Council of Scotland, 3rd Series, Vol. VIII 1683–84* pp. 218-220.
8. Jacobites – the name given to supporters of the Stuart dynasty, after Jacobus, the Latinised form of James. Jacobitism was a political movement aimed at restoring the Roman Catholic King James VII & II, and his heirs, to the thrones of Scotland, England and Ireland.
9. James Francis Edward Stuart, the "Old Pretender" who attempted to reclaim the throne with the 1715 Jacobite rebellion; followed by his son, Charles Edward Stuart, the "Young Pretender", 'Bonnie Prince Charlie', who led the 1745 uprising which ended in defeat at Culloden in April 1746.
10. Stanley, Arthur Penrhyn: *Lectures on the History of the Church of Scotland*, Scribner, Armstrong & Co., 1872 Lecture III, p. 132.
11. The Bill of Rights, 1689, confirmed the deposition of James VII & II and the accession of William and Mary; it guaranteed the Protestant succession, and laid down the principles of parliamentary supremacy.
12. Henderson G D: *The Church of Scotland*, The Saint Andrew Press, 1970 p. 95. Locke had been influenced by Sebastian Castellio, a Protestant refugee in Geneva, about 1540, who had fallen out with Calvin. Castellio argued that it was simply wrong in principle to kill a person for their beliefs, a point of view that was out of step with the then current thinking.
13. The James Lamb who led the psalm singing at the Hill of Beath conventicle.
14. Melville, Evan ed. *Records of the Privy Council of Scotland, 3rd Series, Vol. XV 1690* p. 419.
15. Wodrow, Robert: *The History and Sufferings of the Church of Scotland, Vol. 1*, 1721 p. 409.
16. *Moray Muniments*: NRAS/217/Box 19/202 and NRAS/217/Box 20/2431.
17. *A List of Subscribers to the Company of Scotland, trading to Africa and the Indies*, Google ebooks (free download).
18. Scott, Hew: *Fasti Ecclesiae Scoticanae, Vol. 5*, Oliver & Boyd, 1925 p. 3.
19. Agreed by the Commissioners of the General Assembly of the Church of Scotland, 9th December, 1698: *A Seasonable Admonition and Exhortation to some who separate themselves from the Communion of the Church of Scotland*, George Mosman, Edinburgh 1699 p. 6.

Appendix 1 Dalgety Kirk and St Bridget

1. Royal Commission on Ancient and Historical Monuments – Counties of Fife, Kinross and Clackmannan, 11th Report (HMSO, 1933) pp. 93ff.

2. Ibid, pp. 93ff.

3. Ibid, pp. 93ff.

4. Towill, Edwin S: *Saints of Scotland*, The Saint Andrew Press, 1978 pp. 29-33.

5. Easson, D and MacDonald, A (eds): *Charters of the Abbey of Inchcolm*, Scottish History Society, 1938 p. 128.

6. Taylor, Simon, with Márkus, Gilbert: *The Place Names of Fife, Vol. 1,* Shaun Tyas, 2006 pp. 265-66.

Appendix 2 Scottish Weights, Measures and Currency

1. Stephen, William: *The History of Inverkeithing and Rosyth*, G & W Fraser, 1921 p. 521.

Select Bibliography, Pamphlets and Sources of Information

APS	Acts of Parliament of Scotland
APGA	Acts and Proceedings of the General Assembly of the Church of Scotland; 1560–1618 & 1638–1842, ed. Duncan Shaw 2004
ABBOTSFORD CLUB	*Ecclesiastical Records: Selections from the Minutes of the Synod of Fife* – MDCXI–MDCLXXXVII (1611–1687); reprint 2011
ARNOT, R PAGE	*A History of the Scottish Miners*, George Allan & Unwin, London 1955
ARNOTT, ROBIN G K	*Of Monks and Ministers*, Dalgety Bay 1992
ARNOTT, ROBIN G K	*Gravestones of St Bridget's Kirk*, Dalgety Bay 1989
BALLINGALL, WILLIAM	*The Shores of Fife*, T & A Constable, Edinburgh 1872
BARBIERI, M	*Gazetteer of Fife*, Maclachlan & Stewart, Edinburgh 1857
BARR, JAMES	*The Scottish Covenanters*, John Smith, Glasgow 1947
BEALE, JAMES M	*A History of The Burgh and Parochial Schools of Fife* (ed. Donald Withrington), Scottish Council for Educational Research 1983
BEVERIDGE, ERSKINE	*Manuscript notes on the churchyard of Dalgety, held in Dunfermline Carnegie Library* 1896
BLACK, G F	*A Calendar of Cases of Witchcraft in Scotland 1510–1727*, Arno Press, New York 1979
BRITISH HISTORY ONLINE	*www.british-history.ac.uk/*
BROWN, K M et al, eds.	*The Records of the Parliaments of Scotland to 1707*, University of St Andrews 2007–14. Records of the Parliament of Scotland until the Union in 1707 have been digitised by

academics at St Andrews University and are available online at: www.rps.ac.uk

BROWNRIGG, WILLIAM	*The Art of Making Common Salt* 1748
BURLEIGH, J H S	*A Church History of Scotland*, Oxford UP 1960
BURNS, THOMAS	*Old Scottish Communion Plate* Large Page edition, R & R Clark, Edinburgh 1892
CHAMBERS, ROBERT	*Domestic Annals of Scotland, from the Reformation to the Restoration* 3rd edition, vol. 2, W & R Chambers, Edinburgh 1874
CHALMERS, PETER	*Historical and Statistical Account of the Town and Parish of Dunfermline Vols. 1 & 2*, Wm. Blackwood, Edinburgh 1844
CORBET, GORDON ed.	*The Nature of Fife*; article – *Landscape and History*, Graeme Whittington & Chris Smout, 1998
COWAN, IAN B	*The Scottish Covenanters 1660–1688*, Victor Gollancz, London 1976
CULLEN, KAREN J	*Famine in Scotland: The 'Ill Years' of the 1690s*, Edinburgh UP 2013
DALGLEISH, GEORGE & FOTHRINGHAM, HENRY STEUART	*Silver, Made in Scotland*, National Museum of Scotland revised reprint, 2008
DICKINSON, W C &DONALDSON, G	*A Source Book of Scottish History Vol. 3* Thos. Nelson, Edinburgh 1954
DONALDSON, GORDON	*Scottish Historical Documents* 2nd edition, Scottish Academic Press, Glasgow 1974
DONALDSON, GORDON	*Scotland, James V–James VII;* the Edinburgh History of Scotland 2nd edition, Vol 3, Oliver & Boyd 1971
DONALDSON, GORDON	*The Making of the Scottish Prayer Book of 1637*, Edinburgh UP 1954
EASSON, D E & MACDONALD, ANGUS eds.	*Charters of the Abbey of Inchcolm*, Scottish History Society 1938
FINLAY, IAN	*Scottish Gold and Silver Work* The Strong Oak Press, pub.1956; revised by Henry Fothringham 1991
FOSTER, WALTER R	*Bishop and Presbytery*, SPCK, London 1958
FOSTER, WALTER R	*The Church before the Covenants*, Scottish Academic Press 1975
FOYSTER, E & WHATLEY, C	*A History of Everyday Life in Scotland*, Edinburgh UP 2010
FURGOL, EDWARD M	*A Regimental History of the Covenanting Armies 1639–1651*, John Donald, Edinburgh 1990
GIBSON, A J S & SMOUT T C	*Prices, food and wages in Scotland 1550–1780*, Cambridge UP 1995
GIFFORD, JOHN	*The Buildings of Scotland – Fife*, Penguin 1988

GOODARE, JULIAN ed.   *Scottish Witches and Witch-hunters*, Palgrave Macmillan, London 2015

GRANT, Capt. Iain   *Letter to the author regarding tides in Dalgety Bay* 2017

HARRIS, TIM   *Rebellion, Britain's First Stuart Kings*, Oxford UP 2014

HENDERSON,
ALEXANDER   *The Government and Order of the Church of Scotland* 1641

HENDERSON, EBENEZER   *The Annals of Dunfermline and vicinity from the earliest authentic period to the present time 1089–1878*, John Tweed, Glasgow, 1879

HENDERSON, G D   *Religious Life in Seventeenth Century Scotland*, Cambridge UP 1936

HENDERSON
MUNIMENTS   *National Records of Scotland*

HEWISON, JAMES KING   *The Covenanters*, John Smith & Sons, Glasgow 1908

HUNTER, JOHN   *The Diocese and Presbytery of Dunkeld 1660–1689*, Hodder & Stoughton, London 1917

HUNTER, THOMAS F   *Mining in West Fife, the Crossgates Area (in particular Fordell Colliery)* 2001

JAMIESON, JOHN   *A Dictionary of the Scottish Language*, Edinburgh UP 1808; abridged version 1846

KIRK, JAMES ed.   *The Books of Assumption of the Thirds of Benefices*, Oxford UP 1995

KIRK, THOMAS
& THORESBY, RALPH   *Tours of Scotland 1677 –1685* (ed. P. Hume Brown), David Douglas, Edinburgh 1892

KJV   *King James VI version of the Bible*

LAMONT'S DIARY   1649–1672 published as *The Chronicle of Fife*, Edinburgh 1810

LANG, THEO   *The Kingdom of Fife*, Hodder & Stoughton, London 1951

LARNER, CHRISTINA   *Enemies of God, The Witch-hunt in Scotland*, Chatto & Windus, London 1981

LARNER, CHRISTINA;
LEE, CHRISTOPHER HYDE
& McLACHLAN, HUGH V   *A Source-book of Scottish Witchcraft*, Glasgow University 1977

LEIGHTON, JOHN M   *History of the County of Fife Vol. III*, Joseph Swan, Glasgow 1840

LIFE AND WORK magazine   *An Old Communion Custom – Fencing the Tables,* article by Rev Thomas Burns, pub. Church of Scotland, December 1924

LINDSAY, IAN   *The Scottish Parish Kirk*, The Saint Andrew Press, Edinburgh 1960

McCALLUM, JOHN   *Reforming the Scottish Parish, The Reformation in Fife 1560–1640*, Ashgate, Farnham 2010

MACDONALD, STUART   *The Witches of Fife, Witch-hunting in a Scottish Shire 1560–1710*, Birlinn, Edinburgh 2002

McMICHAEL,
ARCHIBALD C   *Fife and Kinross*, Hugh Henry 1881

McRAE, ALISDAIR	*How the Scots Won the English Civil War*, The History Press, Stroud 2013
MAKEY, WALTER	*The Church of the Covenant 1637–1651*, John Donald, Edinburgh 1979
MARTIN, Dr PAULA	Letter to the author, *'Dalgety as possible fermetoun and removal of village houses'* 2015
MAXWELL, W D	*A History of Worship in the Church of Scotland*, The Baird Trust Lecture, Oxford UP 1955
MERCER, A	*The History of Dunfermline*, John Miller, Dunfermline 1828
MELVILLE, JAMES	*The Diary of Mr James Melville*, The Bannatyne Club, Edinburgh 1829
MITCHELL, A F	*The Westminster Assembly*, The Baird Trust Lecture pub. 1882
MORAY MUNIMENTS	Courtesy of Hon John Stuart, Earl of Moray, in conjunction with the National Archives of Scotland
MURDOCH, ROBIN & LEWIS, JOHN	*Excavations at the St Monans saltpans 1990–96* (as article in The Salt and Coal Industries at St Monans, Fife in the 18th & 19th Centuries, with Drs Colin & Paula Martin) 1999
NEF, JOHN U	*Rise of the British Coal Industry Vol. 2*, Routledge 1966
NORMAND, L & ROBERTS G	*Witchcraft in Early Modern Scotland* 2000
OMAND, DONALD ed.	*The Fife Book*; article: Towns and Villages, Dr Paula Martin 2000
OXFORD DICTIONARY OF NATIONAL BIOGRAPHY	online at: www.oxforddnb.com
PAMPHLET	*Papers lately delivered in to the Honourable Houses of Parliament by the Commissioners of the Kingdom of Scotland, concerning The Proceedings of the Scottish Army and their Intentions; signed Lauderdale, A Johnston, C Erskine, H Kennedy & R Barely* London 1646
PAMPHLET	*A True Relation of what is discovered concerning the MURTHER of the Archb[p] of St Andrews and of what appears to have been the occasion thereof* Unattributed and undated (but thought to have been published in London in1679)
PAMPHLET	*A Seasonable Admonition and Exhortation to some who separate themselves from the Communion of the Church of Scotland. Unanimously agreed unto by the Commissioners of the General Assembly, December 9, 1698 and published by their appointment*, printed by George Mosman, printer to the Church and its Assemblies, Edinburgh 1699
PROCEEDINGS OF THE SOCIETY OF ANTIQUARIES OF SCOTLAND	Vol. 112, National Museum of Antiquities, Edinburgh 1982
PATRICK, MILLAR	*Four Centuries of Scottish Psalmody*, Oxford UP 1949
ROYAL COMMISSION on ANCIENT MONUMENTS in SCOTLAND	*Fife, Kinross and Clackmannan*, Edinburgh 1933

REGISTERS OF THE
PRIVY COUNCIL
OF SCOTLAND: 2nd Series Vol VI 1635–1637 ed. P Hume Brown 1905

3rd Series Vol I 1661–1664 ed. P Hume Brown 1908

3rd Series Vol XV 1690 ed. Evan W M Balfour Melville 1967

REID, HARRY   Reformation, the dangerous birth of the modern world, The Saint Andrew Press, Edinburgh 2009

REID, STUART   Battles of the Scottish Lowlands, Pen & Sword Military, Barnsley 2004

ROBERTSON, FORBES W   Early Scottish Gardeners and their plants 1650–1750, Tuckwell Press, East Linton 2000

ROSS, JOHN M   Four Centuries of Scottish Worship, The Saint Andrew Press, Edinburgh 1972

ROSS, WILLIAM   Aberdour and Inchcolme, David Douglas, Edinburgh 1885

ROSS, WILLIAM   Glimpses of Pastoral Work in Covenanting Times, James Nisbet, London 1877

ROW, JOHN   The Kirk of Scotland 1558–1639, The Wodrow Society, Edinburgh 1842

RYRIE, ALEC   Protestants, Wm. Collins, London 2017

SCOTT, HEW   Fasti Ecclesiae Scoticanae Vol 5 1925

SETON, GEORGE   Memoir of Alexander Seton, Earl of Dunfermline, Wm. Blackwood, Edinburgh 1882

SIBBALD, ROBERT   The History, Ancient and Modern, of the Sheriffdoms of Fife and Kinross with the Descriptions of Both (revised edition), R Tullis, Cupar 1803

SIMPSON, ERIC   Dalgety, the Story of a Parish, Dalgety Bay Community Council 1978

SIMPSON, ERIC   Dalgety Bay: Heritage and Hidden History, Dalgety Bay and Hillend Community Council 1999

SINCLAIR, SIR JOHN   The Statistical Account of Scotland, Wm. Green, Edinburgh 1795

SMOUT, T C   A History of the Scottish People 1560–1830 2nd edition, Wm. Collins, London 1970

SMOUT, T C   Scottish Trade on the Eve of the Union 1660–1707, Oliver & Boyd, Edinburgh 1963

SPOTTISWOODE, JOHN   The History of the Church of Scotland, R Norton, London 1685

STEPHEN, WILLIAM   The History of Inverkeithing and Rosyth, G & W Fraser, Aberdeen 1921

STEVENSON, ROBERT   The Communion in Dunfermline in the 17th Century, A. Romanes, Dunfermline 1900

STEVENSON, WILLIAM   The Presbyterie Booke of Kirkcaldie, James Burt, Kirkcaldy 1900

TAYLOR, J W   Historical Antiquities of Fife Vol. II 3rd edition
TAYLOR, SIMON
with Márkus, Gilbert   The Place Names of Fife Vol 1 2006; Vol 5, Shaun Tyas, Donington 2012

"THE SCOTSMAN" newspaper	Letter from Rev Thomas Burns, 22nd July 1897
TODD, MARGO	*The Culture of Protestantism in Early Modern Scotland*, Yale UP 2002
THOMSON, P D	*Parish and Parish Church,* The Baird Trust Lecture, Thos. Nelson, Edinburgh 1935
TOWILL, EDWIN S	*Saints of Scotland*, The Saint Andrew Press, Edinburgh 1978
UNIVERSITY OF EDINBURGH	*Survey of Scottish Witchcraft Database* (compiled by Julian Goodare, Lauren Martin, Joyce Miller and Louise Yeoman) 2003
WADDELL, PETER H	*An Old Kirk Chronicle, being a history of Auldhame, Tyninghame, and Whitekirk in East Lothian, from session records, 1615–1850* 1893
WALKER, J RUSSELL	*Pre-Reformation Churches in Fifeshire*, Mould & Todd 1895
WEBSTER, ARCHIBALD	*Scottish Population Statistics*, 3rd Series, Scottish History Society 1952
WHATLEY, CHRISTOPHER A	*The Scottish Salt Industry 1570–1850*, Abertay Historical Society 1987
WHATLEY, CHRISTOPHER A	*That Important and Necessary Article, The Salt Industry and its trade in Fife and Tayside c. 1570–1850*, Abertay Historical Society 1984
WHATLEY, CHRISTOPHER A	Letter to the author, *Salt pans at St David's* 2015
WIKIPEDIA	Free encyclopaedia
WILKIE, JAMES	*Bygone Fife from Culross to St Andrews*, Wm. Blackwood, Edinburgh 1931
WILKIE, JAMES	*The History of Fife*, Wm. Blackwood 1924
WODROW, ROBERT	*The History and Sufferings of the Church of Scotland* 1836
YOUNG, ANDREW	History of Burntisland, 2nd Edition, Fifeshire Advertiser 1924

Acknowledgements

I owe a debt of thanks to my wife, Nan, for her support and forbearance, and her helpful comments, during the research for this book, particularly during the period of the Covid-19 pandemic. I wish to thank Eric Simpson and Maureen Wilson for their criticisms and suggestions in early drafts; Dr Simon Taylor, Glasgow University, for his insightful comments and helpful pointers; Professor Christopher Whatley, University of Dundee and Dr Paula Martin, maritime archaeologist, for their kind and positive responses to my questions; Capt. Iain Grant, master mariner, for his comments on shipping and tides in Dalgety Bay; the staff in the libraries of the National Library of Scotland; National Mining Museum of Scotland; Edinburgh Central Library and Fife Cultural Trust's libraries. Thanks are also due to the staff at Troubador Publishing for their support, advice and patience.

I am grateful for the very generous assistance provided by staff at the following institutions and for permission to use images under licence:

Air Images Ltd
British Library
Dunedin Public Art Gallery, New Zealand
Historic Environment Scotland
National Galleries of Scotland
National Library of Scotland

National Museums of Scotland
National Records of Scotland
National Register of Archives of Scotland
UK Coal Authority
University of St Andrews Library

For permission to use extracts from published material, I am grateful to Edinburgh University Press; SPCK; The History Press; The Random House Group; The Saint Andrew Press; The Society of Antiquaries in Scotland; Yale University Press with permission of The Licensor through PLSclear; UK Coal Authority.

Other references and illustrations: all references to The First Book of Discipline come from the version edited by James Cameron. The Dalgety Kirk bell is from J Russell Walker's, *Pre-Reformation Churches in Fifeshire,* 1895; Communion cup illustration and makers' marks are from Thomas Burns, *Old Scottish Communion Plate,* large page edition, 1892; the drawing of the Bell Pit is from *A Short History of the Scottish Coal-mining Industry* pub. by The National Coal Board, Scottish Division, 1958. For the photograph of the Royal Arms of Scotland in Fordell's Lodgings (taken c.1920, photographer unknown) I am indebted to Mr I Joliffe of Falkland.

I have endeavoured to locate all copyright holders and any omissions are inadvertent. Any errors which remain are entirely mine.

All photographs, unless otherwise indicated, are © the author.

Index

 Matador

For exclusive discounts on Matador titles,
sign up to our occasional newsletter at
troubador.co.uk/bookshop